P9-CQR-289

DATE DUE

OCT - 6 1997			
OCT 6 1997			
GAYLORD			PRINTED IN U.S.A.

MEASURING SOCIAL JUDGMENTS

MEASURING SOCIAL JUDGMENTS

The Factorial Survey Approach

PETER H. ROSSI
STEVEN L. NOCK
Editors

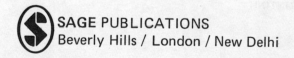

SAGE PUBLICATIONS
Beverly Hills / London / New Delhi

For information address:

SAGE Publications, Inc.
275 South Beverly Drive
Beverly Hills, California 90212

SAGE Publications India Pvt. Ltd.
C-236 Defence Colony
New Delhi 110 024, India

SAGE Publications Ltd
28 Banner Street
London EC1Y 8QE, England

Printed in the United States of America

Library of Congress Cataloging in Publication Data

Main entry under title:

Measuring social judgments.

Bibliography: p.
Contents: The factorial survey approach / Peter H. Rossi and Andy B. Anderson—Household social standing / M. Bonner Meudell—Family social status / Steven L. Nock—[etc.]
1. Social surveys—Methodology—Addresses, essays, lectures. 2. Factorial experiment designs—Methodology—Addresses, essays, lectures. 3. Factor analysis—Addresses, essays, lectures. 4. Sampling (Statistics)—Addresses, essays, lectures. I. Rossi, Peter Henry, 1921- . II. Nock, Steven L.
HN29.F28   300'.7'23   82-674
ISBN 0-8039-1816-X   AACR2

FIRST PRINTING

CONTENTS

To the memory of Paul Felix Lazarsfeld,
pioneer social researcher and creative
contributor to current social
research lore and science

ACKNOWLEDGMENTS

Many persons took part in the development of the factorial survey approach. The dedication of this volume acknowledges the debt the senior author owes to Paul F. Lazarsfeld and his insightful comments that sparked this line of development and shaped its growth. At various points, cogent advice on technical issues was provided by Frederick W. Mosteller and George W. Borhnstedt. All of the authors of chapters in this volume contributed to the common task of improving and testing the factorial survey approach. In addition, Eleanor Weber-Burdin brilliantly helped all of us through difficult points in the preparation of factorial object samples and in the analyses of resulting data. Robert K. Lazarsfeld, now in the Mathematics Department of Harvard University, developed the Fortran program that generates the factorial object samples, while serving as a research associate on this project. Others participated in the work at various times—William Sampson, Guillermina Jasso, Christine Bose, Jeffrey Passell, Paul M. Siegel, and Robert W. Hodge.

Much of the work reported in this volume was supported by NIMH Grant MH 24254, "Experimental Studies of Social Status," for which we are extremely grateful.

We hope those that have helped us are delighted to be acknowledged, especially since we claim that the faults of the work are ours alone.

P.H.R.
S.L.N.

PREFACE

The factorial survey approach described in this volume has been evolving gradually over the past several decades. It began with an attempt to broaden the empirical scope of the term "prestige" from occupations alone to households and families, following the reasoning that socioeconomic stratification was an ordering of households and perhaps lineages. The approach was foreshadowed in the senior author's Ph.D. thesis in which an effort was made to formulate the local community studies of social class into the current framework of psychometric theory and practice. Following a suggestion made by the thesis advisor, Paul F. Lazarsfeld, the thesis suggested that household status positions be examined by using a factorial design in which the characteristics of households be systematically rotated in the form of vignette descriptions of hypothetical households.

Early trials of the vignette approach (Rossi, 1951)[1] seemed very unpromising because in full factorial designs so few characteristics could be systematically rated. Progress was made when it was realized that no one respondent-judge need rate all the vignettes in a full factorial design. All of the studies reported in this volume were undertaken following that important change in approach.

A second important development was the realization that the technique was not specific to the field of social stratification but generally applicable to a wide variety of substantive areas involving the judgment of complex objects. Many of the applications in this volume—child abuse, sexual harassment, and so on—followed from the insight that in areas of social judgment people's evaluations were of complex social objects that varied from one another on a variety of dimensions. Indeed, the current view is that factorial surveys are appropriately applied in the study of substantive areas in which there is presumed to be some kind of social component to the judgment of all kinds of objects.

In this larger view of factorial surveys, this approach is an appropriate one in the study of human choices when the alternatives are complex bundles that vary in many ways. We believe that despite the bewildering complexity of such choice processes, the choices made are lawful. That is, persons share with each other latent principles that govern which attributes of such objects are relevant and how such attributes should be weighted in coming to a summative judgment. To share in this context means not necessarily complete agreement but rather statistical tendencies to behave in their choices in some ways rather than others. We also believe that there may be systematic differences in such principles that mark off one subgroup of a population from another or that mark off types of individuals. Uncovering the shared and idiosyncratic principles of judgments is the objective of factorial surveys.

In simplest terms, factorial surveys consist of providing individuals with contrived hypothetical situations/objects which are to be evaluated according to some process being studied. The construction of such situations/objects follows factorial experimental protocals which ensure orthogonality of all components of the situations/objects. Individuals then respond to a *sample* of all possible contrived situations/objects. It is this latter component of factorial surveys which most strongly marks it as a departure from factorial experiments.

The factorial survey method presumes that the researcher possesses some knowledge of the evaluation process being studied. That is, factorial surveys help one *model* a decision process, but the resulting model depends on the original specification of the process by the researcher. One cannot discover that X is important to a decision process if X was not included in the original specification of that process. As such, factorial surveys will be most fruitfully applied to problems of evaluation which are understood at least tentatively.

This volume presents examples and discussions of the method as it has been applied in diverse applications. The essays chosen illustrate the gradual development of the method over a period of almost a decade, and the reader will soon appreciate the several directions that have been pursued to bring us to this point in the development. Some indication of the degree of development that has occurred in the past few years is found in the chapter by Berk and Rossi. The authors report a study of the sentencing process for convicted criminal offenders first published in 1977. Then they comment on how such research might be "redone" in light of recent factorial survey developments.

The first chapter (Rossi and Anderson) serves as an introduction and elaboration of the method. This chapter may be viewed as a report of the state of the art. The reader will note that subsequent chapters utilize varying degrees of sophistication in applying the factorial survey method, some of which were based on early and incomplete understanding of the method. Even the terminology used has changed as the method has evolved. The most obvious terminological difference between early and later applications is that "factorial objects" (the elements evaluated by respondents) are referred to as "vignettes" in earlier research. We debated the merits of revising all essays to conform to the terminology introduced by Rossi in Chapter 1 against the merits of retaining the original presentation used by authors in first reporting their research. Since one of our goals is to convey the continual evolution and development of the method, we decided on the latter approach.

It was not possible to organize the chapters in a sequence corresponding to the stage of our understanding of the method when the research was conducted or reported. This is because much of the research reported here was conducted at about the same time. Different researchers, however, took different approaches in applying the factorial survey method; some with greater or lesser success. The accumulation of these successes, dead ends, false starts, and mistakes has guided the development of the method, which we hope to convey by the selection of essays in this volume.

The chapters by Meudell, Nock, and Liker discuss research conducted to unravel the process of evaluating the "prestige" or "social standing" of American households. This was one of the first issues to which factorial surveys were applied. Much effort was spent on the design and format of the factorial objects ("vignettes") and the selection of theoretically meaningful factorial dimensions (attributes) to be included on them. Meudell shows how dimensions of extraordinary complexity are specified as components of the prestige evaluation process and how such dimensions are handled analytically.

Two persistent concerns have consumed much of our attention. The first has been the extent to which individuals agree about how they make their evaluations. Nock illustrates several approaches to investigating this issue, as do Rossi and Anderson. We anticipate that this will be an issue to which major attention will be devoted in future developments of the method, as we still lack an agreed-upon technique for studying the problem. The second concern has been the extent to which the factorial object world evokes responses similar to what would be evoked by the "real world." Liker compares prestige evaluations made of hypothetical factorial objects (hypothetical households) with those made of real families and finds remarkable congruence over the evaluation processes applied to both. Still, however, there are some differences, and understanding these will be essential for any researcher using factorial survey methods.

While prestige or social standing is a well-known dimension in social science and has been operationalized and quantified many ways, the research by Alves shows that the factorial survey method allows modeling of social processes which have heretofore eluded rigorous empirical investigation. His research on income fairness evaluations shows that notions of equity and justice are complex social evaluations subject to empirical modeling.

In some applications, the issue is how and why certain conditions and situations alter the meaning of behavior. Garrett asks when and why certain putative child-rearing behaviors come to be defined as child abuse. Similarly, O'Brien asks when certain alcohol drinking behaviors come to be seen as "problem" drinking or alcohol abuse.

Each substantive area investigated required some modification of the method, yet most of the differences seen among the reports of research in this volume reflect specific interests of the researchers. In fact, the method imposes few constraints on the researcher in terms of what may be studied. The diversity of topical areas investigated to date attests to the wide applicability of the method. Yet, as Rossi notes in the conclusion to Chapter 1, there are yet many technical and substantive issues which must be resolved as the factorial survey method is further developed. Future use will undoubtedly lead to fundamental refinements and modifications. The purpose of this volume is to stimulate research that will contribute to those developments.

NOTE

1. A senior honors thesis by Lawrence Mann attempted the approach with ambiguous findings. A more extended attempt by the senior author in collaboration

with Paul M. Siegel and R. W. Hodge in the mid-1960s also foundered on the overly simple vignettes that were used.

REFERENCE

Rossi, P. H., 1951, The Application of Latent Structure Analysis to the Study of Social Stratification. Columbia University.

1

THE FACTORIAL SURVEY APPROACH
An Introduction

PETER H. ROSSI
ANDY B. ANDERSON

The chapters in this volume are concerned with developing an empirically based understanding of certain types of human judgments or evaluations. To evaluate or to judge here means to put a value on some object, placing that object in an ordering. Individuals and human groups are constantly evaluating, placing values implicitly or explicitly on actions, objects, other persons, other groups, institutions, ideas, and so on. Life itself may be viewed as a series of judgment tasks evaluating the sets of alternatives that present themselves at every turn.

The purpose of this book is to explain and illustrate a new method—factorial surveys—for uncovering the principles that lie behind such human evaluations. Factorial surveys are so named because they combine ideas from balanced multivariate experimental designs with sample survey procedures. Few of the constituent parts of the factorial survey technique are totally new; factorial experiments have been around and used for almost a century and sample surveys for at least half that time. The unique feature of the method lies in combining certain features of these existing methods into a powerful tool for the study of human evaluation processes.

The combination of existing techniques has properties that enhance the usefulness of its components. Surveys must usually contend more or less successfully with the multicollinearity of the real world. That is, for example, race and socioeconomic status are usually so closely related in any American community that it is difficult and often impossible to separate the influence of one from the influence of the other. In an experimental or constructed world, factors can be built as orthogonal. In the usual factorial experiment only a few dimensions and only a few levels within each dimension can be used in each experiment, a disability that lessens considerably the resemblance between factorial experiments and real-world conditions. Orthogonality in experiments is often bought at the price of oversimplified experimental conditions.

But factorial surveys are not so limited. The factors in such survey designs can be made essentially orthogonal, making it possible to observe their effects uncontaminated by the usual overlapping in the real world. And relatively large numbers of factors and levels within factors can be used, enhancing the resemblance between real and experimental worlds. Factorial surveys more faithfully capture the complexity of real life and the conditions of real human choices and judgments and at the same time provide the ability to identify clearly the separate influences of the many factors that go into such judgments and choices. In short, from the experimental tradition, the factorial survey borrows and adapts the concept of factor orthogonality and from the survey tradition it borrows the greater richness of detail and complexity that characterizes real-life circumstances.

The problems to which factorial surveys are addressed are longstanding in the social sciences. It is obvious that humans evaluate continually, and it is equally obvious that such judgments are neither totally independent nor totally idiosyncratic. That is, a person tends to make judgments that are in some sense consistent, and each individual does not follow completely idiosyncratic rules in making judgments. In short, there is prima facie evidence that human evaluations are in part socially determined (that is, shared with others) and in part governed by individuality, the mix varying from topic to topic.

Another way of putting these assumptions is to say that we believe human judgments in most areas are structured and that a critical question for social scientists is how best to uncover the structures that underlie such judgments. There are several specific meanings to the idea that human judgments are structured. First, we believe there are a relatively small number of characteristics of objects to which persons pay attention in making judgments about those objects. Thus in choosing among automobiles, not all characteristics of cars are salient. By and large, car buyers pay attention to a relatively small set of characteristics of the cars they choose among, while there may be a seemingly infinite number of ways in which one car differs from another. Second, we also believe that for many domains judgments are socially structured, that there is more or less agreement among persons on how much weight should be given to relevant characteristics and on how such characteristics should be combined in order to make judgments. Thus for example, car buyers generally may weigh fuel efficiency as more important than driver comfort. The third meaning of structure is that each individual tends toward consistency in his or her own judgments, departing in a relatively regular way from the socially defined consensus on how such judgments should be made. Thus one individual may weigh fuel efficiency more or less heavily than is typical for all car buyers.

Although the first meaning of structure in human judgment given in the last paragraph appears as an assumption in the conceptualization of factorial surveys, the other forms of structure are measured empirically and can exist as matters of degree, and hence a set of judgments can be more or less structured (compared to other sets of judgments on other topics). The social component of judgment structure is represented in factorial surveys by a set of weights attached to the characteristics of objects being judged and the calculus or model that represents how such weights are combined in arriving at summary judgments. This is a general expression which models judgment processes that are common to the individuals being studied on the topic in question, the social component in judgments.

The individual component is assumed to have internal consistency as well that can be expressed as relatively constant and consistent deviations of each individual from the general (social) tendencies expressed in the social model described above.

We stress that the procedures used do not guarantee that either the social or individual components of judgments will be present or present to some predetermined extent in any given problem. Rather, it is quite possible that there may be no structure at all in a set of judgments or that a given set of judgments manifests either strong or weak structures. Indeed, one should expect that presented with a set of completely unfamiliar objects (for example, food from an exotic cuisine), individuals may share little in common with each other in their judgments and may be inconsistent in the judgments they make about the objects.

Persons as Evaluators

Human existence may be viewed in part as threading one's way through a succession of choice points, the outcomes of which are

mostly trivial but also a few critical ones having important consequences for subsequent life experiences. Each such choice point
involves making implicit or explicit judgments about the relative
desirability of the alternatives involved. One can divide human
existence into time units so small that individuals are constantly
making choices about what to do in the next time interval, a
circumstance that completely contradicts human experiences.
Choices are being made continually, but most do not surface to be
experienced as self-conscious choosing. The very trivial choices are
made "automatically"; even the less trivial, such as choosing which
street to take to work, may be settled automatically by activating
long-standing decisions about which is the "better" way to go,
decisions which have become habits.

Those choices that surface as deliberate weighing and evaluation
of alternatives tend to have more important consequences for the
future. Deciding whether or not to take a particular job, to marry a
particular person, to buy this car or that house, and similar decisions
may involve explicit weighing of the positive and negative aspects of
each alternative, attempting to arrive at an expected net balance that
would clearly point in one direction or another. In some cases, the
choice process does not appear to the individual as deliberation, but
rather as an intuitive "flash" in which one choice suddenly is
revealed as the most appropriate. Whether or not a choice is
experienced as deliberate is not critical for present purposes; all that
is necessary is that choices are made in a situation in which there
exists alternative courses of action.

Psychologists have developed standardized techniques for uncovering principles of judgments for classes of objects which differ
only with respect to a single dimension. For example, objects of the
same size but of different weights may be used in a weight judging
task in which certain task conditions are experimentally manipulated
(such as placement of a standard or comparison weight) and judgments about relative heaviness elicited. The task of modeling such
judgments is relatively simple in the typical one-dimensional experiment described above. The modeling task becomes more complicated when the objects differ with respect to many attributes.
Judgments about social objects typically involve objects that have
many traits on which they vary. When many dimensions, each those
with many levels, are used, the techniques and experimental designs
of the psychophysics laboratory break down. Perhaps the social

objects judgment problem is best presented through an illustration.

In deciding which house to buy among the alternatives available at a point in time in a housing market, a potential buyer may be presented with a set of houses that range in purchase prices, costs of upkeep and taxes, locations, structural designs, neighborhoods, interior conditions, distances to frequently visited destinations, and so on. If all of the relevant characteristics of houses were perfectly correlated, decision making could be simplified by adopting a rule, for example, to be guided by price. But the housing market is considerably more confusing, for within the same price range houses vary considerably in size, location, structural design, and so on.

Hence, making housing decisions implies explicit or implicit subdecisions on what is more or less important and what features can be traded off to obtain more important and more desirable features. In other words, the specific features of a house are combined in some way to arrive at an overall evaluation that allows comparisons with other houses.[1]

The judgments made—among houses or anything else—are rarely made completely *de novo*. That is, such choices are guided at least in part by the existence of more or less fixed preference schedules among objects and actions belonging to relatively homogeneous classes. Thus one may have a more or less fixed preference schedule for foods in which some are consistently ranked above others, a preference for ranch-style houses over Cape Cod cottages, an ordering of television programs, and so on, each preference schedule consisting of an ordering of objects belonging to a class in terms of their desirability, goodness, or some other evaluative dimension. Were only one preference schedule activated at a time in the making of complex choices, then it would be easy to understand decisions made; one of the main problems is how preference schedules concerning different qualities or classes of objects are combined for a single decision involving the several schedules that are activated. Thus a preference for free-standing single-family homes may conflict with a preference for easy access to relatives and friends.

To re-emphasize a point made earlier, the issue for social science presented by the seeming heterogeneity of judgments is to discern what may be the underlying order to such judgments. In other words, what information is used in making judgments. How may such information be used? And how do individuals differ in the ways in which information of different sorts is combined?

The ultimate origins of preference schedules are not an issue in this context, but one may speculate that some are determined by biological makeup (as is likely for the panhuman preference for meat over cereals), some are largely socially determined (for example, the widespread American preference for beef over lamb), and others are forged out of the particular experiences of individuals (as, for example, an individual's preference for beef stew over pot roast). We can also assume that such preference schedules are not fixed forever; styles and fashions change, and individuals are obviously influenced by such changes. In addition, individuals may shift their preferences independently, perhaps out of experience with past choices or for some other reason.

To some degree each individual may be viewed as having an idiosyncratic set of preference schedules; indeed this is the basis of the common observation that there are differences in taste. Yet the features common to all preference schedules must be considerable, accounting in large part for observable uniformities in market behavior, media listening and viewing ratings, and similar phenomena. Indeed, it is problematic whether or not the interindividual similarities in preference schedules dominate interindividual differences. Hence, it may well be that cultural differences in food preference schedules dominate the total amount of variance in individual food preferences.

This can be expressed more formally by letting each judgment, J_i, be as shown in 1.0.

$$J_i = b_0 + b_1 X_{i1} + \ldots + b_k X_{ik} + e_i \qquad [1.0]$$

The object is characterized by a set of variables $X_1, X_2, \ldots, X_k$. Given specific values of these variables, there will be a predicted judgment of $\hat{J}_i$, usually based on an OLS solution to the regression of J_i on the object dimensions. That conditional expectation $\hat{J}_i$ is equivalent to $(b_0 + b_1 X_{i1} + \ldots + b_k X_{ik})$, and in regression theory it is sometimes referred to as the systematic component. The residual, e_i, represents the deviation of an individual judgment, J_i, from that predicted given the X_k characteristics of the object and the best-fitting estimates of the b coefficients. If the model is correct and if all individuals rendering judgments are in agreement about the proper judgment given any particular set of object characteristics, the error term will be zero. Of course, in practice error terms represent a variety of influences: individual errors or idiosyncracies, measurement error, the influence of variables omitted from the equation, intrinsic uncertainty, the consequences of specification error, and others. But under the assumption that only individual deviations from the social calculus are involved, we can view the expression for a judgment as being comprising two parts, one part a function of the characteristics and the socially agreed-upon weights attached to the characteristics and one part representing individual deviations from that concensus. To the extent that social concensus prevails, Σe_i^2 will be small and the resulting regression equation will have a high R^2 value and the b coefficients will represent the concensus weights. In addition, $1-R^2$ will represent, among other things, the individual deviations from concensus. In practice, to disentangle individual deviations from all the other things in the residual requires additional analysis using variables characterizing the judges, for example, to increase the explained component of J_i. The point here is not how we do this, but only that this formulation offers a way to estimate the social and individual components of social judgments elicited by factorial surveys.

Modeling the Social Component of Judgments, J_j

We will define the "social components" of judgments to be the best estimates of individual judgments and judgment processes that can be made by pooling the judgments made by individuals in a population (or more usually by a sample of a population). Assuming that each object is being judged as having more or less of some value, and that each object can be described in terms of a limited number of dimensions, we can estimate an expected rating for each object by modeling how the individuals in the population studied used the dimensions to arrive at their judgments. The regression solution is shown in 1.0 because of its simplicity and also because there is some evidence that persons use an additive principle in arriving at their overall judgments of complex objects (Anderson, 1974).

Note that the formulation in 1.0 does not prejudge whether the dimensions are quantitative variables (for example, income) or qualitative (such as sex). Qualitative variables can be represented as binary variables (dummy variables), in which case the associated b coefficient is the increment (or decrement) in the estimated judgment that is received by an object that has the characteristic in question.

Dimensions, X, may also be formulated as interaction terms between pairs of other dimensions if nonadditivity is suspected, but this usually compromises orthogonality.

Other representations of social judgment processes are also possible. For example, given that the rating scales used are often short and hence subject to truncation bias (as in the example discussed later in this chapter), logistic regression forms may be more appropriate in particular cases. Indeed, the full repertorie of multivariate methods may be employed, the selection being governed by substantive judgments about which best represents the ways dimensions and their interactions are combined to make judgments.

If the set of judgments that go into the estimation of the parameters of 1.0 are actual judgments of concrete objects, then one can expect that the dimensions of the objects will be more or less correlated. For example, more expensive houses will tend to be larger, set on larger plots, be in better repair, be more likely to have such amenities as air-conditioning and double-glazed windows. Similarly, judgments of convicted criminals would involve criminals whose characteristics (dimensions) are highly intercorrelated. Hence the estimates to be derived from the analysis of real-world judgments are likely to be rendered unstable by the multicollinearity among the dimensions of the objects being rated. And there is no generally appropriate way to ascertain the separate and distinct contributions of correlated independent variables.

The factorial survey approach solves the problems caused by such real-world multicollinearity by constructing sets of objects to be rated whose dimensions are uncorrelated or orthogonal or approximately so. How this is accomplished will be described in detail in later sections of this chapter. For the time being, however, the reader should bear in mind that the parameters of 1.0, when derived from a factorial survey, are not affected (or only minimally so) by collinearity among the dimensions that describe objects to be rated.

In addition, the factorial survey approach standardizes the judgments made. Real-world judgments on housing purchases may well be dichotomous: Either a house is purchased or it is not. Or criminal court sentences may be probation, dismissal, a declaration of innocence, sentences of varying lengths as well as to different kinds of jails and prisons. In a factorial survey the judgments are made in the same way for all objects that are judged and range along a continuum.

Modeling Subgroup Variation in Judgments

While equation 1.0 models the overall judgment processes to be found within a sample, it does so at the expense of ignoring structured ways in which sample members may vary in such processes. In particular, subgroups within the sample—characterized by gender, race, socioeconomic level, region, or some other characteristic—may vary in a number of ways, as follows:

1. *Judgment Thresholds:*	Subgroups may vary in average levels of judgments rendered. For example, women might judge all examples of possible sexual harassment as more serious than men, or

$$\bar{J}_q \neq \bar{J}_m \quad \text{where q and m are subgroups}$$

2. *Judgment Variance:*	Subgroups may differ in the variability of their judgments, or

$$\sigma^2_{J_q} \neq \sigma^2_{J_m}$$

3. *Judgment Error:*	Subgroups may vary in the extent of stochastic error, or

$$1 - R^2_q \neq 1 - R^2_m$$

4. *Judgment Processes:*	Subgroups vary in the weights given to different dimensions, or

$$b_{kq} \neq b_{km}$$

Subgroup variations in judgment thresholds can be easily discerned by adding variables identifying respondents' characteristics to equation 1.0, as in 2.0 below:

$$J_i = b_0 + \sum_{p=1}^{k} b_k X_{ik} + \sum_{p=k+1}^{R} b_R C_{iR} + e_i \qquad [2.0]$$

where the various C_R are characteristics of the individual respondents such as age, sex, education, or other variables thought to influence judgments. Since the constructed factorial objects defined by the X_k are mutually orthogonal to the C_R, the addition of the C_R terms to the equation should leave the b coefficients attached to the X_k relatively unchanged. The only effect should be a reduction in Σe^2; therefore, the statistical tests will be more powerful (that is, they will have a lower probability of a Type II error). In effect, we have produced a decomposition into the social and individual components. From the original equation 1.0 we can construct a residual $e = J_i - \hat{J}_i$, and now e_i can be further reduced by entering the C_R terms into the equation as shown in 2.0. The C_R terms will be approximately orthogonal to the X_i but will not necessarily be orthogonal to each other.[2] Some of these characteristics may be qualitative, as in sex or race, in which case the associated b coefficient is the increment or decrement to expected ratings given by the subgroups defined by that qualitative characteristic. Thus the b coefficient attached to being male ($C_i = 1$ if male), for example, would show the increment or decrement to the judgments given by males, as contrasted to females. In other cases in which the characteristic may be quantitative variables, the associated b coefficients indicate the rate of change in the judgments with each unit increase in the characteristic in question. Thus with each added year, people may regard crimes in general as more serious (or less serious).

Discerning whether there are subgroup differences in the variances of ratings requires dividing the sample into the relevant subgroups and computing the variances of ratings so segregated.

Under some circumstances, an investigator might want to remove interindividual or intersubgroup mean and variance differentials from the judgment ratings. Standardizing ratings by setting each individual mean equal to zero and each individual's variance to 1 will accomplish the desired standardization. Note that a few of the studies described in the chapters that follow employ standardization, decisions made on substantive grounds.

Several alternative strategies are available to estimate other subgroup differences. In the case of categorical subgroups, such as sex or race, one may simply do separate regressions of 2.0 within each subgroup. The resulting b_k coefficients compared across subgroups indicate the extent to which different dimensions' weight are employed by, for example, blacks and whites in arriving at judgments. The b_k coefficient differences across subgroups indicate the extent to which within-subgroup characteristics C_R add or subtract from the overall judgment. Thus, it may well be the case that older respondents rate crimes more seriously in one subgroup and less seriously in another subgroup.

Comparing R^2 across subgroup equations also allows comparisons of the amounts of error in judgment across subgroups. For example, a finding that college graduates have much the same b coefficients as high school graduates but higher R^2 indicates that both groups weigh dimensions alike but that college graduates make fewer "errors" in applying weights as they make their judgments.

An alternative strategy would be to construct interaction terms between factorial object dimensions and respondent characteristics, as in 2.1 below:

$$ J_i = b_0 + \sum_{p=1}^{k} b_{k_i} X_k + \sum_{p=k+1}^{k} b_R C_R + \Sigma b_s I_s + e_i \qquad [2.1] $$

where X_k is a vector of vignette characteristics, X
     C_R is a vector of respondent characteristics, C
     I_s is a vector of interaction terms I formed
        between pairs of X and C
     e_i is the usual stochastic error term

Equation 2.1 has the advantage of being more versatile but the disadvantage of the usual difficulties encountered in using interaction terms: The equation becomes unwieldy, and multicollinearity is increased.

Modeling Individual Variations in Judgment

The line between subgroups and individuals becomes somewhat fuzzy as the sizes of subgroups become very small. Indeed, an extreme form of equation 2.1 would be to enter a dummy variable for each individual capturing the extent to which each respondent varies from the total sample in threshold judgments.[3]

Individual variation in judgment principles, however, can be more directly modeled by computing equation 2.0 across the judgments of each individual, producing as many regression equations as there are respondents in the sample studied. Of course, this can be done only if each individual rates somewhat more objects than there are X dimensions, a usual feature of the vignette studies.

Under this interpretation, equation 2.0 becomes modified as shown in 2.2:

$$\hat{J}_{ij} = b_0 + b_1 X_1 + b_2 X_2 \ldots + b_k X_k \qquad [2]$$

where $\hat{J}_{ij}$ is the estimated rating for object j for individual i and i is fixed

b_0 is the intercept term for individual i

b_k are the weights given by individual i in that person's ratings

Since equation 2.2 is computed only over the ratings made by each individual, the parameters computed refer only to his or her rating principles. $R^2{}_i$ computed for equation 2.2 indicates the amount of wriggle or error in the judgments of individual i. Thus a rigidly structured set of judgments for an individual who always applied the same weights in the precise way suggested by the model to every judgment would lead to an $R^2{}_i$ approaching 1.0, and a person making random judgments would produce a corresponding value approaching 0.0.

The b_k coefficients for an individual may be used to characterize that individual. The vector of coefficients, b_k, when entered into a factor matrix in which rows are individuals and columns are b_k coefficients, may then be factor analyzed, Q-factor fashion, to arrive at typologies of individuals characterized by similarities in the ways in which they make judgments.[4] There are other ways of accomplishing the empirically based grouping, such as cluster analysis or nonmetric multidimensional scaling.

An alternative form of 2.2 is given below in which individuals are characterized by the ways in which they differ from the pooled judgments of a sample as follows:

$$D_{ij} = J_{ij} - \hat{J}_j = b_{i0} + b_{i1} X_1 + b_{i2} X_2 \ldots + b_{ik} X_k + e \qquad [2.3]$$

in which i is not allowed to vary and in which the coefficients have interpretations which refer only to individual i

Equation 2.3 transforms the ratings into differences from the estimated value of a rating, as based on the total sample (J_j), those differences being regressed on the X_k characteristics of the factorial objects. The b_{ik} coefficients resulting from 2.3 are then interpretable as individual variations from the social judgment principles. In further analyses, these coefficients may be treated in the same way as those resulting from the application of 2.2.

Studying Actual Judgments

It would appear that "real-life" judgments would be the most appropriate data for researchers to use in attempting to implement the ideas laid out in the previous section. Thus, for example, in a study of how criminal punishments are made it might appear to be relevant to examine the actual sentencing decisions of judges in a criminal court; indeed, any of the superior courts in even medium-sized cities would produce a superabundance of cases of sentencing decisions for study. However, studying such judgments presents a number of real difficulties: First, the distributions of cases and their characteristics that would come before the typical superior court are not the most useful. For example, one of the problems criminologists often pose is whether judges are sensitive to class or race in their sentencing behavior or whether they are responding more to the "legal" characteristics of the cases before them (that is, nature of evidence, credibility of witnesses, and so on). In any typical run of cases before the courts, there are very few of the critical cases that would enable one to obtain substantial amounts of empirical evidence on the issue; there are few, if any, middle-class burglars or college graduate muggers or female rapists. In short, in the real world, the various relevant characteristics of criminal cases tend to be correlated.

A second characteristic of real-world judgments is that they tend to be constrained by factors that may have little to do with the objects being judged. Thus, for example, judges cannot give any sentence to convicted criminals but are guided by limits set in the criminal code. Similarly, home purchasers cannot buy any house on the market, only those within income constraints usually as judged by local mortgage lenders. Preferences for spouses are constrained by legal prohibitions against polygamous marriages, the necessity for mutual consent on the part of both parties, and so on. Hence judgments as expressed in real-world choices tend to be constrained by what may be regarded as situational elements which are extraneous to the judgment.[5]

A third characteristic of real-life choices is that they are often rare events in the lives of individuals, especially those choices in which special interest may reside. Ordinarily, an individual makes few spouse choices in a lifetime, a few more housing choices, considerably more automobile purchases, and so on. An important implication of the general formulation of the previous section is that we need many observations on choices made by individuals in order to be able to uncover underlying principles.

All of these considerations argue for moving away from the observation of actual choices or evaluations made in real-life situations to a contrived but enriched set of choices in which individuals are asked to make many judgments on sets of social objects that include combinations of characteristics that are rarely encountered in "real-life" choice circumstances.

The Concept of "Factorial Object Universe"

In order to observe fully the ways in which the several dimensions that describe an object are used in making judgments about that class of objects, we would want judgments of all possible combinations of values of those dimensions. The full set of such combinations defines a "factorial object universe. To clarify the discussion which follows, we establish the following definitions:

Dimension—a quality of social objects or a variable characterizing such objects that can vary in kind or amount, such as sex, income, distance, and criminal actions.

Levels—the specific values that a dimension may take. For example, "Male" is a level of the dimension "Sex," "$10,000" is a level of the dimension "income," "burglary" is a level of the dimension "criminal actions."

Object—a unit being judged that is described in terms of a single level for every dimension. An "object" may consist of this statement: "A male who earns $10,000 per year and who has been convicted of burglary."

Judgment—rating, rank, or other valuation given by a respondent to an object.

Factorial Object Universe—the set of all unique objects formed by all possible combinations of one level from each of the dimensions.

Factorial Object Sample—an unbiased sample of the objects in a factorial object universe.

Respondent Subsample—an unbiased sample of a factorial object universe that is given to a single respondent for judgment.

To simplify the discussion, the adjective "factorial" is often dropped in the discussion that follows; hence "object sample" or "object universe" should be understood as referring to factorial object universes and factorial object samples.

The number of objects in a factorial object universe is easily calculated, given the number of dimensions, k, and the number of levels, q, within each dimension, as, $\prod_1^k \pi_{qk}$. Thus if the factorial survey is designed as a study of the status judgments of families, characterized by one of 10 levels of income, one of 24 occupations of breadwinners, and two races, the total number of unique objects in the factorial object universe is $(10)(24)(2)=480$. It can also be easily appreciated that the sizes of factorial object universes can get very large. For example, if we add to the previous example a dimension of family size with 10 levels, we increase the universe to 4,800, and if we also add occupations for breadwinners' spouses (an additional 24 levels), the size of the universe of increased in 115,200. It is this exponential increase of the size of factorial object universes that makes impractical the traditional application of factorial designs to studies of judgments.

There are several critically important characteristics of a factorial object universe. First, the dimensions are approximately orthogonal, or $r_{k,s}=0.0$ (where $s\neq k$), each level in a dimension appearing equally frequently with each level in every other dimension. It follows from this characteristic that unbiased factorial object samples and respondent subsamples will also tend asymptotically toward orthogonality among dimensions, varying from that characteristic within the limits of sampling error.

Second, the distributions of levels along any dimension, k, will be rectangular; that is, any level within a dimension will appear in the factorial universe as frequently as any other level within that dimension. Indeed, if there are q levels within a dimension, then each level will appear with a probability equal to 1/q.[6] Again, this characteristic of the factorial object universe is reproduced asymptotically in both object samples and respondent samples. In these two respects, a factorial object universe is very different from the "real world" in which distributions of, for example, family income are far from rectangular and in which there is a strong positive correlation between, family income and breadwinners' occupations. However, it is precisely this difference from real-world situations which constitutes an advantage, since persons who are asked to judge factorial object populations are thereby asked to make judgments that reveal more clearly the weightings and preferences used as the bases for such judgments.

It is the approximate orthogonality among dimensions that makes it possible to disentangle the separate effects upon judgments of dimensions that are ordinarily (in the real-world context) correlated. Rectangularity allows observations to be made along all segments of a dimension, such that the response of judgments to variations in a dimension can be estimated more efficiently as to both size and form.

A "factorial object sample" is an unbiased sample of the members of a "factorial object universe" that preserves the essential characteristics of the object population—namely, that the correlations among dimensions asymptotically approach zero as the size of the sample increases and that the distribution of objects along any of the dimensions tends asymptotically toward rectangular. We will argue that because such samples have the same properties (asymptotically) as the populations from which they were drawn, analyses of such samples will result in estimates that asymptotically converge on population parameters. The application of sampling makes it possible to handle many dimensions and many levels.

A "respondent subsample" is a subsample of the above drawn in a random manner for the purpose of eliciting judgments from a given respondent. Thus individual respondents are given relatively small subsamples of factorial objects that can be put together with other respondent subsamples to form relatively large samples of factorial object populations.

The Judging Task

In one type of factorial design experiment with repeated measures, each respondent is asked to judge each of the factorial objects in a factorial object universe. For example, a simple study in which two status dimensions are being studied, educational attainment in three levels and occupation in three levels, there are nine distinct factorial objects, as follows:

Education	Occupation
High	High
High	Medium
High	Low
Medium	High
Medium	Medium
Medium	Low
Low	High
Low	Medium
Low	Low

The judgment task set for each respondent might be to rate each unique factorial object according to its "social status" or "prestige standing." The numerical form of the judgment made may also vary, from magnitude estimation methods as recommended by Stevens (1957) to simple two- or three-point rating scales.

Given a sufficient number of respondents who have judged the factorial object universe, described above, the modes of analysis are fairly straightforward. In the experimental tradition, ANOVA would be appropriate along with appropriate counterpart multiple regression methods. (We will return to the topic of analytic methods later.)

While the simple example holds for small factorial object universes up to about 50 unique objects, it becomes an impractical procedure whenever factorial object universes become as complicated as one would like. For example, the *Dictionary of Occupational Titles* records more than 30,000 distinctly different job titles, and the decennial census detailed occupational codes recognize about 600 occupational titles, many of which are residual catchalls such as "clerks, typists and other clerical workers not elsewhere classified." Educational attainment might be viewed in terms of successive years of accomplishment ranging from 0 years of schooling through as many as 20 years, or in terms of finishing recognized units of schooling—for example, "completed elementary school" or "completed junior college."

If a factorial object universe is defined as comprising 40 distinct occupational groupings and 16 educational attainment levels, then there are 640 unique factorial objects in the factorial object population. Even this falls far short of the full detail of a world in which there are many jobs and in which status is affected in addition by ethnicity, consumption patterns, income, and other characteristics. Even the simple factorial object universe of size 640 is not practical as a judgment task, let alone factorial object populations that comprise millions of unique factorial objects.[7]

However, there is no strong argument that requires each respondent to rate every factorial object in the set. Fractional replication methods are often used in experimental designs and have much to recommend them, especially for relatively small factorial object universes. For very large factorial object universes, random sampling of the objects can be used, with each respondent-judge being given an independently drawn random sample of factorial objects, respondent subsamples, as defined in the last section. (Lest the reader's mind boggle at the vision of drawing random samples from the factorial object sets in the tradition of colored balls drawn from urns, the actual methods of drawing samples are much simpler, requiring only access to a reasonably sized mainframe computer.)

Analyzing Judgments

If each of n respondent rates separate respondent subsamples of m factorial objects, the resulting data are $nm=N$ judgments, J_i. Since adding random samples to random samples simply produces larger random samples, it makes sense to pool the judgments, producing a single sample of judgments of size N.

If we proceed to draw each respondent subsample by simple random sampling (with replacement), each of the respondent subsamples will rarely contain identical objects. Indeed, for very large object universes, the probability that any unique object will appear in a subsample of size m is m over the size of the factorial object universe, a very small number. Nor is it likely that any two respondents will both rate any given object. However, any two respondent subsamples will resemble each other in orthogonality and in the proportions of objects manifesting any given level—both features, of course, being identical only within the limits of sampling error. A factorial object sample that is made up by pooling the m judgments made by each of the n respondents is also a simple random sample, but now of size $N=nm$, with sampling errors that are largely a function of the sample size.

The task of analyzing the resulting factorial object sample has been described in OLS terms in the previous section. Hence one solution to the analysis task is to select the appropriate forms from among equations 2.0 to 2.3 and to specify those equations in terms of the particular data set involved. An illustration of such an analysis is given in the next section of this chapter.

It should be noted, however, that the OLS formulation has been chosen mainly for simplicity and because there is some theoretical reason for believing that judgments at least in some domains are represented reasonably as additive combinations of weighted dimensions and levels within dimensions. However, one need not be completely fixed on the OLS formulation. There are circumstances when it would make sense on theoretical grounds to choose to transform dimensions in order to model nonlinear or multiplicative relations of dimensions to judgments. We will see in the example shown in the next section that a logistic representation is also a reasonable way to analyze that particular data set.

Although the object sample may be drawn in an unbiased fashion, the corresponding samples of judgments are not independent of each other. The fact that each respondent produces m judgments and that it is likely that such judgments may be affected by response sets within each respondent means that some degree of intrarespondent correlation may be present. In one of the chapters of this volume, the authors test their data set for such correlations and contrast results for data subsets in which such intrarespondent correlations cannot be present.[8]

Although the factorial objects to be judged are presented in random order to each respondent, there is also the potential for serial correlation to develop among the judgments of individual respondents. For example, because the first few factorial objects presented to a respondent for judgment by chance may contain factorial objects that are very much alike, a respondent may decide to shift his or her frame of reference in judging, alternating between being generous and strict. Such a serial order dependency among judgments may appear in some data sets, although in the examples contained in this volume serial order correlations within respondents appear not to be present to any appreciable extent.

Perhaps the best way to discuss further the analysis process is to present a specific empirical example. We turn to such an exercise in the next section.

Measuring the Social Definition of
Sexual Harassment: An Example of
the Factorial Survey Approach

The Substantive Issues

One of the major applications of the factorial survey approach to the measurement of social judgments will be to uncover variations in the social definitions of phenomena that change. Currently, our society is redefining relations between spouses or between spouses and children and developing new standards for what should be considered child or spouse abuse. For persons responsible for the administration of law or for the formulation of new legislation or administrative regulations, the issues in particular cases often become whether the official is enforcing his or her own personal (and idiosyncratic) notions of what constitutes, for example, spouse abuse or whether he or she is simply carrying out the consensus of some larger constituency. In such circumstances factorial surveys can provide data on what are the social definitions of child abuse or spouse abuse, possibly to provide guidance to legislators attempting to bring law into line with popular consensus or to advocates who want to change social definitions to provide legitimacy for certain actions. Several such studies will be discussed in detail in the chapters that follow, including studies of the social definition of child abuse, acceptable levels of drinking among college students, and appropriate punishments for convicted felons.

One such area of current controversy concerns the social definition of sexual harassment. At the one extreme, some support the view that any and all contact across gender lines within certain contexts should be free of any sexual content. The contexts which should be free of any sexual content include the work place, schools, and other public places. At the other extreme, there are those who draw the line between acceptable and unacceptable behavior at the use of threats and force, regarding sexual advances unaccompanied by the use of or threat of use of power and/or force as acceptable cross-gender behavior in such contexts.

The issue of sexual harassment and its definition arises more and more frequently in schools and work places as persons who consider themselves to have been victims of sexual harassment advance such complaints as the bases of requests for punitive actions to be taken against alleged offenders. Indeed, in some institutional settings the number of complaints filed with grievance bodies has been growing so rapidly that there is considerable pressure to develop more or less formal codes of conduct to serve as guides to members about how one should behave and also to provide guidance to grievance bodies about when serious violations of appropriate standards have occurred.

One of the institutional settings in which the issue of sexual harassment has surfaced is the University of California at Santa Barbara. A few extremely unpleasant cases of males forcing their attentions on women, usually students, led the administration to appoint a committee to investigate complaints about the prevalence of sexual harassment and to suggest standards of conduct. The committee report was met with mixed reactions; on the one hand, there were those who praised the committee for defining the university context as normatively free from sexual overtones and for asserting that any departure from that standard is an instance of sexual harassment. On the other hand, there were those who asserted that the committee went much too far ahead of current opinion in the university community.

To cast some light on the issue, Professors Richard Berk and Marilyn Brewer undertook a factorial survey designed in collaboration with students enrolled in a graduate seminar on evaluation research.[9] Consultation on design and analysis issues was provided by the senior author and Eleanor Weber-Burdin at the Social and Demographic Research Institute.[10]

Defining the Factorial Object Set

The major task in the design of a factorial survey is to decide on what dimensions and levels to use. Since the factorial object population is defined as the set of all possible combinations of levels across dimensions, whatever is decided about dimensions and levels within dimensions also sets what is to be the factorial object universe.

Deciding on what should be included as a dimension or a level is an issue that can be decided only by drawing upon existing substantive knowledge. Thus, a factorial survey approach to the sentencing decisions of criminal court judges would draw on studies of how judges make their decisions and on the theoretical literature on sentencing. In the case of sexual harassment, there are few empirical studies and some polemical literature. In addition, since the controversy had arisen locally, Berk and Brewer and their collaborators had fairly good ideas of the points of disagreement among disputing parties.

Although the issue of sexual harassment in principle is one which could affect both genders as victims and as aggressors, in practice the vast majority of complaints are brought by women against men. Furthermore, the issue often has been posed as the inappropriate exercise of institutionally based power. Hence while sexual harassment might conceivably occur between persons defined in any possible combination of authority relations, most instances consist of a person of high status making inappropriate use of his position and derived power to obtain sexual favors from a woman of lower status in the organization.

Recognizing that the main interest in defining sexual harassment lies in relationships involving a higher-status male and a lower-status female, the first major design decision was to focus exclusively on relationships involving men in superior and women in inferior power positions. Accordingly, two dimensions were defined as follows:

Dimension A: Status of Male
Levels
    1   Single graduate student
    2   Single graduate student TA
    3   Married graduate student
    4   Married graduate student TA
    5   Single 30-year-old professor
    6   Married 30-year-old professor
    7   Single 45-year-old professor
    8   Married 45-year-old professor
    9   Single 65-year-old professor
    10 Married 65-year-old professor

Dimension B: Status of Female
Levels
    1   Single graduate student
    2   Freshman
    3   Senior
    4   Married graduate student

Note that Dimensions A and B contain information on the marital status of all of the male statuses and for some of the female statuses. This information was added because making sexual advances might be seen by some as more appropriate for single males vis-a-vis single females than otherwise.

It is important to bear in mind that the decisions that led to the two dimensions defined above might easily have taken different directions under other investigators. For example, three dimensions might have been used, one defining the power relationship, another describing sex, and a third the marital status of a person. The fully crossed combinations of these three dimensions would have allowed, for example, some of the objects describing women acting aggressively toward men and women in positions of power exercising such power (implicitly) in cross-sex relationships. In addition, the objects would also contain instances in which within-sex harassment would be at issue, a wrinkle that would have changed the character of the study considerably. These considerations are not discussed here in order to dispute the judgments that were actually made in the design of the study; rather, they are raised to demonstrate that the design of a factorial object universe is to be undertaken carefully and with special consideration to the substantive issues involved.

The gender of the males in Dimension A was designated by generating a set of male names to be attached randomly to each description. A set of female names was similarly generated to be attached to Dimension B.[11]

Reasoning that whether or not a given act might be seen as harassment could depend on the previous relationships between the males and females involved, a third dimension was created to capture the previous relationship of the two persons involved. The relationship was stated in terms of the woman's relationship to the man, as follows:

Dimension C: Woman's Relationship to Man
   Levels
      1   Had rarely had occasion to talk to
      2   Had gone out several times with
      3   Often had occasion to talk with
      4   Had been regularly dating
      5   Had been close friends with
      6   After being asked, had declined to go out with

A fourth dimension concerned the context in which the alleged harassment took place. What might seem clearly harassment in the context of an office or in the coffee shop may be somewhat ambiguous in the context of a party. Dimension D was defined as follows:

Dimension D: Social Setting
Levels
1   When class had ended she approached him
2   After class he asked her if she could stay a minute
3   On the way out of class they started talking
4   She went to his office after class
5   She went to his office because he had asked to see her
6   As she was walking to her next class she bumped into him
7   While in the library, they ran into each other and started talking
8   Between classes they were in the coffee shop
9   They were at a restaurant
10 They were both at a party

Another set of "extenuating" circumstances claimed by some as explaining why some acts were misinterpreted as "harassment" had to do with the extent to which the woman in question seemed to invite a sexual advance. Hence Dimension E, described below, included statements that suggested different levels of receptivity to sexual advances on the part of the woman involved.

Dimension E: Woman's "Receptivity"
Levels
1   She seemed worried and asked about grades
2   She asked about grades but did not appear concerned
3   She talked about some ideas she had from class
4   She said that she enjoyed and looked forward to his class
5   She invited him to a party she was having
6   She said it was nice to see him outside of the stuffy classroom
7   She said she enjoyed talking with him and hoped they would be friends
8   During their conversation her language became quite suggestive
9   While they talked, she frequently touched his arm
10 As they talked, she repeatedly brushed up against him
11 She made it obvious she would do anything for a good grade
12 Blank text

Note that level 12, "blank text," indicated that one of the dimension levels is the omission of any description from that dimension. In this case a fixed proportion of all factorial objects (8.3 percent) would contain no statement of the woman's alleged receptivity.

The remaining three dimensions all concern the male's behavior toward the female student, respectively classified as verbal behavior, physical acts, and degrees of threat. These three dimensions define together the sequence of events that might constitute harassment in the views of some of the subjects.

Dimension F: Male's Verbal Behavior
   Levels
      1   He asked her about her other courses
      2   He remarked that she was making good progress in class
      3   Straying from the subject, he remarked that she reminded him of an old girlfriend
      4   He suggested that they go out sometime to dinner and a movie
      5   He asked her to go home with him
      6   He said he looked forward to working with her
      7   He suggested that they go to a place where they could speak more privately
      8   He told her a dirty joke
      9   He said "Your personality is absolutely magnetic"
      10   He said her hair was extremely attractive
      11   He said he thought she'd be great in bed
      12   He talked about his last lecture

Dimension G: Male's Physical Acts
   Levels
      1   He reached out and straightened her hair
      2   He held her hand and said "I'm glad you're taking my course"
      3   Meanwhile he playfully poked her in the ribs
      4   He put his arm around her waist and squeezed
      5   He put his arm on her shoulder
      6   He forced her to a secluded area and attempted to have sex with her
      7   He moved closer to her
      8   He started to fondle and hiss her
      9   He forced her down, grabbing at her clothes
      10   Blank text

Dimension H: Male's Threat
   Levels
      1   He promised he would do everything to help her
      2   He warned her that "Your success in class depends on many factors."

3 He said that he could substantially improve her grade if she
   cooperated
4 He then threatened to lower her grade if she didn't have sex
   with him
5 Blank text

It is the total set of all combinations of these eight dimensions
which defined the factorial object set. Because some of the combinations of Dimension A and Dimension B would describe persons of
equal status—that is, graduate student males and graduate student
females—all such equal status combinations were omitted.[12] The
number of unique factorial objects in the universe so defined is
calculated[13] to be 21,565,440.

Defining the Judgment Rating Task

Given the study's objective, each of the factorial objects given to a
respondent ideally was to be judged as either describing an instance
of sexual harassment or not describing such an instance. Of course,
while dichotomous judgments of this kind may be desirable, real-
world judgments ordinarily are not that clear-cut; sexual harassment
judgments are likely to share that characteristic as well, with specific
incidents being more or less clearly sexual harassment or not sexual
harassment. Correspondingly, respondents were provided with a
continuum on which to place their judgments ranging from 1 to 9,
with integer steps in between, anchoring the continuum by equating 1
with the statement "definitely not harassment" and 9 with "definitely
harassment."

As we will show in a later point in this section, the scale used was
too short to accommodate the differentiations subjects perceive
among the factorial objects they were asked to rate. As a consequence,
judgments made tended to bunch toward the 9 and 1 ends of the scale.

Generating Factorial Object Respondent Subsamples

Each subject was to be asked to judge a subsample of 25 factorial
objects drawn from the factorial object universe described earlier.
Ideally we prefer to draw each subsample object independently on
each draw, producing a simple random sample of factorial objects.
The method actually used accomplishes that end by constructing
each factorial object independently from the dimensions involved.

A computer program was devised[14] which generates respondent subsamples of factorial objects from dimension lists. The program picks a value (level) at random from Dimension A, then a level from Dimension B, and so on through the last dimension in that factorial object set. Each such cycle through the dimensions in the factorial object population in question produces an additional subsample object. A run of m cycles produces a factorial object respondent subsample.

In addition to picking factorial object respondent subsamples, the program also produces a printout describing each of the objects drawn for each respondent, along with a coded tape which describes in coded form each of the objects in each respondent subsample. The printout can then be used as a self-administered questionnaire or as a schedule in a face-to-face or telephone interview. The coded tape can serve as a basic data tape with the addition of judgment responses given by each respondent to each of the factorial objects in his or her subsample.

The method of collecting the judgments in the Santa Barbara study was by self-administered, mailed questionnaires, a mode suitable for a highly literate population that is accustomed to filling out question-naires. Other modes of data collection have been used, as described in other chapters of this monograph. In many of the studies the objects have each been printed on a blank IBM card, with each respondent being handed his or her subsample as a stack of such cards to be sorted into bins or envelopes each marked with a number representing a point on a continuum. The program described earlier can be modified to print on such cards or on pages of varying sizes.

In all administrations undertaken up to this point, respondents were asked to read each object and then to make their judgments. Obviously, respondents who cannot read or who read with difficulty would find the task difficult to accomplish, but most respondents can rate and/or sort a subsample of 50 to 60 such objects quite easily. (The average time for sorting 60 objects is 20 minutes.) There is no reason to believe that the objects cannot be read to respondents, but there is every reason to believe that doing so would lengthen the time needed for administration by a factor of two or greater.

Because subjects were to be conducted by mail with a self-administered questionnaire, the size of respondent subsamples was set relatively low, at 25. It was feared that larger subsamples would lead to a formidably large questionnaire that might lead many subjects to refuse even to start the rating task.

The factorial objects were incorporated into a computer-printed questionnaire, each factorial object printed as indicated in the following example:

CINDY M. A MARRIED GRADUATE STUDENT
OFTEN HAD OCCASION TO TALK TO
GARY T. A SINGLE 65-YEAR-OLD PROFESSOR
THEY WERE BOTH AT A PARTY.
SHE SAID THAT SHE ENJOYED AND LOOKED FORWARD TO
    HIS CLASS.
HE ASKED HER ABOUT HER OTHER COURSES.
HE SAID THAT SHE COULD SUBSTANTIALLY IMPROVE HER
    GRADE IF SHE COOPERATED.

DEFINITELY NOT   DEFINITELY
HARASSMENT   HARASSMENT
    1   2   3   4   5   6   7   8   9

A judgment was recorded by the subject by circling one of the numbers on the rating scale printed below each factorial object (as shown above).

Sampling Respondents

Undergraduate students at the University of California at Santa Barbara constituted the respondent universe about which generalizations were to be drawn. A sample of 400 was drawn using random numbers from lists of undergraduates registered in the spring 1980 quarter. Undergraduates in the sample were contacted initially by phone by one of the members of the evaluation research seminar, told that a questionnaire would be sent to them through the mail, and urged to fill out the questionnaire. Completed questionnaires were returned by campus mail to the principal investigators.

All told, 273 questionnaires were completed and returned, yielding a response rate of 68 percent. There appears to be a slight response bias by sex; men were slightly less likely to return completed questionnaires.[15]

Distribution of Judgment Ratings

As shown in Table 1.1, the distribution of ratings of sexual harassment judgments is decidedly bimodal, constituting a shallow J-

TABLE 1.1   Distribution of Sexual Harassment Ratings

Rating		Percent
"Definitely Not Harassment"	1	12.8
	2	7.8
	3	6.0
	4	6.3
	5	8.0
	6	8.1
	7	10.3
	8	10.4
"Definitely Harassment"	9	29.5
No rating given		.6
		100% = (5850)**

Average Rating*	= 5.86
Standard Deviation*	= 2.92
Median Rating*	= 6.56

*Computed without cases in which no ratings were received.
**Based on first 234 questionnaires returned.

distribution. Almost 30 percent of the judgments cluster in the extreme rating of 9 as objects that respondents saw as "definitely sexual harassment." There is also some clustering at the opposite extreme, with almost 13 percent of the respondents' judgments falling at 1, "definitely not harassment." The least used rating was 3, garnering only 6 percent of the judgments.

Despite the minor cluster at 1, most of the judgments are on the high side, as indicated by an average of 5.86 and median of 6.56.

Several alternative explanations, not mutually exclusive, can be drawn upon to help understand why the judgment ratings were thus distributed. First, it should be noted that the levels in each of the dimensions tend to be more frequently on the sexual harassment side, with relatively few neutral or "nonharassment" statements constituting the levels that make up most of the dimensions. This means that the typical factorial object generated using the levels defined tended to suggest some degree of sexual harassment. Second, the rating task set for the subjects stressed to the respondent to make a determination of the degree of definiteness of sexual harassment in a particular incident. In a sense, asking for degrees of "definiteness" is not a very sensible task. Some respondents may have interpreted the scale as asking for the seriousness of the offense and others as

asking how sure they were about their judgment. In either case, however, the meaning of a rating of 9 or 1 is somewhat obscure. Third, the
rating scale may have not been fine enough to allow respondents to
express perceived differences among factorial objects which they
might have wanted to express. Hence the rating scale may have
truncated judgments, resulting in the pile-up of judgments at the two
extremes. In other words, respondents may have felt that some of the
objects described incidents which deserved ratings that were higher
than 9, desiring thereby to express an opinion that the incidents in
question were perhaps aggravated instances of sexual harassment.
Correspondingly, some respondents may have wanted to use ratings
below 1, indicating that some incidents were the opposite of sexual
harassment but represented, perhaps, courtly behavior.

The resulting distribution of ratings will make it difficult for all the
assumptions that undergird the use of ordinary least squares to be
fulfilled. We will indicate further how other multivariate models can
be used to obtain closer fits to the data. However, for illustrative
purposes we will use the usual linear regression model.

OLS Results

Each of the levels that define the factorial object set has been
expressed as binary (dummy) variables and used as independent
variables in the ordinary least squares regression (using equation
1.0) of the judgments made on factorial object characteristics, as
shown in Table 1.2. The resulting regression coefficients (shown in
column b) express the extent to which judgments are affected by the
presence of a particular level in a factorial object that is being rated.
Thus, the first regression coefficient in the table states that when the
male in an object is described as a "single graduate student," that
object on the average has a score lower by .4244 than a reference
object which is the conjunction of all the omitted categories.[16] In
short, regardless of which other levels are included in a factorial
object, the actions and statements of single graduate students are less
likely to be regarded as "definitely sexual harassment."

Note that all the coefficients for levels of status for males are
negative, indicating that incidents involving all statuses shown are
less likely to be regarded as sexual harassments than reference
objects. Of course, only two shown are statistically significant, and
even these are not very large. In short, while the status of the male
described in a factorial object modifies harassment judgments, the
adjustments are slight.

Even less of an impact on sexual harassment judgments is made by
Dimension B, consisting of four status levels describing the woman

TABLE 1.2   Regression of Sexual Harassment Judgments on Dimensions
and Levels: Santa Barbara Undergraduate Sample
(levels coded as binary dummy variables)

Dimension and Level	b	SE
Dimension A: Status of Male[a]		
Single graduate student	-.4244**	.1495
Single graduate student TA	-.2481	.1482
Married graduate student	-.1271	.1500
Married graduate student TA	-.4297**	.1456
Single 30-year-old professor	-.1872	.1073
Married 30-year-old professor	-.0798	.1063
Single 45-year-old professor	-.1041	.1073
Married 45-year-old professor	-.1320	.1061
Single 65-year-old professor	-.0273	.1073
Dimension B: Status of Female[b]		
Single graduate student	-.0131	.0777
Freshman	.0100	.0831
Senior	.0100	.0843
Dimension C: Woman's Prior Relationship to Male[c]		
Had rarely had occasion to talk to	-.2207*	.0945
Had gone out several times with	-.6348***	.0941
Often had occasion to talk with	-.3310**	.0953
Had been regularly dating	-1.1680***	.0949
Had been close friends with	-.4876***	.0938
Dimension D: Social Setting[d]		
When class had ended she approached him	.0685	.1187
After class he asked her if she could stay a minute	.1118	.1207
On the way out of class they started talking	.0981	.1213
She went to his office after class	.0898	.1193
She went to his office because he had asked to see her	.2165	.1215
As she was walking to her next class she bumped into him	.1477	.1217
While in the library, they ran into each other and started talking	-.0179	.1202
Between classes they were in the coffee shop	-.0493	.1201
They were at a restaurant	-.0361	.1207
Dimension E: Woman's Receptivity[e]		
She seemed worried and asked about grades	.2737*	.1306
She asked about grades, but did not appear concerned	.0786	.1336
She talked about some ideas she had from class	.1478	.1318
She said that she enjoyed and looked forward to his class	.0920	.1311
She invited him to a party she was having	-.1806	.1313
She said it was nice to see him outside of the stuffy classroom	.1020	.1311
She said she enjoyed talking with him and hoped they would be friends	-.0264	.1316
During their conversation her language became quite suggestive	-.8992***	.1302
While they talked, she frequently touched his arm	-.5210***	.1324
As they talked, she repeatedly brushed up against him	-.9743***	.1323
She made it obvious she would do anything for a good grade	-1.1467***	.1328

(continued)

TABLE 1.2 Continued

Dimension and Level	b	SE
Dimension F: Male's Verbal Behavior[f]		
He asked her about her other courses	.2416	.1331
He remarked that she was making good progress in class	.3608**	.1339
Straying from the subject, he remarked that she reminded him of an old girl friend	.9717***	.1334
He suggested that they go out sometime to dinner and a movie	.9454***	.1357
He asked her to go home with him	1.3182***	.1318
He said he looked forward to working with her	.7065***	.1372
He suggested that they go to a place where they could speak more privately	.8189***	.1346
He told her a dirty joke	.9692***	.1321
He said "Your personality is absolutely magnetic"	.6478***	.1353
He said her hair was extremely attractive	.9056***	.1353
He said he thought she'd be great in bed	1.8774***	.1332
Dimension G: Male's Physical Acts[g]		
He reached out and straightened her hair	.7221***	.1064
He held her hand and said "I am glad you're taking my course"	.4227***	.1111
Meanwhile he playfully poked her in the ribs	.6341***	.1097
He put his arm around her waist and squeezed	1.1505***	.1107
He put his arm on her shoulder	.4686***	.1200
He forced her to a secluded area and attempted to have sex with her	3.1521***	.1107
He moved closer to her	.0004***	.1128
He started to fondle and kiss her	1.8046***	.1105
He forced her down grabbing at her clothes	3.1154***	.1101
Dimension H: Male's Threat[h]		
He promised he would do everything to help her	.4315***	.0830
He warned her that "Your success in class depends on many factors"	2.2912***	.0820
He said that he could substantially improve her grade if she cooperated	2.7001***	.0823
He then threatened to lower her grade if she didn't have sex with him	4.1821***	.0810
Intercept	3.2567***	.1949

$$R^2 = .5018$$
$$N = (5812)$$

*p = .05 or less
**p = .01 or less
***p = .001 or less

[a.] Omitted level is "Married 65-year-old professor."
[b.] Omitted level is "Married graduate student."
[c.] Omitted level is "After being asked had declined to go out with."
[d.] Omitted level is "They were botn at a party."
[e.] Omitted level is blank text—that is, no levels from this dimension appear on a given percent of the factorial objects.
[f.] Omitted level is "He talked about his last lecture."
[g,h.] Omitted level is blank text.

in the sexual harassment incident. Whether the woman in question was a graduate student, a freshman, or a senior made no difference in the judgments of the respondents. Nor did the setting in which the incident took place make any difference, as the nonsignificant coefficients for all the levels of Dimension D indicate.

Note that while there may have been good reasons for the designers to add these dimensions to the factorial object universe, the empirical findings indicated that, by and large, respondents ignored them in making their judgments. Hence the factorial survey method provides information on dimensions and levels that do not belong to the substantive domain in question. In other words, any irrelevant dimension or level added to a factorial universe can be expected to yield b-coefficients that are essentially zero.

In contrast, all the remaining dimensions do influence sexual harassment judgments. The significant coefficients computed for each level of Dimension C indicate that the more intimate the relationship between the male and the female had been in the past, the less likely the incident was to be regarded as sexual harassment. At the extreme, if the two had been dating regularly, the sexual harassment judgment was shifted more than one point on the sexual harassment scale toward "definitely not harassment."

The significant coefficients for Dimension E indicate that if the woman involved in an incident makes statements or acts in a fashion that might be construed as indicating either sexual interest or availability, then the sexual harassment ratings are shifted toward the "definitely not harassment" end. In contrast, the positive significant coefficient for "She seemed worried and asked about grades" apparently means that expressing vulnerability increases slightly the chance of an incident being seen as sexual harassment.

The remaining three dimensions all concern the actions of the males shown in the incidents. Especially critical are the levels of Dimension H, expressing degrees of threat. The statement indicating "He threatened to lower her grade if she did not have sex" shifts the sexual harassment judgment more than 4 units toward the harassment side.

Dimensions F and G, respectively verbal and physical behavior of the males shown in incidents, also affect sexual harassment judgments. Almost any verbal statement increased the likelihood that the incident in question would be considered sexual harassment. Similarly, any physical gesture that involved touching or moving closer also influenced judgments more to the "definitely sexual harassment" side.

TABLE 1.3   Regression of Sexual Harassment Judgments on Effect-Coded
Dimensions: Santa Barbara Undergraduate Sample

	b	SE	β
A: Status of Male	1.0260***	.2792	.0361
C: Woman's Prior Relationship to Male	.8339***	.0642	.1209
E: Woman's Receptivity	1.0113***	.0617	.1539
F: Male's Verbal Behavior	.9714***	.0563	.1604
G: Male's Physical Behavior	.9635***	.0250	.3593
H: Male's Threat	.9777***	.0170	.5362
Intercept	5.861***	.0170	
$R^2 =$	.498***		
$N =$	(5812)		

*p = .05 or less
**p = .01 or less
***p = .001 or less

NOTE: Dimensions B and D had no significant raw coefficient and hence are deleted from the table.

Note that the levels included in an incident accounted for a large proportion of the variation in the ratings given, as shown by the fact that R^2 is slightly more than .50. None of the applications discussed in the chapters that follow will show R^2 as large. We suspect that the high R^2 for the sexual harassment study indicates that this is a topic in which there is a fair amount of consensus about what is important and that this is a population that can easily process the amount of information that was put into each of the objects.

A more concise way of expressing the analysis is shown in Table 1.3. In that table we have created quantitative variables out of each of the dimensions by giving each level a value that is equal to the regression coefficients shown in Table 1.2.[17] Table 1.3 also contains standardized regression coefficients for each of the dimensions, providing an index that permits comparisons of the several dimensions according to the contribution of each to the judgments.

The technique of recoding a set of dummy variables into a single quantitative variable by using the b-coefficients is sometimes referred to as "coding proportional to effect." (See the citation in the technical appendix.) The resulting variables will "explain" the same proportion of the variance in Y as did the original set of dummies. Thus R^2 remains unchanged. However, the b-coefficients attached to the new variables are not interpretable. In fact, they should all equal 1 apart from rounding error and sampling-induced departures from orthogonality when more than one dimension is recoded in the same equation. The β^2, however, can be interpreted as an index of importance, and, if complete orthogonality were maintained, the $\Sigma\beta_\kappa^2$ would equal R^2 and each β_κ^2 could be interpreted as the proportion of the variation in Y "accounted for" by each of the κ dimensions. See the technical appendix for a discussion of other uses of coding proportional to effect.

The standardized regression coefficients shown in the last column bear out the discussion earlier in this section. First, Dimension H, Male's Threat, has the largest coefficient, followed by Dimension G, Male's Physical Behavior. The remaining important dimensions, C, E, and F, have coefficients about the same size, indicating roughly equal contributions to sexual harassment judgments.

Gender Subgroup Differences

While there is considerable evidence in Tables 1.2 and 1.3 that respondents largely agree with each other on what constitutes sexual harassment, it is possible that systematic disagreements may characterize subgroups among the subjects. It should be recalled that subjects are undergraduates at the University of California at Santa Barbara and hence are relatively homogeneous with respect to most socioeconomic measures. Perhaps the most relevant source of potential disagreement is gender; what may be regarded as sexual harassment by women may be seen as ardent wooing on the part of males.

Gender differences may take one or both of two forms: First, there may simply be differences in the intercepts, with females regarding all incidents described in the factorial objects as more likely to be sexual harassment. Second, men and women may disagree about what constitutes sexual harassment and hence weigh levels and dimensions differently.

In Table 1.4 the analysis of Table 1.3 has been run separately for males and females.[18] Note that the coefficients for males are similar to those for females, and in no case are there any inversions in size order among coefficients. In short it appears that men and women are weighing the dimensions in about the same ways.

There is a gender difference in intercept, however, with the intercept for women being .46 higher than that for men. Typically,

50

TABLE 1.4 Regression of Sexual Harassment Judgments on Effect Coded Dimensions: Separately for Male and Female Subjects of Santa Barbara Undergraduate Sample

	Male Respondents			Female Respondents		
	b	SE	β	b	SE	β
A: Status of Male	1.1101*	.5630	.0369	1.1091**	.3211	.0399
C: Woman's Prior Relationship to Male	.6988***	.1248	.1504	.8954***	.0761	.1291
E: Woman's Receptivity	.9936***	.1178	.1503	1.004***	.0717	.1536
F: Male's Verbal Behavior	.9394***	.1065	.1574	.9773***	.0665	.1611
G: Male's Physical Behavior	.9792***	.0491	.3526	.9691***	.0290	.3624
H: Male's Threat	1.020***	.0334	.5444	.9590***	.0197	.5339
Intercept	5.5165***	.0532		5.9730***	.0317	
$R^2 =$	.491***			.502***		
N	(1614)			(4158)		

$*p = .05$ or less
$**p = .01$ or less
$***p = .001$ or less

TABLE 1.5 Regression of Sexual Harassment Judgments on Effect-Coded Dimensions and Respondent Characteristics: Santa Barbara Undergraduate Sample

	b	SE	β
I. Dimension			
A: Status of Male	1.0142***	.2781	.0357
B: Status of Female	.0310	.3491	.0009
C: Woman's Prior Relationship to Male	.8336***	.0639	.1208
D: Social Setting	.4161*	.2096	.0184
E: Woman's Receptivity	1.0122***	.0609	.1540
F: Male's Verbal Behavior	.9604***	.0561	.1586
G: Male's Physical Behavior	.9634***	.0248	.3593
H: Male's Threat	.9794***	.0169	.5371
II. Respondent Characteristics			
Sex (Female = 1, Male = 0)	.4513***	.0603	.0694
Having been a victim of sexual harassment[a]	.3989***	.1346	.0276
Having a personal friend who has been the victim of sexual harassment[a]	.5077***	.0745	.0634
Age (Years)	-.0042	.0060	-.0065
Intercept	5.6904***	.3619	
R^2 =	.507***		
N =	(5762)		

*p = .05 or less
**p = .01 or less
***p = .001 or less
[a] Dummy variables constructed from the answers to the first two alternatives in the following question, "Which of the following statements best describes your personal experience with what you feel to be sexual harassment at UCSB?"
   (1) "I have been a victim of sexual harassment while at UCSB."
   (2) "I have not been a victim of sexual harassment myself, but a close friend of mine has been a victim of sexual harassment and has told me personally about it."
   (3) "I have not been a victim of sexual harassment myself and I do not know directly of any incidents of sexual harassment among my close personal friends."

compared to men, women rate each incident about half a point more likely to be sexual harassment.

These findings suggest that it would be appropriate to add gender as a respondent characteristic to the analysis of Table 1.3 along with other respondent characteristics (as in equation 2.2). Not many such characteristics appear on the questionnaire distributed to the Santa Barbara students. We ended up with four such characteristics in the analysis shown in Table 1.5, including gender, experience personally with sexual harassment, knowing someone who has experienced sexual harassment, and age.

The findings of Table 1.5 are as follows: First, the background information does not add much explanatory power to the equation of Table 1.3, R^2 increasing by less than .01. Second, the b-coefficient attached to gender is close to the intercept gender difference shown in Table 1.4, as one might have expected. Women give sexual harassment judgments that tend to be .45 points higher than men's ratings. Third, the sexual harassment experiences, direct or indirect, increase the ratings, about .4 for personal experience and about .51 for experiences related by a friend. Of course, since few persons have directly or indirectly experienced sexual harassment, these personal characteristics do not contribute much overall. Finally, age apparently makes little difference in the ratings, as one might expect for a sample of undergraduates among whom age differences are not very large.

Individual Differences in Sexual Harassment Judgments

The analyses of the previous section brought to light a consistent difference between men and women in their views of sexual harassment, with women giving almost half a point greater judgment on the average to objects, net of all the characteristics of the objects in question. In addition, personal or indirect experience with sexual harassment also increased the ratings given.

Now we turn to the task of detecting individual differences in the ways the objects were rated. There are various ways to go about the task of analyzing individual differences. Perhaps the most comprehensive approach would be to run each person's regression separately and obtain a vector of estimated b-coefficients representing each individual's weights. If the research task were concerned primarily with variation in the judgment calculus and not in the consensus weights, this effort is worth considering. The distribution of the individual b_k^* around the group b_k could be examined and each b_k could be used in a formal test of the null $b_k^* - b^k = 0$. Or more general tests for pooling, such as the Chow test, can be used. Case-by-case consideration of the b_k^* vector is tedious, and most social research applications will find it unnecessary. If there is substantial variation in the individual weights, it usually will be more practical to group individuals on the basis of the similarity of the b_k^* profiles. This can be accomplished in a variety of ways discussed previously: cluster analysis, Q-factor analysis, nonmetric multidimensional scaling, profile analysis, and others. These groupings might then be compared on the basis of their members' characteristics. Or, if the goal is to permit estimation of a single equation, dummy variables can be used to code group membership, and interaction terms formed by multiplying group dummies by the X_k object characteristics can be used to estimate weighting differences. This technique is sometimes called "slope dummies" and is represented in equation 2.1.

A variety of other, less standard methods also have been used to examine individual differences. In one approach, a residual, D_{ij}, is calculated by finding the difference between the estimated social judgment given to an object, $\hat{J}_{ij}$, and the judgment given by an individual i, to an object, J_{ij}. Regressions are then computed for each of the respondents over the objects he or she has rated. This was done for the sexual harassment data, and the resulting estimates are shown in Table 1.6 for three individual respondents.

Table 1.6 was computed by OLS computations for the following equation for each individual, i.

$$D_{ij}=(J_{ij}-\hat{J}_{ij})=b_0+b_1X_1+ \ldots +b_5X_5+e$$

in which X_1 through X_5 are the effect coded dimensions, Prior Relationship, Woman's Receptivity, Male's Verbal Behavior, Male's Physical Behavior, and Male's Threat, respectively, as defined previously

The three persons represented in each of the columns of Table 1.6 were picked from among the first four persons on the data tape and are not represented as anything other than three illustrations.

The R^2s for each individual represent, among other things, the extent to which each person's difference from the computed estimates from the sample can be accounted for by the designated characteristics of the 25 vignettes rated by that person and idiosyncratic weightings. A low value of R^2 then suggests that the individual's residual for each object (the deviation between the judgment and the judgment predicted by the aggregate regression) cannot be explained by the individual's object set and/or weighting differences. Such would appear to be the case for Individual A, whose R^2 and b coefficients do not reach statistical significance at least at the .05 level. Individuals B and C, in contrast, do have some significant coefficients, and their R^2s reach a size to which some attention might be paid. Individual B tends to weigh the dimension Male's Physical Behavior more heavily than the sample, while Individual C weighs more heavily the Woman's Receptivity dimension. Note that the sign

TABLE 1.6   Regression of D_{ij} Values on Factorial Object
            Characteristics for Selected Individual
            Respondents: Santa Barbara Study

Independent Variables	Dependent Variable is $D_{ij} = (J_{ij} - \hat{J}_{ij})$		
	Individual A	Individual B	Individual C
	b/SE	b/SE	b/SE
Prior Relationship	.2831	-2.172	-.529
	(4.43)	(2.61)	(3.73)
Woman's Receptivity	2.120	1.222	4.39***
	(1.08)	(.657)	(.897)
Male's Verbal Behavior	.9166	1.37	-1.05
	(1.62)	(.907)	(.710)
Male's Physical Behavior	.3369	.828*	-.629
	(.399)	(.314)	(.533)
Male's Threat	-.2121	-.017	-.084
	(.353)	(.261)	(.278)
Intercept	-.544	.242	.715
	(.493)	(.338)	(.381)
$R^2 =$	.307	.437*	.634**
$N =$	(25)	(25)	(25)

*Means p = .05 or less
**Means p = .01 or less
***Means p = .001 or less

of the coefficient indicates that the more receptive a woman's actions
appear, the higher the difference between Individual C's rating and
that of the total sample. Of course, using residuals as dependent
variables can be risky; they are a combination of various influences
and errors. Still, in the process of exploring individual differences, it
is sometimes informative to treat these deviations from consensus as
things to be explained.

The results of Table 1.6 perhaps might be of interest to a
counsellor concerned with providing guidance to the individuals in
question. In order to provide general research findings, we have to
find some way of explaining individual variation in rating principles.
In order to do so, we have computed coefficients for each respondent
and used those coefficients as dependent variables in the analysis
presented in Table 1.7. Unfortunately, the Santa Barbara study did
not contain many ways of characterizing individuals that could be
used as independent variables. Hence the analyses of Table 1.7 must

TABLE 1.7 Regression of Regression Coefficients for Individual Respondents on Selected Respondent Characteristics: Santa Barbara Study (N = 232)

Dependent Variables		Independent Variables			Intercept	R^2
		Female Respondent	Personal Experience with Sexual Harassment	Knows Someone Sexually Harassed		
R^2	b =	.0556**	.067	−.003	.246	.04*
	SE =	(.021)	(.047)	(.047)	(.024)	
Intercept	b =	.445**	.398	.578**	−.054	.10***
	SE =	(.133)	(.297)	(.164)	(.606)	
b_C	b =	.079	−.552	−.259	−.203	.02
	SE =	(.159)	(.355)	(.196)	(.725)	
b_E	b =	.055	−.026	−.065	.673	.005
	SE =	(.181)	(.408)	(.226)	(.834)	
b_F	b =	.055	−.026	−.065	.723	.006
	SE =	(.153)	(.342)	(.190)	(.699)	
b_G	b =	−.001	−.064	−.008	.174	.002
	SE =	(.073)	(.163)	(.090)	(.332)	
b_H	b =	−.062	−.235*	.008	−.063	.03
	SE =	(.052)	(.117)	(.064)	(.238)	

*p = .05 or less
**p = .01 or less
***p = .001 or less

be regarded as simply illustrative of how this analysis might be conducted.

In Table 1.7 the coefficients resulting from individual-level regressions of D_{ij} on object dimensions are used as dependent variables, each in its turn. As independent variables, only three are available, respondent sex, and personal or indirect experiences with sexual harassment. Of the seven regressions run, only two present information that warrants attention. First, in the row containing coefficients for the regression of R^2 on respondent characteristics we note that the coefficient for sex is positive, indicating that women respondents tend to have higher individual R^2s, by about .06, indicating the women make on the average "surer" judgments (that is, with less error) than men. Second, as the second row of Table 1.7 shows, women tend to have higher intercepts, by about .445, indicating that women shift their judgments upwards, as compared to men. In addition, knowing someone who has experienced sexual harassment shifts the intercept upwards by .578. Note that these are results that have been preshadowed by the findings related in Table 1.5 and are about the same size as the subgroup effects, defined by the same variables. In this case, because we do not have many independent variables to use in the analysis, the individual-level results shown in Table 1.7 are not revealing beyond those that have already been detected in subgroup analyses.

The remaining coefficients in Table 1.7 are either not statistically significant at the .05 (or better) level or hover close to that level. But of the remaining 24 coefficients only one is significant at the .05 level, about what one would expect by chance. The significant coefficient appears to show that persons who have had personal direct experiences with sexual harassment weigh *less* the dimension of Male Threat in their judgments, a finding that appears suspect on prima facie grounds. These suggestions do not exhaust the ways of exploring individual differences and are intended only to illustrate the range of options open to the researcher concerned with individual variation.

Correcting for the Effects of Truncation

In Table 1.1 the distribution of sexual harassment ratings suggested that the range of ratings provided to respondents was too short because judgments piled up on the two extreme ratings, 9 and 1. This further suggests that the response functional form is better represented

TABLE 1.8   Logistic Regression on Selected Factorial
Object Characteristics: Santa Barbara

Independent Variables	b	Logistic Equation Approximate SE	OLS b
Regularly dating	-.575***	.049	(-.825)
Her language suggestive	-.565***	.066	(-.795)
Do anything for a grade	-.696***	.068	(-1.026)
She would be good in bed	1.000***	.070	(1.120)
Attempted sex	2.525***	.134	(2.72)
Fondled and kissed her	1.058***	.069	(1.422)
Forced her down	2.376***	.122	(2.708)
Warned about grades	1.306***	.048	(2.090)
Cooperation improve grade	1.579***	.051	(2.496)
Sex or lower grade	3.186***	.115	(3.990)
Intercept	-.644***	.027	(3.057)
R^2 =	.493***		(.452)
N =	(5965)		

Logistic form used =
$$J_{ij} = 8/(1+e^{-(b_0 + \Sigma b_j C_j)}) + e$$

***p = .001 or less

by a logistic curve than a straight line. In the logistic regression form estimated judgments take an S-shape form, with the left tail asymptotically approaching a minimum and the right a maximum. Since the rating scale administered to the respondents could not exceed 9 or go below 1, the logistic form more closely fits the circumstances facing raters than a linear representation.

A logistic regression was computed by Richard A. Berk and is shown in Table 1.8 for a selected number of the dimensions and levels used earlier in this section.[19] The logistic form used was as follows:

$$J_{ij} = 8/(1+e^{-(b_0 + \Sigma b_j C_j)}) + e$$

where J_{ij} are the judgments made by individual i of object j
b_0, b_j are regression coefficients
and C_j are levels represented as dummy variables

The first column of Table 1.8 presents the logistic coefficients with the corresponding OLS coefficients shown in the last column. All of the coefficients shown in the table are significant, not a surprising finding given that the levels used were chosen as among the strongest as shown in the OLS regression of Table 1.2.

The logistic form fits the data somewhat better as the higher R^2 for the logistic form indicates, picking up an additional 4 percent explained variance. The coefficients also tend to resemble the OLS coefficients, although comparisons are difficult since the logistic coefficients change as values of the several variables are changed. It should be noted, however, that none of the signs differ and that the size rank order of the coefficients is identical across the logistic and the OLS equations.

In short, even though the logistic expression more clearly fits the data, given the greater cost of the logistic expression and the greater flexibility of the OLS, one may well prefer the latter, at least as a first approximation. Perhaps the most important lesson to be learned from Table 1.8 and from the distribution of ratings shown in Table 1.1 is the importance of allowing respondents the opportunity to express their judgments as clearly as possible. A scale that is too short will produce ratings that are difficult to represent in the convenient OLS form.

Future Developments in Factorial Surveys

This monograph presents a fair sampling of how factorial surveys have been used over the last decade. The examples vary considerably in their complexity and sophistication, representing stages in the development of this new technique. There can be little doubt that if factorial surveys prove to be useful, additional developments may make the examples in this monograph mainly of interest to social research historians. Indeed, there are several developments that can be anticipated at this point and on which we can expect to see some technical research in the future.

The applications of factorial surveys have been mainly to substantive issues in social normative judgments. That is, the research has attempted to discern the variety of social definitions in substantive areas in which it is clear that social consensus is changing, as, for example, in studies of sexual harassment definitions, child abuse, drinking problems, and the like. Another kind of substantive issue has been to simulate judgments in areas where norms conflict, as in the case of distributive justice judgments of household income or the sentencing of convicted criminals. We believe that the technique has wide applicability and can be extended to other substantive areas. Consumer purchase decisions appear to be one substantive area to which factorial surveys might be profitably applied. Indeed, at this writing, Professor Anne Shlay of Cornell University is designing a factorial survey for the study of housing preferences in which respondents make judgments about descriptions of housing systematically varying in size, location, price, and other characteristics that differentiate among housing typically offered on the local market in question. Other types of consumer decisions, especially when the products offered on the market vary widely, would also appear to be amenable to study through factorial surveys.

An extremely critical issue is whether or not the judgments made in response to factorial surveys illuminate actual decisions made by persons in nonhypothetical circumstances. Does the study of sentencing under factorial survey conditions illuminate the ways in which actual sentencing decisions are made? Is the artificiality of factorial object universe orthogonality an obstacle to the extrapolation of such judgments to real-life situations? One of the chapters of the volume addresses this issue with respect to status judgments with mixed conclusions. Considerably more can be done to cast some empirical light on this issue.

There are also technical questions that need to be answered. First, there is good reason to suspect that dimensions and levels cannot be added to the design of factorial surveys without running the risk of providing so much information to respondents on each object that errors begin to swamp the effects of structure in the resulting judgments. It may well be the case that levels can be extended indefinitely but that dimensions are limited by the information-processing abilities of respondents. Thus, for example, it may not matter whether one uses a few age groups or represents age in single years, but the number of different dimensions—age, sex, race, region, and so on—used in an object universe is so limited. In any event, methodological research on the effects of adding levels and dimensions is needed.

A second technical issue of great importance centers on the appropriate ways to collect judgments. As we have seen in the example of this chapter, there are occasions when nine-point scales are inappropriate. Experimentation with alternative judgment devices is called for, especially with adaptations of magnitude estimation procedures, with extended rating scales, with multiple rating scales, and other devices.

A final technical issue concerns the size of the rating task. Respondent subsamples have ranged up to size 60 in the examples given in this monograph. Clearly, for analyses that focus on individual differences in rating principles, larger respondent sub-samples would be desirable, but there is the danger that the task might increase error when expanded and hence that there may be a tradeoff between error and precision in the estimates of individual-level parameters. There is, furthermore, the issue of intraindividual correlation, whose presence in judgments is undoubtedly a problem that has received insufficient attention. Other statistical issues are discussed in the technical appendix.

In sum we believe that factorial surveys will turn out to be a useful and enriching addition to the tools of social science research. While the studies described in this volume provide, we believe, sufficient evidence of the promise of factorial surveys, it is also clear that only future uses will be able to provide the necessary evidence.

Technical Appendix

This chapter was written as a general introduction to factorial surveys. It was intended to provide a look at the basic characteristics of the technique. The remaining chapters are substantive applications. The introduction was not intended as a technical manual for generating and analyzing factorial surveys. Even so, a few more technical matters deserve mention. To some extent, a technical chapter is premature. Although work under way is concerned with particular statistical issues associated with using factorial surveys, most work to date has dealt exclusively with substantive applications. Some work has been done, however, and in this section we intend to make readers aware of the direction the technical studies are taking or are anticipated to take.

Analysis

The dominant analytic model used to date in factorial surveys has been a single linear additive equation estimated using OLS. The reasons are obvious. Each judgment is a quantitative result (usually) of a set of qualitative and quantitative characteristics. The characteristics are fixed and measured (or produced) without error. Order is random within the individual and across individuals. The OLS assumptions would appear to be (1) met directly, or (2) to be plausible first assumptions, or (3), as in the case of the normality of ε_j, to be assumptions against which OLS is robust. In the event that the assumption(s) of spherical disturbances is violated, the equation can be estimated using generalized least squares. In the event that the model seems incorrect in form (that is, nonlinear and/or nonadditive), it is ordinarily possible to rewrite the expression by adding higher-order terms or interactions or by taking logarithms of the variables or by using other standard methods.

Still, additional work needs to be done, especially in three areas. First, the error structure needs to be better understood. Particularly in the case of analysis at the level of individual regressions, there is a possibility of violating the assumptions about the distribution and independence of the error terms. Second, more work is needed on the problem of integrating individual regressions with the aggregate regression. On the surface, this appears to be a special case of the problem of pooling cross-sections and time series. Here, however, the cross-sections are individuals and have no order through time, as is the case in the typical econometric pooling problem. One standard approach to the pooling problem has already been discussed. It is possible to use individual dummies and slope dummies (individual dummies times the factorial object variables). This technique has the effect of permitting each individual to have his or her own intercept and regression coefficients. However, unless the independent variables are few in number, the resulting equations become unmanageably large and multicollinear. Reducing individuals to homogeneous groups and using quantitative independent variables will make this approach more feasible. Other approaches to the pooling problem, such as the components of variance models, have not yet been investigated.

A third area needing attention concerns the class of judgment models. To this point, the models have assumed that a judgment is a linear combination of traits or items of information. N. H. Anderson has considered a larger class of models that includes averaging models and that permits the introduction of contrast effects. Anderson's theory of information integration will be mentioned later. The point here is only that a larger class of judgment models exists and that they can be used in the analysis of factorial surveys.

A brief addition is needed to the discussion of the generation of factorial objects. Much of the discussion, and the example, assumed independent variables coded as dummy variables. While this is often the case, it should be noted that factorial surveys often contain quantitative variables such as income or years of education in family prestige studies, the amount of money stolen in crime seriousness studies, the price of a product in marketing applications, or the probability of getting away with a crime in deterrence research. In applications using quantitative variables, the analysis is particularly straightforward, and the resulting partial regression coefficients can be interpreted as the expected increase (or decrease) in the judgment scale for each unit change in the quantitative variable statistically holding constant the other independent variables. If all the independent variables are factorial dimensions, they will be approximately orthogonal and the addition/deletion of a variable will not substantially change the coefficients of the other terms.

In previous sections we discussed the relationships between factorial dimensions as being independent and uncorrelated. Of course, the two are not equivalent. We are primarily concerned with them being uncorrelated, but in fact they will be independent and this is a sufficient condition to make them uncorrelated. If the two variables are quantitative, then their independence follows directly from the nature of the object generator. Suppose dimension A with four levels and dimension B with five levels. Each level is equally likely to be selected from A and from B, and the two selections are independent. That is, for example, $P(A_1)=1/4$ and $P(B_3)=1/5$ and $P(A_1 \cup B_3)=1/4 \times 1/5=1/20$. Because the two selections (generations) are independent, the conditional probability $P(B_3| \ A_1)=P(B_3)$ and so on for every pair of levels from A and B. At a less formal level, one can envision the A x B plane; because of the nature of the generator, the points selected from this plan will be uniformly spread throughout the plane, the only constraint being that they lie at preselected (fixed) values of A and B.

In the case of qualitative variables coded as dummy variables, the relationship is only slightly more complicated. Again, suppose two dimensions, A and B, this time qualitative. Suppose four levels of A coded as three dummy variables and five levels of B coded as four dummy variables. We will refer to A and B as conceptual variables or dimensions. It should be obvious, then, that dummy variables within a conceptual variable are not uncorrelated. In fact, for groups of equal size it can be shown that the correlation between two dummy variables from the same conceptual variable will be equal to $r_{ij}=-1/(g-1)$ where g is the number of groups. However, two dummy variables from different conceptual variables will be independent. Moreover, the two conceptual variables will be independent. Although a formal proof is available, the easiest way to see the independence of the conceptual variables is to visualize an A x B contingency table. A chi-square test for independence will be based on the calculation

$$\chi^2 = \Sigma \ \frac{(0-E)^2}{E}$$

where E, the expected frequency for each cell, is the product of the row probability times the column probability times the total sample size. The product of the row and column probabilities gives the cell probability *under the assumption of independence,* and the probability is converted to an expected frequency by multiplication by the sample size. As previously shown, the factorial object probabilities are the product of their separate dimension probabilities, and hence for factorial surveys the object frequencies should depart from the expected frequencies only by chance. Consequently, the conceptual variables (dimensions) are independent.

Relationship to N. H. Anderson's
Information Integration Theory

Information integration theory cuts across a variety of areas within psychology. Judgments or perceptions of any kind may be viewed as a response to several stimuli or pieces of information. Anderson's work has examined carefully the importance given different items of information and the rules for combining the different items to render a single judgment (Anderson, 1974). In a typical experiment a subject will be given several pieces of information about an object and will be asked to render a summary assessment about the object. Applications have been found in many areas, including traditional psychophysics and a variety of areas of social psychology.

Factorial surveys developed independently of information integration theory, but they are quite similar to Anderson's additive model. The primary difference is in the design. Anderson typically uses a fully crossed factorial design, which means that only a few variables can be used, each having only a few levels. The factorial design is compelling because the independent variables can be kept orthogonal and nonadditivities (interactions) can be estimated. Factorial surveys also maintain dimensional independence (or approximately so); more important, they permit many more levels and dimensions to be used. This gain, we believe, is one of the most important contributions of factorial surveys.

Experiments in the information integration tradition usually are analyzed using factorial analysis of variance, and this permits a direct assessment of interaction effects. In fact, each specific cell's nonadditive component can be calculated. Factorial surveys have more difficulty with interactions because any specific cell is likely to be empty or nearly empty. However, lower-order interactions can be estimated, and if a more fine-grained look at the response surface is required, an enhanced design can be used. So far no factorial surveys have used the enhanced designs. But there is no reason why something like the Box-Draper evolutionary operationism approach (1969) cannot be used. Specific areas of the design space could be selected for more intense investigation, and objects could be generated to provide the closer look. This could be done a priori or as part of a sequence of projects in which each succeeding survey is used to plan the next, each becoming progressively more refined and giving increasingly detailed information about the response surface.

Rescaling Qualitative Variables

When qualitative categories can be viewed as falling along a single underlying continuum, they may be placed on that continuum by using the regression coefficients attached to the dummy variables coding the categories.

For example, in studies of family prestige, occupations may be coded as dummy variables but may be considered to fall along a single occupational prestige dimension. If family prestige is regressed on the dummy variables coding occupations, the resulting partial regression coefficients can be used to scale occupations. With the mean of the deleted occupation becoming the constant, every other category can be given the scale value of $b_0+b_kX_k$ where b_k is the partial regression coefficient attached to each of the k categories.[20] This is sometimes called coding proportional to effect (see Boyle, 1970; Wertz and Linn, 1971; Lansing, 1971; Andrews, Morgan, and Sonquist, 1967). The result is that a single new quantitative variable replaces the set of dummies, and the R^2 due to the dummies remains unchanged. The resulting variable can be used as an independent variable in a regression, but its raw regression coefficient will be of no use since it will be 1.00 (or approximately so) by construction. However, the β^2 (the square of the standardized partial) can be interpreted as the proportion of the variation in the dependent variable accounted for by the scaled variable. This is similar to the approach used in MCA. This technique is particularly useful when the number of dummy variables is large and unwieldy. Since the dimensions in factorial surveys are mutually independent, the rescaling is not sensitive to adding or deleting variables. Of course, an adjustment must be made to the degrees of freedom since k constraints, not 1, have been placed on the data by estimating the coefficient on the new variable. Clearly, there should be an assumption that a single underlying continuum exists, that we know the order of categories along the dimension, that the continuum is related linearly to the dependent variable, and that the categories fall along the dimension in proportion to their effect on Y.

For reasons that are beyond the scope of this chapter, the rescaling technique can be viewed as fundamental measurement. This is an area currently under investigation. At first sight, the method seems to have the look of someone attempting to pull himself up by his own bootstraps. Measurement, we are taught early, is done prior to analysis not during analysis. A growing number suggest the contrary, arguing that measurement is often done best in the context of the theory in which the measurement is to be used and that the rescaling approach is a promising advance in that direction. There are, of course, a number of problems associated with this claim, and it is not the purpose of this comment to undertake the argument, only to note the development of this view.

The argument is made in more detail in Anderson's work on functional measurement (1974) among others. Anderson's scaling is based on marginal means from factorial designs, but the argument for using the data for scaling the independent variables is the same.

NOTES

1. To economists who assert that market price embodies an assessment of the bundle of characteristics that make up a specific product, the judgments people make are manifested in the prices they are willing to pay. Thus housing economists have computed "hedonic indices" for housing prices which express the features of housing in terms of the increments (or decrements) in price received for a house that has each specific feature. These hedonic indices are computed by regressing market prices on the specific features of housing. The underlying model here is quite similar to that used in factorial surveys, with price paid being equivalent to a judgment or evaluation. However, factorial surveys manipulate the traits so as to maintain approximate orthogonality among characteristics. In the housing market, many characteristics of houses are highly correlated; hence, it becomes more difficult to assess unique contributions of each characteristic (Follain and Malpezzi, 1980).

2. This is accomplished by constructing the objects by random selection of each level from each dimension. The process will be described in more detail in a later section.

3. This approach is somewhat fatuous because it would simply tell us that individuals vary one from the other and would not explain sources of the differences. In addition, this interpretation of equation 2.1 would use up many degrees of freedom.

4. No empirical examples in factorial surveys of the Q-factor approach currently exist.

5. Of course, what is regarded as intrinsic to a judgment realm and what is regarded as extraneous is somewhat arbitrary. The prices of housing may be regarded as an "intrinsic" characteristic or as an expression of choice and hence part of a judgment.

6. In practice the distributions of cases among levels may be changed from rectangular for good substantive reasons without disturbing orthogonality. For example, if the given content is given to two levels that is, the same content appears in both, then the probability of the content in question appearing as a level is $2/q$. As will be shown in some of the examples given in the chapters that follow, nonrectangular distributions of levels may be justified for substantive reasons.

7. Lest the reader suspect we are making up numbers, simply consider a factorial object population made up of 10 dimensions each with 10 levels or $10^{10} = 10,000,000,000$ unique factorial objects.

8. Accomplished by taking several samples consisting of one judgment drawn randomly from each respondent's sample.

9. We are grateful to our Santa Barbara colleagues for permission to use these data for illustrative purposes.

10. In addition, Alan Neustadtl and Paul Bobrowski, graduate students in the Department of Sociology at the University of Massachusetts, participated in the design of the study and did much of the work of producing the samples of factorial objects for administration at the University of California, Santa Barbara.

11. Sixteen male names and 17 female names were so used, each as a first name and an initial as a last name (Robert B. and Rita L., for example). In effect these lists of

names acted as additional dimensions, since each list was allowed to combine freely with the appropriate status. The names are not considered dimensions, however, mainly because they play no substantive roles, expect to provide variety in the names that designate that Dimension A pertains to males and Dimension B pertains to females.

12. It should be noted that the introduction of prohibited combinations compromises the orthogonality of the factorial object population and derivitively the resulting factorial object sample. Hence care should be used in making such prohibitions, especially extensive ones that would introduce serious collinearity among dimensions. In the examples presented in this volume, the effects of minor extent prohibitions are shown to increase correlations among dimensions from essentially zero to about .2 to .3. In this particular case the correlation between the two dimensions in question in the factorial object sample was .30.

13. Calculated as $\overset{k}{\pi}_{qk} - G$.
where π_{qk} is the product of the q levels in the k dimensions and G is the number of prohibited combinations of the 2 levels involved.

14. The program was written by Robert K. Lazarsfeld in FORTRAN for use on a CDC Cyber 74 computer system. Input for the program includes dimensions and levels along with restrictions on combinations allowed. Output can be printed cards, pages of questionnaires, or other formats. Copies of the program and documentation are available for the costs of reproduction and handling from the senior author.

15. Men were sampled using a considerably smaller sampling ratio, designed to produce twice as many women as men in the final sample size.

16. The reference object in this case describes "a married professor over 65," "a married graduate student," "after being asked had declined to go out with," "they were both at a party" with no statement on the woman's receptivity, "he talked about his last lecture" with no statement about the last two dimensions. Note that the reference object contains no actions and no threats being made by the male described, which makes the reference object perhaps among the least likely of all objects to be regarded as sexual harassment.

17. Actually, each level was given the value by which the sexual harassment judgments given to factorial objects with that level differed from the overall sexual harassment judgment grand mean.

18. In addition, it would also be sensible to run Table 1.2 separately for the two genders. Actually, this was done (although not reported here) in order to see whether or not there were any outstanding differences in the regression coefficients computed for each of the levels. No such differences appeared.

19. Levels are represented as dummy variables. Levels used were chosen for use here if the OLS solution (as in Table 1.2) produced b-coefficients which were greater than 1.0, a decision made to reduce the costs of computation. In addition, the ratings were changed to range between 0 and 8 by subtracting one from each rating.

20. The choice of a constant is arbitrary. One can use the grand mean of Y (as does MCA) or the mean of the lowest-ranking group or any other selected point.

REFERENCES

Anderson, N. H., 1974, "Information integration theory: a brief survey," in D. H. Drantz et al. (eds.) Contemporary Developments in Mathematical Psychology. San Francisco: W. H. Freeman.

Note: N. H. Anderson's work is spread throughout many different journals and books. This article and its bibliography provide a good overview.

Andrews, Frank, James Morgan, and John Sonquist, 1967, Multiple Classification Analysis. Ann Arbor: Institute for Social Research, University of Michigan.

Box, George E. P. and Norman R. Draper, 1969, Evolutionary Operation. New York: John Wiley.

Boyle, Richard P., 1970, "Path analysis and ordinal data." American Journal of Sociology 75 (January): 461-480.

Follain, James R. and Stephen Malpezzi, 1980, Dissecting Housing Value and Rent: Estimates of Hedonic Indices for 30 Metropolitan Areas. Washington, DC: The Urban Institute.

Lansing M., 1971, "Techniques for using ordinal measures in regression and path analysis," in H. L. Costner (ed.) Sociological Methodology. San Francisco: Jossey-Bass.

Stevens, S. S., 1957, "On the psychophysical law," Psychological Review 64: 153-181.

Wertz, C. F. and R. L. Linn, 1971, "Comments on Boyle's 'Path Analysis and Ordinal Data.' " American Journal of Sociology 76 (May): 1109-1112.

2

HOUSEHOLD SOCIAL STANDING
Dynamic and Static Dimensions

M. BONNER MEUDELL

Empirical research in the area of social stratification has typically focused on static determinants of social status, including variables such as occupation, education, and income. On a conceptual level, these variables represent objective positions within social structural hierarchies. For example, occupations are usually classified within an occupational prestige hierarchy in which each occupation is assigned a value or position reflecting its location along the prestige continuum. It is because these variables are positions that they reflect the more unchanging, static aspects of social status. Although there is little debate concerning the relevance of such positions, the heavy reliance on them has led to a neglect of other components of social position. In particular, dynamic information which pertains to incumbents' performances vis-a-vis their positions has been virtually ignored.

This lack of empirical attention concerning the dynamic or performance[1] area in social stratification research is attributable, in part, to the strong concentration that has been placed on the status attainment process. For many, the focus on quantifying inter- and intragenerational shifts in occupations has meant acceptance of the Duncan SEI occupational prestige score as the standard measure of social status (Haug, 1972). This trend, which has been viewed as implicitly theory-laden in a functionalist direction (Horan, 1978), has resulted in a de-emphasis on the examination of alternative conceptualizations of social status. Conspicuously missing has been concern with dynamic factors and their relation to social standing despite the *theoretical* emphasis that has been placed on this dimension of social status.

The theoretical distinction between static and dynamic aspects of social status was presented clearly in the work of the functionalist theorist, Kingsley Davis (1942). Defining static data as the invidious values attached to any position in a given social structure, he pointed out that such values are independent of both the particular individual occupying the position and the success of that individual in fulfilling the requirements of the position. In contrast, the dynamic dimension refers to individuals' concrete behaviors and contains an element of novelty and unpredictability. In emphasizing the dual sense in which social standing is actually evaluated, Davis stressed the necessity of separating the two dimensions when studying the process empirically.

Parsons employed a similar dichotomy in his theoretical analysis of social stratification. He noted (1954) that every unit in a system of action is treated both as an object having ascertainable qualities and as an entity performing the functions of a role. The former relates to the static dimension and the latter to the dynamic dimension.

Role theory elaborates this distinction further (Sarbin, 1966; Biddle and Thomas, 1966). According to this perspective, the social world comprises a network of variously interrelated positions or roles. Attached to each position are sets of expectations concerning how incumbents are to behave or to enact their roles. Role theorists pay major attention to the degree to which an individual conforms to the requirements of a particular status—in other words, how well an individual performs in relation to her or his static positions. In attempting to connect social structure and role behavior through the concept of role expectations, role theorists have emphasized both the form and content of social roles. The implications are clear for social stratification research. Form may be viewed as reflecting the static dimension and content, the dynamic dimension.

This research examines the role of dynamic factors in the determination of social standing. Specifically, this research considers such factors as they affect social standing evaluations of households. To accomplish this objective, a vignette technique is employed.

Methodology

The data collection procedure is a technique developed by Rossi and associates (1974) and is based on the use of vignettes. Each vignette consists of brief statements describing a household that is being evaluated. All households consisted of a husband and wife. Information included on the vignettes represent both the static and the dynamic dimensions. The dependent variable and the specific vignette variables are described below.

Dependent Variable

The dependent variable in this study is social standing, which is conceptually defined as the location of a social unit along a continuum representing desirability and goodness. That households are evaluated as higher or lower on this continuum is supported by a long history of both theoretical (Parsons, 1954; Weber, 1947) and empirical (Warner and Lunt, 1941; Reiss, 1961) research. The operational definition of social standing is an actual evaluation of a vignette on a nine-point scale ranging from "highest social standing" to "lowest social standing." For purposes of analysis each point on the scale is treated as an equal interval. In recognition of the possibility that respondents may have been idiosyncratic in their use of this scale (that is, in the range of scores and variability of scores) however, a standardized version of the dependent variable is also used.

Static Independent Variables

Occupation. Since the 1920s empirical research has consistently revealed a high degree of consensus regarding the prestige of occupations (Counts, 1925; Smith, 1943; North and Hatt, 1947). Further, these prestige evaluations have remained consistent over time (Hodge et al., 1964) and across different societies (Hodge et al., 1966). Also, incumbents' characteristics, such as sex, have had only minor effects on the estimated prestige score (Bose, 1973). The stability in these evaluations indicates that the performance of the incumbent is not being measured or taken into account, but rather the position itself is being evaluated. For this reason, the occupational prestige score is an appropriate representative of the static dimension.[2] Vignettes described an occupation for both husband and wife.

Education. Educational attainment, the second static variable, has been viewed in a theoretical sense as a major factor in the determination of status. Weber considered a formal process of education as one of the bases of social status (1947). Parsons indicated the static nature of education when he noted that "probably the best single index of the line between 'upper middle' and the rest of the middle class is the expectation that children will have a college education," stressing that education is an entitlement rather than an indication of learning or performance (1954: 433). In this perspective education is viewed as a static position rather than a dynamic performance.

Early community studies (Warner et al., 1949; Hollingshead, 1949) and status attainment research (Blau and Duncan, 1967) have also treated educational position as an essential static element of social status. More recent stratification research (Rossi et al., 1974; Nock and Rossi, 1978) has continued to support the notion that education has an independent influence on social status.

In short, there is good reason to view educational level as a determinant of social status. Further, it is considered to be a static variable because knowledge that individuals have completed a certain level of schooling places them in a position (for example, high school graduate or college graduate) without providing information regarding their performances within these positions.[3] Vignettes described an educational attainment for both husband and wife.

Dynamic Independent Variables

Selection of the dynamic variables was a more difficult task for two reasons. First, unlike the static variables, the effects of the dynamic components have not been thoroughly explored in prior social stratification research. Without this legacy of empirical findings on which to draw, it is much less clear which variables best represent the dynamic dimension.

Second, there is a high degree of diversity implicit in the concept of social performance. The manner in which people perform with respect to the expectations of their different static positions is varied and can be communicated in a multitude of ways. Thus, in attempting to understand the effects of the dynamic dimension on social status it is important to choose indicators that tap as many aspects of the performance concept as possible. The following variables were selected to provide the broadest coverage of the dynamic dimension possible.

Attributes. The first dynamic variable, which deals with attributes and personal qualities, was selected because it implicitly or explicitly describes the way individuals perform. That is, by providing a more complete personal description, this variable indicates how a person is likely to behave in a variety of situations (Phillips, 1963). The attribute data refer either to the fulfillment of expectations attached to specific roles or to performances in a more general context. Both vignette members are described by such attributes. The information is classified into the following four categories:

(a) work attributes
    work-related behaviors and characteristics that suggest how well an individual is performing in an occupational position;
(b) social attributes
    personal interests and interpersonal relations that indicate how a person performs individually, as a friend, and as a family member;
(c) emotional attributes
    mental and emotional stability information that implies how well an individual handles problems and, thus, how well he or she performs in a variety of positions;
(d) deviant attributes
    illegal or negatively sanctioned behavior that reveals individuals' tendencies toward immoral, unconventional behaviors and performances.

These categorizations are helpful in studying the effects of the attribute data on family social standing. However, it should be pointed out that an attribute representing a specific category may also provide insight into the quality of performances associated with other attribute categories. For instance, certain work-related attributes may also provide dynamic information regarding social attributes. For this reason, these categories are used only heuristically in the analysis.

Affiliational Ties. The second indicator of the dynamic dimension deals with affiliational membership. Previous research in the area of associations has focused mainly on the relationship between quantity of affiliational ties and social class (Hyman and Wright, 1958, 1971; Babchuck and Booth, 1969). Our interest, however, is not with the number of ties but rather with the performance information that is provided by each particular association. Affiliational ties are viewed as dynamic data because they furnish insight into the way a person performs in a variety of roles, such as concerned citizen or parent. By using a wide range of affiliations, the effects of both favorable and unfavorable performances are available. Each vignette member is assigned an affiliation.

Leisure-Time Activities. The final dynamic variable reflects life-style behaviors by describing leisure-time activities. It is considered to be dynamic because it pertains to the way people perform during their free time. Leisure activities and lifestyles have frequently been linked to social class (Veblen, 1934; Clarke, 1956; Catton, 1972; Reissman, 1954; Brudge, 1969; Noe, 1971). And while previous research supports the idea that social status and leisure-time activities are related, little has been done to explicate this connection further. The current research is an attempt to clarify this issue by exploring the impact of specific leisure-time activities on social standing. Each vignette family is described by a leisure-time activity.

The dynamic characteristics described above are nominal variables, and in order to assign values appropriate for the analytic approach, a scaling technique based on dummy variable regression analysis was used. Vignette ratings were regressed on the set of nominal categories and the resulting slopes assigned to respective categories as scale values. Except for certain constraints imposed to prevent highly implausible combinations, the values of the vignette variables were randomly selected.[4] This random design resulted in the vignette characteristics being fairly independent of one another, a feature which greatly reduces the problem of multicollinearity and allows for a more accurate interpretation of the different predictor variables' effects on household social standing.

Unit of Analysis

The unit of analysis is the household, comprising the wife and the husband. Families have been viewed as important in theoretical works of sociologists (Weber, 1947; Parsons, 1954; Barber, 1957; Turner, 1970). In addition, many community studies have used the family as the unit of analysis (Warner and Lunt, 1941; Hollingshead, 1949; Lynd and Lynd, 1929). Knowledge about an individual's family is readily accessible information which is useful in determining social status. Because of the logical, empirical, and theoretical support, the household is treated as the appropriate object of study.

Sample

A national area probability sample of 506 noninstitutionalized adults was used in this study. In a personal interview, each respondent evaluated a set of 50 vignettes on the dimension of household social standing. This produced 24,787 rated vignettes.[5] In addition to the rating task, basic demographic and socioeconomic information was obtained from each respondent.

Analysis and Findings

The expectation is that both the static and the dynamic variables are influential in predicting household social standing. To examine this issue, bivariate and multiple regression analysis techniques are used.

Bivariate Relationships of Dependent and Independent Variables

The bivariate relationships presented in Table 2.1 indicate that the correlation between social standing and each of the nine characteristics is positive and significant, suggesting that each of the vignette variables contributes, in some degree, to the social standing accorded a household. These results show that the respondents are assimilating all vignette information in the rating process, rather than simply relying on one or two of the hypothetical household's characteristics. If the latter situation had been the case, we would expect some of the coefficients to be negative or not significant.[6]

Although all the vignette data are used in the rating process, it is also apparent that these variables have unequal impact on the household social standing. In order to explore this issue more thoroughly, multiple regression analysis techniques are utilized.

Effects of Static and Dynamic Variables on Social Standing

Table 2.2 presents the results of regressing household social standing on the total set of nine vignette characteristics. This equation allows an examination of the overall pattern of relationships among the hypothetical household characteristics and social standing.

The R^2 of .232 indicates that the independent variables explain a moderate proportion of the variance in the dependent variable. This value is in keeping with the results of the previous vignette studies that have utilized similar amounts of vignette data (Nock and Rossi, 1978, 1979). Each vignette characteristic is statistically significant, though in some cases the substantive effect is small.

TABLE 2.1 Bivariate Correlations among Vignette Characteristics and Social Standing

	WE	HE	WOCC	HOCC	WAT	HAT	WAF	HAF	FL
Static									
Wife Education (WE)									
Husb. Education (HE)	.00								
Wife Occupation (WOCC)	.25	.02							
Husb. Occupation (HOCC)	.02	.28	.09						
Dynamic									
Wife Attribute (WAT)	.00	.00	.01	.00					
Husb. Attribute (HAT)	.01	.00	.00	.00	−.01				
Wife Affiliation (WAF)	.02	.00	.00	.01	.00	.00			
Husb. Affiliation (HAF)	.00	.04	−.01	.01	.00	.01	.01		
Family Leisure (FL)	.00	.01	.00	.00	.01	.01	.00	.00	
*Social Standing**	.12	.14	.15	.21	.24	.28	.10	.11	.04

*All correlation coefficients between social standing and each vignette variable are significant at the .05 level of probability.

76

TABLE 2.2 Regression of Social Standing on Static and Dynamic Variables

Vignette Variables	b	Beta	T*
Static			
Wife Education	.024	.084	14.6
Husb. Education	.023	.083	14.4
Wife Occupation	.008	.112	19.4
Husb. Occupation	.011	.176	30.2
Dynamic			
Wife Attribute	.010	.240	43.2
Husb. Attribute	.010	.276	49.6
Wife Affiliation	.010	.100	18.0
Husb. Affiliation	.009	.100	18.0
Family Leisure	.007	.036	6.4

$R^2 = .232$
$N = 24,787$

*Each coefficient is significant at the .05 level of probability.

Focusing on the static data, an interesting relationship between the spouses' characteristics emerges. Specifically, a comparison of the effects of their educational levels reveals that the husband and the wife have nearly equal impact on the social standing accorded their family, with the ratio of the slopes for wife's education to the husband's equaling 1.01 (.084/.083=1.01).[7] This indicates that, with respect to education, the attainment of the wife is as important as is her husband's in explaining household social standing.

Such equivalency is not found for occupations. Still, however, the wife's occupational prestige makes a substantial contribution in the determination of family social standing. The ratio of the wife's beta to the husband's is .64 (.112/.176=.64). These ratios are most striking when viewed in the context of prior stratification literature. Social status research has often de-emphasized or entirely omitted the wife's characteristics when determining the status of the family. However, these results are consistent with others' in pointing to the importance of the wife's education and occupation in the determination of family social standing (Rossi et al., 1974; Nock and Rossi, 1978, 1979; Sampson and Rossi, 1975).

Shifting to a comparison of the relative impact of education and occupation, the ratio of husband's education beta to husband's occupation beta produces a value of .47, indicating that the former static characteristic counts roughly half as much as the latter. Previous vignette studies have found comparable ratios in the range .25 to .35 (Nock and Rossi, 1978; Sampson and Rossi, 1975). The break with earlier vignette results is even clearer when we examine the betas of the wife's education to occupation ratio, which equals .75. The highest previous ratio was .47 (Sampson and Rossi, 1975).

Overall, these findings suggest greater equality among the static characteristics in their contributions to social standing than has been found by other researchers.

The question is why, compared with previous social standing research, the two spouses' static characteristics are more equal in importance. One possible explanation, which is discussed more thoroughly below,concerns the importance of the dynamic data. In the earlier research, the static information was found to be the most important determinant of social standing. Although other characteristics have also been influential, their effects have not been comparable to those of either the spouses' occupations or educations. However, as will be shown, the dynamic characteristics which were included on the vignettes were as important, if not more so, than the static data. This depreciation of the static variables' impact vis-a-vis other vignette variables may account for the narrowing gap between the static variables' coefficients. It appears that as the static variables begin to account for proportionally smaller amounts of variance in social standing overall, the relative differences among them in their individual importances are reduced.

To investigate this issue further, the impact of the dynamic data on the evaluation of household social standing is investigated. An examination of the relative influences of the dynamic variables reveals that the effects of the two spouses' affiliational characteristics are equal. The attribute betas for the husband and wife, while not being equal, are quite similar (ratio of husband to wife=.87). Thus, as was true for the static characteristics, the effects of the two spouses' dynamic variables do not differ greatly, if at all.

Further examination of the dynamic performance data shows that the wife's attribute information is more important than is that about her affiliation (ratio=2.4). The comparable ratio for the husband is 2.8. Family leisure activity is the weakest contributor to household social standing, as evidenced by its beta being roughly one-seventh the size of the attribute betas and one-third the size of the affiliation betas.

The magnitudes of these *dynamic* variables' betas make it clear that the attribute variables predominate. Affiliational ties have notable import, but the family leisure activity has only a minimal impact.

In exploring the effects of the vignette variables, one of the more interesting questions deals with the relationship between the static and the dynamic data. That is, how do the characteristics which represent these two dimensions compare in their relative influence on social standing? An examination of the ratios of the variables' betas reveals the major impact spouses' attribute characteristics have on the dependent variable. Comparing attribute and occupation effects, one notes the ratio for husbands is 1.6 and for wives the effect is 1.4 the magnitude of the husband's occupational prestige beta. This finding is striking because the husband's occupational prestige has traditionally been the major, and often times sole, determinant of household social standing. Both attribute betas are more than twice the size of the wife's occupation beta and roughly three times the size of each spouses' educational level beta. These two effects dominate all others in the analysis. The affiliation variables are also important factors, although to a lesser extent. Again, the family leisure activity characteristic does not appear to be substantively important.

The major implication to be drawn from these comparisons is the importance of the dynamic characteristics in the determination of household social standing. With the exception of family leisure, the dynamic variables appear to have as much, or more, effect than more traditional static variables. Thus, rather than being ignored or having primarily idiosyncratic influences on the dependent variable, the characteristics representing the dynamic dimension appear to be integral in the rating process. Recognizing that this type of information is important, we now turn to a more detailed examination of the particular manner in which these dynamic characteristics affect the hypothetical families' social standings.

A Closer Examination of the Effects of the Dynamic Data

To obtain a clearer understanding of the effects of the dynamic dimension, four separate dummy variable regression equations were run, one each for the wife's and the husband's attributes and affiliational ties. The family leisure-time dummy variable regression is excluded from this segment of the analysis since it explained less than .1 percent of the variance in the dependent variable.[8]

These separate equations formed the basis of the scaling procedure, and by focusing on them it is possible to delineate the impact of the specific attributes and affiliational ties. This, in turn, provides a more accurate picture of the relationship between the dynamic dimension and the evaluation of household social standing.

Attribute Data. The attribute data, which were included to provide information concerning how family members fulfilled the requirements of their various positions, are presented in Table 2.3 and 2.4. Table 2.3 presents for the wife and Table 2.4 for the husband the results of regressing household social standing on the 30 attribute dummy variables. The righthand column in each table indicates which of the four heuristic categories—work, social, emotional, or deviant—the particular attribute characteristic represents.

A review of the general findings in these tables reveals R^2 values of .057 for the wife and .075 for the husband. Because of the near independence between the two sets of dummy variables, the combined explained variance resulting from knowledge of both spouses' attribute data is approximately 13 percent. This finding is striking since it represents *more than half* of the total amount of explained variance (13%/23%=.57). The indented attribute values do not have significant b-coefficients, showing that certain types of attribute data do not, from a statistical perspective, influence the determination of household social standing.

An examination of the variation in the magnitude of the b-coefficients indicates, for both spouses, that the increase in status resulting from the most positive attribute characteristic is much less than the decrease in status associated with the most negatively evaluated characteristic. Wife's attributes may potentially cost the household three times as much as they might enhance it, and husband's, four times as much. In short, of the selected attribute characteristics, there is more penalty associated with those which are viewed as negative than reward gained by those which are favorable.

Comparisons between the ranges of the spouses' b-coefficient values indicate that while the positive end of the continuum is similar, the negative range is greater for the husband. The most

TABLE 2.3   Regression of Social Standing on Wife Attribute Dummy Variables

Attribute*	b	Category
is known for having integrity and honesty	.20	social
is a warm and loving person	.18	social
enjoys classical music	.17	social
has a great deal of self-confidence	.17	work-related
is highly respected by friends	.17	social
is successful as a spouse and parent	.14	social
is very well organized	.12	work-related
has a good imagination	.11	work-related
speaks well	.10	work-related
plays the violin quite well	.10	social
is creative and artistic	.09	work-related
has a good sense of humor	.08	social
is often called on for personal advice	.07	social
has an easygoing manner	.06	social
has a lot of ambition	.03	work-related
no attribute included on vignette	intercept	
is a very nervous person	-.12	emotional
is often depressed	-.15	emotional
sees a psychiatrist weekly	-.20	emotional
often takes tranquilizers	-.21	emotional
tends to drink too much at parties	-.25	emotional
has spent some time in a mental hospital	-.27	emotional
reads a lot of pornography	-.30	deviant
has a gambling problem	-.31	deviant
drove while license was suspended	-.35	deviant
is rumored to have had several extramarital affairs	-.39	deviant
has bribed a public official to obtain favors	-.45	deviant
has passed worthless checks involving less than $100	-.52	deviant
has neglected to care for children	-.62	deviant
has engaged in homosexual acts with consenting adults	-.63	deviant
caused an auto accident while driving drunk	-.64	deviant

$R^2 = .057$

*Indented attributes are not significant at the .05 level of probability; all others are.

unfavorable characteristic associated with the wife had the effect of reducing the standardized household social standing a magnitude of .64 compared to the husband's most unfavorable attribute characteristic having the potential negative impact of .78. Husbands' negative attributes are more costly than comparable attributes of the wife.

With respect to the categories of attribute data, for both spouses all the significant social and work data have a positive impact on

TABLE 2.4   Regression of Social Standing on Husband Attribute Dummy Variables

Attribute*	b	Category
is very well organized	.18	work-related
is highly respected by friends	.14	social
is a warm and loving person	.14	social
is known for having integrity and honesty	.13	social
enjoys classical music	.11	social
is successful as a spouse and parent	.11	social
has a good sense of humor	.09	social
has an easygoing manner	.09	social
speaks well	.08	work-related
is often called on for personal advice	.08	social
has a lot of ambition	.06	work-related
is creative and artistic	.05	work-related
has a good imagination	.04	work-related
plays the violin quite well	.02	social
no attribute included on vignette	intercept	
has a great deal of self-confidence	-.01	work-related
often takes tranquilizers	-.21	emotional
is a very nervous person	-.21	emotional
is often depressed	-.25	emotional
sees a psychiatrist weekly	-.25	emotional
has spent some time in a mental hospital	-.29	emotional
tends to drink too much at parties	-.39	emotional
drove while license was suspended	-.39	deviant
has a gambling problem	-.43	deviant
reads a lot of pornography	-.48	deviant
is rumored to have had several extramarital affairs	-.50	deviant
has bribed a public official to obtain favors	-.56	deviant
has passed worthless checks involving less than $100	-.68	deviant
caused an auto accident while driving drunk	-.68	deviant
has engaged in homosexual acts with consenting adults	-.75	deviant
has neglected to care for children	-.78	deviant

$R^2 = .075$

*Indented attributes are not significant at the .05 level of probability; all others are.

household social standing, while all significant emotional and deviant data are negative in their influence.

Comparing those categories with positive effects (social and work) social attributes garner more social standing than do work attributes. That is, the social data, which indicate how a person performs individually, as a friend, and as a family member, have the strongest positive impact on the dependent variable. Specifically, for the wife, all but one of the six most positive characteristics are social attributes. A similar pattern is shown for the husband, with five of the six most positive attributes being social attributes. These results suggest that, with respect to *improving* family social standing, the social variables are slightly more important than the work-related ones.

In general, the relative ordering of the two spouses' particular types of social and work-related information are similar. However, an interesting exception concerns the work-related characteristic of "has a great deal of self-confidence." When applied to the wife, this attribute is strong and positive, ranking fourth among all attributes and improving the household prestige by .17. However, for the husband the characteristic does not even have a significant effect. This suggests that the popular conceptualization of the male role includes being self-confident; as a result, this attribute is not viewed as special. In contrast, the female is viewed as exceptional when she is identified as possessing this characteristic, and family social standing is accordingly enhanced.

Examining the emotional and deviant attribute characteristics, we find that for both of the spouses, all b-coefficients are significant and negative. Also, these two categories of attribute data cluster together for both of the spouses, with the deviant characteristics having the most negative impact on household social standing.

The emotional characteristics were included to indicate mental and emotional stability and to provide information concerning how a person handles problems or performs in a variety of situations. As expected, the more severe the characteristic, the stronger its negative impact on social standing. With respect to ordering, a general congruence between the two spouses exists. For both wife and husband, the two emotional characteristics of "having spent time in a mental hospital" and "drinking too much at parties" receive the strongest negative sanctions.

For the deviant data, which indicate an individual's tendencies toward immoral, unconventional behavior, there is also similarity in their impact for the two spouses. The particular behaviors of "neglecting to care for children," "engaging in homosexual acts," and "causing an auto accident while driving drunk" have the strongest negative impact on the household social standing.

Affiliational Ties. Data on affiliational ties were included on the vignettes because they provide insight into how people perform vis-à-vis the requirements of various positions. For example, by knowing

TABLE 2.5   Regression of Social Standing on Wife Affiliation Dummy Variables

Affiliation*	b
association to help fund cancer research	.17
active with the college's alumni organization**	.17
town's Junior Chamber of Commerce	.13
organization which helps senior citizens	.13
church-related association	.11
volunteer work with the American Red Cross	.08
organization to aid in stamping out a disease	.07
extremely conservative political party	.07
organization aimed at preventing cruelty to animals	.07
tennis club	.06
bowling league	.06
PTA	.06
active with Boy Scouts of America	.06
organization promoting antiabortion laws	.04
community service organization	.03
local art museum	.03
labor union	.02
country club	.02
Veterans' Association	.02
neighborhood association	.01
meditation group	.01
Republican Party	.01
Democratic Party	.01
card-playing club	.00
no affiliation included on vignette	intercept
civil rights organization	-.01
chess club	-.04
Socialist Party	-.14
Alcoholics Anonymous	-.16
radical political organization	-.23
Communist Party	-.46

$R^2 = .010$

*Indented affiliations are not significant at the .05 level of probability; all others are.
**This affiliation is not considered significant because it is not independent of the educational-level variable (see text).

that an individual is active in the PTA, it is possible to infer something about his or her performance in the role of a parent. An examination of the set of specific affiliations included in the household indicates which performances are highly rewarded, as well as those that are negatively sanctioned. Tables 2.5 and 2.6 present the results of regressing household social standing on the wife's and the husband's affiliational tie dummy variables.

TABLE 2.6   Regression of Social Standing on Husband Affiliation
Dummy Variables

Affiliation*	b
active with college alumni organization**	.30
labor union	.16
association to help fund cancer research	.15
organization which helps senior citizens	.14
PTA	.12
organization aimed at preventing cruelty to animals	.11
active with Boy Scouts of America	.11
church-related association	.09
organization promoting antiabortion laws	.09
country club	.08
tennis club	.08
volunteer work for the American Red Cross	.08
town's Junior Chamber of Commerce	.07
Veterans' Association	.07
Democratic Party	.07
community service organization	.05
organization to aid in stamping out a disease	.05
neighborhood association	.04
bowling league	.04
chess club	.02
card-playing club	.01
Republican Party	.01
no affiliation included on vignette	intercept
extremely conservative political party	-.01
meditation group	-.04
local art museum	-.07
Alcoholics Anonymous	-.09
Socialist Party	-.10
civil rights organization	-.11
radical political organization	-.18
Communist Party	-.44

$R^2 = .010$

*Indented affiliations are not significant at the .05 level of probability; all others are.
**This affiliation is not considered significant because it is not independent of the educational-level variable (see text).

An overview of the tables shows that the explanatory power of these data is not large. Each spouse's affiliational ties account for approximately one percent of the unexplained variance, suggesting that although the contribution of this information is statistically significant, its substantive impact is not great.

Unlike the situation with the attribute dummy variables, the majority of these b-coefficients are *not* significant. This finding applies to both spouses, with 22 (73 percent) of the wife's and 17 (57 percent) of the husband's not being statistically significant, implying that a small set of affiliational ties are responsible for most of the effect on household social standing.

An examination of the ranges of the b-coefficient values shows that the most positive affiliational tie for the wife raises social standing ratings by .17 and the most positive for the husband by .16. The negative impact was greater than the positive, with maximum b-coefficients equaling -.46 for the wife and -.44 for the husband. As with the attribute data, the loss of status resulting from negatively defined information is greater than the gain from positive information.

To understand why certain affiliational ties have more impact, underlying factors which provide a common link among the significant ties were sought. The first factor relates to one's performance, both positive and negative, in the role of concerned citizen. Exceptional performances in this role result from affiliational ties that reflect important societal values and from affiliational ties that represent a break from stereotypic expectations.

The positive impact resulting from either spouse's involvement in groups aimed at funding cancer research or helping senior citizens demonstrates the importance of societal values in performance as a concerned citizen. Both cancer and the plight of the elderly have been socially defined as serious problems. As a result, the household's social standing is increased when the husband or the wife displays exceptional performances by working to resolve these problems. An examination of the nonsignificant affiliational ties, however, indicates that in order to warrant this reward the societal problems must be clearly articulated. Thus, involvement with an organization with diffuse goals such as one aimed at stamping out a disease, or the American Red Cross, do not produce significant boosts in the dependent variable.

Another societal value that results in a significantly positive performance involves the church. It appears that being associated with a church-related organization implies exceptional performance as a church member, and due to the importance of this institution, this performance increases the household social standing when either spouse is involved.

In addition to the positive impact which results because the organization is viewed as important, performance in the concerned citizen role may be significant because the individual is not normally expected to be performing in this role. For example, membership in the town's Junior Chamber of Commerce has significant effects only for the wife, suggesting that role expectations exist which make her involvement in this organization exceptional. Such involvement on the husband's part may be considered more consistent with the stereotypic male role and, as a result, is not viewed as exceptional.

In a similar way, involvement with organizations aimed at preventing cruelty to animals or focused on promoting antiabortion laws are traditionally connected with the woman's role and, as such, may be considered as normal performance when associated with the wife. However, the husband's involvement in these organizations is considered atypical and thus carries status-enhancing consequences.

Shifting to the lower end of the continuum, it is apparent that negative performances in the role of citizen are being sanctioned. For both spouses, involvement with leftist political organizations accounts for the strongest downward pull on household social standing. These ties reveal a poor performance as an American citizen. In fact, being active in these organizations may be viewed as both not fulfilling expected requirements and also working against national goals and values. The most dramatic impact is Communist Party affiliation, which reduces household social standing by .46 when associated with the wife and .44 when associated with the husband. Less negative in its effect is the political affiliation of "radical political party." Although more vague in its intent, it also infers unpatriotic performances on the part of its members, as indicated by b-coefficients of -.23 and -.18 for the wife and husband, respectively.

The third political affiliation which is negatively sanctioned for both spouses is the Socialist Party. It is interesting that although membership in this organization has negative consequences, they are not as negative as those due to Communist Party membership.

For the husband only, an association with a "civil rights organization" is significantly negative. This perception possibly results because this organization has an identification with civil disobedience, as well as reflecting a liberal orientation, thus implying that the husband is not performing well as a law-abiding and patriotic citizen.

A second underlying factor in the explanation of significant affiliational ties concerns performance in the parental role. Again, the impact of stereotypic expectations is apparent. Specifically, for the husband involvement with either the PTA or the Boy Scouts of America produces a positive significant increase in the dependent variable, yet neither is significant when associated with the wife. It

seems that for the wife affiliational involvements that are commonly
identified with the position of mother do not represent special
performances. For the husband, however, these involvements represent a distinguished performance as father.

A third factor relates to the work role and is represented by labor
union membership. This affiliation is the most positively significant
affiliational tie for the husband, although it does not produce a
significant impact when associated with the wife. It appears that, for
the husband only, labor union affiliation portrays a notable performance with respect to his occupational position. It is interesting,
however, that the household is not being positively rewarded when
the wife is so affiliated, indicating that requirements of a woman vis-
a-vis her occupational position are perceived as different from a
man's. The outcome is that the family is rewarded for the husband's
extra efforts in the area of organizing and supporting his fellow
workers, while a comparable performance on the part of the wife
results in no household status gains.

The final underlying factor reflects overall performance information in the affiliational tie of Alcoholics Anonymous. This is the only
negative affiliation which does not have a political connotation. It is
interesting that membership in this organization in which people are
attempting to rehabilitate themselves lowers family social standing.
It appears that members of society see the ability of an alcoholic, or a
previous alcoholic, to perform well in various positions or roles as
jeopardized because of the problem. As a result, for both the husband
and the wife efforts to correct problem drinking are not rewarded but
are actually penalized.

Summary and Implications

The impact of these findings is far-reaching. To begin with, the fact
that the respondents readily incorporated the data concerning both
spouses in the evaluation process provides further support for the
importance of the wife's characteristics. This finding is a clear
critique of more limited measures of social standing which omit such
data. Researchers must increase their sensitivity to the characteristics of the wife when attempting to develop composite social standing
indicators.

Another major finding is the salience of dynamic data in the determination of household social standing. Although this dimension has been overlooked in empirically based measures of social standing, the results of the current study reveal its importance. Dynamic data actually contribute more than the static dimension. The best predictors of the dependent variable are not the standard occupation or education data, but rather the husband's and wife's attribute data. Thus, previous singular reliance on occupational prestige as the surrogate for social standing is called into question. Such a reliance on a single characteristic is apparently too simplistic a method to represent the complex concept of social standing.

These findings indicate that although the overwhelming majority of social status measures have concentrated on the static characteristics of individuals and families, dynamic data are crucial in the determination of social standing and should not be overlooked. In attempting to incorporate dynamic information into the measurement process, however, new and special problems are soon encountered.

First, unlike the static characteristics, such as educational levels and occupational prestige, the possible dynamic traits seem infinite. Thus, although there is great variety in types of occupations, there are limits. Also, occupations have been organized into prestige levels, which makes investigation of them easier. In contrast, dynamic data cover a vast spectrum of affiliations, attributes, and performances. The particular data included in this study only begin to expose the dynamic variables that may influence status judgments. It may be possible to impose categorizations on the myriad of dynamic data; however, more research into the effects of these characteristics is necessary before this task can be accomplished.

Another problem associated with the investigation of dynamic data concerns the number of these characteristics that can be associated with an individual. This is rarely a problem with the static data. Usually individuals are employed in one or possibly two occupations. They also have a single educational level. This is not the case with dynamic characteristics. Several attributes, affiliational ties, and other kinds of dynamic data can be associated with a single family member. Also, this information may be conflicting, in that it reflects both positive and negative performances. By presenting a selected set of dynamic traits the researcher has implicitly deemphasized the remaining multitude of unmentioned dynamic data.

Any attempts to incorporate such dynamic information in social status measures must face the difficult questions of how much and what type of information is relevant.

Despite the problems inherent in examining the dynamic aspects of status, our findings clearly substantiate their importance. Because such performance data play a critical role in the evaluation of the hypothetical household's social standing, it is probable that these data are also incorporated in status evaluations of actual households. The inclusion of such information may make the measure of social standing more complicated. However, our findings indicate that dynamic data should not be ignored if the goal of the research is to obtain accurate, valid judgments of social standing.

Appendix A

Occupations

Physician	Factory Assembly Line Supervisor
College Professor	
Lawyer	Key Punch Operator
Electrical Engineer	Car Dealer
City Superintendent of Schools	Post Office Clerk
Manager of a Factory Employing more than 200 People	Carpenter
	Typist
High School Teacher	Cotton Farmer
Registered Nurse	Plumber
Hospital Lab Technician	Telephone Operator
Advertising Executive	Supervisor of Telephone Operators
Accountant	
Building Contractor	Welder
Hotel Manager	Wholesale Salesperson
Electrician	Auto Mechanic
Police Officer	Inspector in a Factory
Tool Machinist	Beautician
Locomotive Engineer	Washing Machine Repairman
Bookkeeper	Truck Driver
Manager of a Supermarket	Cashier
Office Secretary	File Clerk

Warehouse Clerk
Housepainter
Textile Machine Operator
Someone Who Sells Shoes in a
    Store
Delivery Truck Driver
Assembly Line Worker

Stock Clerk
Parking Lot Attendant
Laundry Worker
Garbage Collector
Living on Welfare
Housewife

Appendix B

Educational Levels

did not finish elementary school
graduated elementary school
finished one year of high school
finished two years of high school

graduated high school
finished one year of college
finished two years of college
graduated college

Appendix C

Family Leisure-Time Activities

spends vacations hiking and
    camping
often visits art museums
spends vacations boating
spends vacations working on
    second jobs
usually stays at home on vacation
    and fixes up the house
plays tennis regularly
spends vacations relaxing at home
spends vacations golfing
usually bowls on the weekends
often takes drives on Sunday
    afternoons
spends their vacations visiting
    relatives

regularly plays bridge
spends vacations traveling in
    their car
spends vacations at resort
    hotels
often attends sporting events
spends vacations traveling in a
    rented camper
spends vacations skiing
goes to the movies a couple of
    times a week
spends vacations watching
    television
usually spends their vacations
    separately

NOTES

1. The terms "dynamic" and "performance" are used interchangeably throughout this chapter.

2. See Appendix A for a complete list of the occupations that were used in the creation of the vignettes.

3. See Appendix B for a complete list of the educational levels that were used in the creation of the vignettes.

4. These constraints included controlling the minimum educational level that could appear with certain professional affiliations and occupations and preventing the difference between the husband's and wife's occupational prestige scores, which range from 8.2 to 81.5, from exceeding 50 points. The occupational title of housewife had a 20 percent probability of being associated with the hypothetical wife. For the dynamic variables, a wife or a husband who was assigned the affiliational tie of "college alumni organization" was assigned a college-level education. Also, each of the five dynamic characteristics had a 25 percent probability of being omitted.

5. The respondents were unable to sort approximately 2 percent of the hypothetical households; however, an examination of the unsorted data revealed no systematic differences from the sorted vignettes.

6. It should be noted that due to the large sample size, the issue of statistical significance is not a major consideration.

7. In the analysis which is concerned with comparisons among different variables, the standardized rather than the unstandardized b-coefficients are examined. This is necessary because the independent variables are measured in different units. Although these standardized coefficients (betas) should be interpreted with some caution because the vignette variables have an artificially imposed, rectangular distribution, they are still useful in comparing the relative contributions of the independent variables.

8. See Appendix C for a complete list of the family leisure-time activities that were used in the creation of the vignettes.

REFERENCES

Babchuck, Nicholus and Alan Booth, 1969, "Voluntary association membership: a longitudinal analysis." American Sociological Review 34: 31-45.

Barber, Bernard, 1957, Social Stratification. New York: Harcourt Brace Jovanovich.

Biddle, Bruce J. and Edwin J. Thomas, 1966, Role Theory: Concepts and Research. New York: John Wiley.

Blau, Peter M. and Otis Dudley Duncan, 1967, The American Ocupational Structure. New York: John Wiley.

Bose, Christine E., 1973, Jobs and Gender: Sex and Occupational Prestige. Johns Hopkins University, Center for Metropolitan Planning and Research, mimeo.

Brudge, Rabel J., 1969, "Levels of occupational prestige and leisure activity." Journal of Leisure Research 1: 262-275.

Catton, William R., Jr., 1972, "Leisure and social stratification," pp. 520-538 in G. W. Theilbar and S. D. Feldman (eds.) Issues in Inequality. Boston: Little, Brown.

Clarke, Alfred C., 1956, "Leisure and occupational prestige." American Sociological Review 21: 301-307.

Counts, George S., 1925, "The social status of occupations: a problem in vocational guidance." School Review 33: 16-27.

Davis, Kingsley, 1942, "The conceptual analysis of stratification." American Sociological Review 7: 309-321.

Haug, Marie, 1972, "Social-class measurement: a methodological critique," pp. 429-451 in G. W. Thielbar and S. D. Feldman (eds.) Issues in Social Inequality. Boston: Little, Brown.

Hodge, Robert W., Paul M. Siegel, and Peter H. Rossi, 1964, "Occupational prestige in the United States, 1925-63." American Journal of Sociology 70: 268-292.

Hodge, Robert W., Donald J. Treiman, and Peter H. Rossi, 1966, "A comparative study of occupational prestige," pp. 309-321 in R. Bendix and S. Lipset (eds.) Class, Status and Power. New York: Free Press.

Hollingshead, August B., 1949, Elmstown Youth. New York: John Wiley.

Horan, Patrick M., 1978, "Is status attainment research atheoretical?" American Sociological Review 43: 534-541.

Hyman, Herbert H. and Charles R. Wright, 1971, "Trends in voluntary association memberships of American adults." American Sociological Review 36: 191-206.

1958, "Voluntary association memberships of American adults: evidence from national sample surveys." American Sociological Review 23: 284-294.

Lynd, Robert S. and Helen Merril Lynd, 1929, Middletown. New York: Harcourt Brace Jovanovich.

Nock, Steven L. and Peter H. Rossi, 1979, "Household types and social standing." Social Forces 57: 1325-1345.

1978, "Ascription versus achievement in the attribution of social status." American Journal of Sociology 84: 541-564.

Noe, F. P., 1971, "Autonomous spheres of leisure activity for the executive and blue collarite." Journal of Leisure Research 3: 220-249.

North, Cecil C. and Paul K. Hatt, 1947, "Jobs and occupations: a popular evaluation." Opinion News 9: 3-13.

Parsons, Talcott, 1954, Essays in Sociological Theory. New York: Free Press.

Phillips, Derek L., 1963, "Rejection: a possible consequence of seeking help for mental disorders." American Sociological Review 28: 963-972.

Reiss, Albert J., 1961, Occupations and Social Status. New York: Free Press.

Reissman, Leonard, 1954, "Social class, leisure and social participation." American Sociological Review 19: 76-84.

Rossi, Peter H., William A. Sampson, Christine E. Bose, Guillermina, Jasso, and Jeff Passel, 1974, "Measuring household social standing." Social Science Research 3: 169-190.

Sampson, William A. and Peter H. Rossi, 1975, "Race and family social standing." American Sociological Review 40: 201-214.

Sarbin, Theodore R., 1966, "Role enactment," pp. 195-200 in B. J. Biddle and
    E. J. Thomas (eds.) Role Theory: Concepts and Research. New York: John Wiley.
Smith, Mapheus, 1943, "An empirical scale of prestige status of occupations."
    American Sociological Review 8: 185-192.
Turner, Ralph H., 1970, Family Interaction. New York: John Wiley.
Veblen, Thorstein, 1934, Theory of the Leisure Class. New York: Modern Library.
Warner, W. Lloyd and Paul W. Lunt, 1941, The Social Life of a Modern Community.
    New Haven: Yale University Press.
Warner, W. Lloyd, Marcia Meeker, and Kenneth Eells, 1949, Social Class in
    America. Chicago: Science Research Associates.
Weber, Max, 1947, The Theory of Social and Economic Organization (A. M.
    Henderson and Talcott Parsons, trans.). New York: Oxford University Press.

3

FAMILY SOCIAL STATUS
Consensus on Characteristics

STEVEN L. NOCK

The social standing allocated to a family depends mainly on the occupational and educational attainments of adult members (Rossi et al., 1974; Nock and Rossi, 1978). To a lesser degree, race and ethnicity are status characteristics (Sampson, 1975; Sampson and Rossi, 1975). Empirical research has firmly established the importance of both types of characteristics—achieved and ascribed. Little is known, however, about the relative importance of such factors or of the way they are evaluated by Americans. This research investigated the relative status value of diverse family characteristics, some achieved and some ascribed.

After presenting the results of this research question, we turn to a detailed consideration of the question of the amount of consensus among Americans in their evaluations of household social standing. For both substantive and methodological reasons, demonstrating a high degree of agreement on how families were evaluated is critical.

The family of origin is one of the few ascriptive groups to which members of modern society belong, and, as such, it is believed to have consequences throughout one's life. It has become abundantly clear from the status attainment studies of the past decade that the social origins of persons have both direct and indirect effects on their status attainment (Blau and Duncan, 1967; Sewell and Hauser, 1975; Jencks et al., 1972).

From the general social stratification literature we find considerable support for a position that asserts that the prestige standing of a family unit is affected directly by the standing of the members' own families of orientation, *independently* of the individual achievements of family members.

The literature is silent on how ascription and achievement elements are combined to arrive at an overall current social standing, but there is considerable agreement that some significant contribution is made by each set of elements.

The present study can be seen as an extension of the status attribution research undertaken by Rossi and his colleagues. In those studies individuals rated short vignettes which described simple nuclear families (husband and wife) in terms of their education and occupation along a nine-point scale of "social standing." These ratings were then regressed on the vignette household characteristics to discern the determinants of household social standing ratings. Later studies enriched the descriptions of vignette families, extending them to include more complex families, race, age of members, number of children, ethnicity, and several other characteristics.

The ascriptive elements of the family (that is, social origins) are indicated in this research by specifying the educational and occupational attainments of each family member's father as well as designating an ethnic or racial category for the family. The achievement elements are represented by the occupational and educational attainment levels of each family member and a statement concerning the migration history of the family.[1]

The selection of these characteristics was directed in part by past research, as well as by the methodological requirements of this study. Both education and occupation have consistently been found to be important determinants of family social status (see Rossi et al., 1974; Nock and Rossi, 1978). In addition to these two, Sampson and Rossi (1975) found that race is important in the attribution of family social status. Complementing such a finding is the early research by Bogardus (1925) and the more recent work by the Triandises (1965) indicating that ethnic titles are relevant in status judgments. Thus, the families studied in this research have their social origins described by characteristics that have been demonstrated to have strong and consistent effects in the determination of family status.

An equal amount of information describes the achievements of family members. In addition to indicating occupational and educational achievements of each member, we have described the family's migration status (migration history and type of area lived in). Where parental achievement is included to indicate the social origins of each person (that is, the social context within which their own achievement occurred), migration status is included to indicate a spatial context within which the individual and joint achievements of the couple occurred. Empirical studies have found considerable differences in individual occupational status according to the size of areas moved to and from. Blau and Duncan noted that "regardless of the size of the community where he now works, the larger the community where he grew up, the better are his chances to achieve occupational success and to move up from the status of his father" (Blau and Duncan in Abrahamson, Mizruchi, Hornung, 1976: 287). The reasons for this are unknown. Thus we know that there is some enhanced achievement value associated with spatial origins. Whether or not there is similarly status value is the question we are asking.

We know that occupations are often different things, depending on the context in which they are found. To be a doctor in a small town is not the same as being one in a large metropolitan area. Thus it may be hypothesized that migration to certain areas (particularly the large city, where one finds the best occupational opportunities) might be seen not only instrumentally but may be, itself, status-enchancing. As such, migration would be properly seen as an aspect of achievement. Twenty-five statements describe residence or migration from or to various types of areas which differ in size (Suburb of a Large City, Large City, and so on).

Method

A national area probability sample of 536 adult noninstitutionalized respondents rated on a nine-point scale the "social standing" of a set of 50 "vignette" descriptions of hypothetical households. Fieldwork was conducted by Audits and Surveys, Inc., a New York-based research organization.[2] A sex quota of 50 percent was imposed. The hypothetical households which respondents rated were described in short vignettes, containing the following information:

I.   Nuclear Family
  1. Occupation of Husband (one of 50 occupations including living on welfare)
  2. Educational Attainment of Husband (fifth grade through college)

3. Occupation of Wife (one of 50 occupations including that of housewife)
4. Educational Attainment of Wife (fifth grade through college)
5. Migration Status—Area of Residence and Migration History (permanent residence in, or migration from and to, one of five types of areas: large city, suburb of large city, small town, small city, country)

II. Family of Origin
1. Husband's Father's Educational Attainment (fifth grade through college)
2. Husband's Father's Occupation (one of 50 occupations including living on welfare)
3. Wife's Father's Educational Attainment (fifth grade through college)
4. Wife's Father's Occupation (one of 50 occupations including living on welfare)
5. Ethnicity, Described by the National Origin of the Nuclear Family (one of 20 ethnicities including Black-American)

Occupation is measured as occupational prestige scores reported in Ornstein (1977). Education is measured as years of education. Hodge, Siegel, and Rossi derived prestige scores for each of 20 ethnic categories in 1964. It is these scores we use to measure enthnicity.

Migration status refers to statements describing the general type of area in which the nuclear couple lives and their history of migration. This variable was constructed by assigning to each statement the regression coefficient associated with it when entered as a dummy variable in an equation predicting ratings of "social standing." This was the "score" used to represent each statement, and thus it reflects the effect each statement has on the estimated ratings of households.

Families or origin are described by reference to each member's father only. While it would have been desirable to describe both families of origin as completely as we did the nuclear family (that is, describing both husband and wife), there are two reasons this was not done.

First, it has been found that at some point the amount of information presented to individuals who are making status judgments becomes burdensome. Thus, the complexity of the vignettes used to

```
┌─────────────────────────────────────────────────────────────────────────┐
│                                                                           │
│     HUSBAND              GRADUATED COLLEGE                                 │
│                          PHYSICIAN                                        │
│                                                                           │
│     HUSBAND'S FATHER     GRADUATED HIGH SCHOOL                            │
│                          CAR DEALER                                       │
│                                                                           │
│     WIFE                 FINISHED TWO YEARS OF COLLEGE                     │
│                          OFFICE SECRETARY                                 │
│                                                                           │
│     WIFE'S FATHER        FINISHED TWO YEARS OF HIGH SCHOOL                │
│                          WASHING MACHINE REPAIRMAN                        │
│                                                                           │
│            THE COUPLE'S NATIONAL BACKGROUND IS ITALIAN-AMERICAN           │
│                                                                           │
│       THE COUPLE MOVED FROM THE COUNTRY TO A SUBURB OF A LARGE CITY       │
│                                                                           │
└─────────────────────────────────────────────────────────────────────────┘
```

```
┌─────────────────────────────────────────────────────────────────────────┐
│                                                                           │
│     HUSBAND              DID NOT FINISH ELEMENTARY SCHOOL                 │
│                          LOCOMOTIVE ENGINEER                             │
│                                                                           │
│     HUSBAND'S FATHER     GRADUATED ELEMENTARY SCHOOL                      │
│                          ASSEMBLY LINE OPERATOR                          │
│                                                                           │
│     WIFE                 GRADUATED ELEMENTARY SCHOOL                      │
│                          TEXTILE MACHINE OPERATOR                        │
│                                                                           │
│     WIFE'S FATHER        GRADUATED COLLEGE                                │
│                          PHYSICIAN                                        │
│                                                                           │
│            THE COUPLE'S NATIONAL BACKGROUND IS POLISH-AMERICAN            │
│                                                                           │
│       THE COUPLE MOVED FROM A SUBURB OF A LARGE CITY TO THE COUNTRY       │
│                                                                           │
└─────────────────────────────────────────────────────────────────────────┘
```

Figure 3.1   Examples of Vignettes

describe families must be kept at a minimum. We believed four additional descriptive elements (both education and occupation of both husband and wife) would make the task tiring and generate error.

Second, the information describing families is contained on a vignette card the size of a standard data card (IBM card). Formatting such vignettes must be done in such a way as to present the information clearly and neatly. Pretests indicated that vignettes containing descriptions of husband's and wife's mothers were difficult to read or evaluate easily.

We do not feel that the omission of this information is greatly problematic. The unit of analysis is the *nuclear* family, and descriptions of the family members' parents serve only to indicate social origin. Thus, while our indicators of social origin could be enhanced, we have chosen those elements we know to be most important to family social standing (husband's occupation and education) and thus believe that we have adequately indicated the ascriptive elements of the study.

Some examples of the vignettes are shown in Figure 3.1. A total of 26,800 vignettes was produced. Of these, useful ratings were obtained for 26,734 (99 percent). Most of the missing vignettes resulted from cards being bent both prior and subsequent to fieldwork.

To explain the determinants of the social standing ratings given to vignettes, we posit a model in which the ratings are a function of the vignette characteristics, characteristics of the respondent, and some interaction of these factors. We employed ordinary least-squares regression as our mode of analysis using the following model:

$$R_i = f\,[(V_i) + (I_{ij}) + (IV_{ij}) + (VV_{ik,ik+1})] + e$$

where

R_i = rating given to vignette i

V_i = coded characteristics of information of vignette i

I_{ij} = characteristics of respondent j who rated vignette i

IV_{ij} = interaction of characteristics of respondent j and characteristics of vignette i

$VV_{ik,ik+1}$ = interaction of vignette characteristic k and vignette characteristic k+1, etc.

e = random error

We refer to two forms of R_i throughout this chapter; the original rating converted to a scale which runs 0 to 100, and the z-score representation of respondent's ratings. We shall employ the mnemonics "HPRES" for the former and "ZPRES" for the latter form of transformed rating. HPRES is simply a conversion of the original nine-point scale to make it comparable with occupational prestige scales which usually run from 0 to 100. ZPRES is the standardized (that is z-score) score of the rating respondents gave to vignettes standardized in terms of the particular respondent's mean and standard deviation(s) of ratings.

TABLE 3.1   Regression of HPRES (Equation 1) and ZPRES (Equation 2) on Vignette Characteristics

Vignette Characteristic	HPRES—Equation 1			ZPRES—Equation 2		
	b	Standard Error b	Maximum Percent Effect[a]	b	Standard Error b	Maximum Percent Effect[a]
Education						
Husband	1.166	.044	14.56	.0506	.002	16.63
Husb. Father	.136	.044	1.70	.0070	.002	2.26
Wife	.623	.044	7.79	.0267	.002	8.87
Wife Father	.109	.044	1.36	.0069	.002	2.27
Ethnicity[b]	.076	.011	3.76	.0036	.000	4.65
Occupational Prestige[c]						
Husband	.483	.010	40.20	.0217	.000	47.30
Husb. Father	.070	.010	5.83	.0028	.000	5.91
Wife	.240	.011	19.97	.0117	.000	25.64
Wife Father	.068	.010	5.65	.0030	.000	6.79
Migration Status[d]	.750	.174	2.90	.0166	.006	1.68
Intercept		-52.13			-3.729	
R^2		.179			.259	
F		915			574	
N		26253			26253	

a. Percent change in predicted score due to variable.
b. Ethnicity scores derived by Hodge, Siegel, and Rossi.
c. Occupational Prestige Scores from Ornstein (1977).
d. Coded from 25 categorical statements.

In contrast to HPRES, ZPRES reflects the possibility that respondents may vary both in their average ratings and the amount of variance in their ratings. Some individuals may rate all vignettes relatively higher or lower than do other respondents while still using the same rating principles. Similarly, some raters may *use more* of the rating scale than do others while agreeing on the rating principles used. ZPRES will remove such differences, giving all raters a mean rating of 0 and standard deviation of 1.

If respondents agreed on the principles they used in making their judgments of the vignette families but differed in terms of the numbers they chose to represent their judgments (for example, one respondent using 2 as the lowest score and another respondent using 3 despite agreement on which families would be given the lowest score), ZPRES will remove the effects of such differences. If such differences exist, ZPRES will better reflect the amount of agreement among respondents in the principles invoked in making status judgments.

Vignette Characteristic Effects

The equations in Table 3.1 are the result of regressing HPRES and ZPRES (equations 1 and 2, respectively) on the characteristics of the vignettes.[3] One of the most remarkable things about these equations is the rather small amount of explanatory power they express. The ten family characteristics explain between 18 and 26 percent of the total variance in rating, depending on the particular version of rating we use. The standard errors are quite small and are, of course, not affected by the amount of explained variance. The small R^2s are partly a function of the rating task itself. With fewer characteristics other researchers have accounted for considerably more variance by computing mean ratings given to identical vignettes (R^2s ranging from .60 to .80). (See Rossi et al., 1974.) We have found that the more information included on the vignette, the more error is generated by the rating task. Similarly, the more vignettes each respondent rates, the more error is generated. Such a large sample virtually guarantees that a simple linear additive model will express only modest amounts of explained variance. We have found that estimating equations *for each respondent* reveals much higher R^2s, even when the structure of equations is unchanged. We take our parameter estimates to be good estimates of the actual empirical importance of the characteristics we are studying. Low R^2s in aggregate equations such as these are not particularly surprising and are certainly not problematic.

It is not at all surprising that all coefficients attain statistical significance with such a large sample—virtually any departure from zero will result in statistically significant estimates. Further, the large sample gives us reason to believe that even the very small slopes accurately portray the true empirical importance of characteristics and are not simply measurement error. Thus it is obvious that some statistically significant variables mean very little in any substantive sense. For this reason, we have calculated the maximum effect each variable *could* have on predicted ratings and expressed this as a percentage of the possible range in variation. This is determined simply by evaluating each variable at its maximum contribution and minimum contribution to the value of the predicted prestige score for the household. For example, the range of estimated HPRES scores from equation 1 in Table 3.2 is 1.56 to 89.62 or 88.06. The slope on ethnicity is .076. Multiplying this by the minimum value of the variable (21.9, the prestige score for the category "Black-American") and the maximum (65.4, the prestige score for the category "British-American") and taking the difference (3.31) and dividing by the range tells us that this variable *could* alter the HPRES estimate by as much as 3.7 percent. These values are labeled "maximum percent effect" in tables.

This procedure is analogous to calculating "elasticities" except that rather than determining the percent change in HPRES or ZPRES due to a one percent change in any variable (as does an elasticity), we calculate the change due to a *maximum* change in any variable.

Determinants of Family Social Standing

Looking now at equation 1 in Table 3.1 we note first that there are considerable differences among the family characteristics in terms of their importance to the predicted values of HPRES—ranging from having a potential contribution of less than 2 percent (wife's father's education) to more than 40 percent (husband's occupation). Obviously, not all characteristics included on the vignettes are substantively important to the estimated value of HPRES.

Surprisingly, national origin (ethnicity) has very little effect. A Black family and a British-American family would differ by only 3.31 points in predicted HPRES, all other things being equal. As with any other characteristic, however, it may be that it is, or is not, important relative only to the other information presented. Thus, for example, ethnicity may not be salient when detailed educational and occupational information is available, but when such information is not available it may indeed be very important.

Race especially and ethnicity to a lesser extent have traditionally been viewed as important ascriptive categories. Our evidence suggests that as we have specified them, they are not all that important. We suggest that the psychodynamics of both race and ethnicity are similar. Both are ascriptive categories which are associated with varying degrees and strengths of stereotypes. However, the important point is that they are *stereotypical* categories. The "ideal world" of our vignettes violates all rules of stereotyping and thus renders these categories useless. While certain restrictions on education-occupation attainment mixes were imposed to eliminate bizarre or anomalous combinations, no such restrictions were imposed on ethnic titles and occupational or educational attainments. If ethnicity and race are equally probable as predictors of great achievements (on those dimensions considered here) as they are of failure, then they apparently serve no purpose in terms of their status value. In the real world, of course, we know that race and ethnicity do act to predict occupational and educational achievements. Apparently such information is what makes race and ethnicty important. That is, ethnicity is not *independent* in its effects. This finding is consistent with that of Sampson and Rossi in their study of the effects of race on family social standing (1975). In their research families were found to be affected by race by an amount equal to 1.75 HPRES points (1975: 208). Whereas our effects are somewhat stronger due to the addition of ethnicity, neither our results nor Sampson and Rossi's suggest much of an effect. As they note "a white/black difference of 1.72 points seems quite small" (p. 208).

Second, we note that migration status is only trivially related to household social standing. As we had specified this item, it indicated migration or lack of it for the nuclear couple. What we find is that while such migration as from city to city may enhance *achievement* empirically, it is not recognized as a status element for the households in our society. We must conclude that even though certain types of spatial origins and migration patterns have definite achievement value in terms of one's occupation, they have no status value in themselves and do not affect the overall social standing of a family. It might be recalled that we had speculated that certain occupations might carry more or less weight depending on the context within which they were found. HPRES values given various occupations and educational attainments were found to be essentially identical in various spatial contexts, indicating that spatial context as thus specified is not relevant in this regard (that is, there was no interaction effect between migration status and achievement characteristics).

Third, we note that for both husband's father and wife's father, educational attainment does not count to any important degree in the reckoning of family social status. From previous studies we know that the importance of occupation is approximately twice that of education in studies such as these. To the extent that parental characteristics indicating social origin *are* significant, parental education is apparently the point of diminishing returns—providing this piece of information to respondents apparently provides no useful information. That is, to the extent that respondents care to know about social origins, their concern does not go so far as to include information about parental educational attainment.

When we look at those characteristics which are important to the reckoning of family social standing, we find few surprises. The most important characteristics are the achieved characteristics of husband and wife. Compared to similar characteristics of parents, we see that the overall significance of social origin appears to be slight. We have already noted that parents' education is not important to family social standing. What are important are occupations and educational attainments of the husband and wife. Occupational prestige is by far the most important characteristic. Given this design, it is possible to ascertain the relative importance of similar vignette characteristics in *this* study by adding their slopes. That is, we can determine the combined effect of husband's and wife's occupation by simply adding the regression coefficients for occupation for each member. The sum of the b's will express the combined effects of the characteristics. Thus, the appropriate sum for occupations comparing husbands and wives with parental effects would be $(b_h + b_w)\Sigma\phi$ vs. $(b_{hf} + b_{wf})\Sigma\phi$ where the subscripts h, w, hf, and wf refer to husband, wife, husband's father, and wife's father, respectively, and ϕ is the symbol for occupational prestige. This is possible in *this* case because for each member of the vignette, ϕ is identical with the same variance.

First, we wish to compare the nuclear couple with parents in terms of the relative importance of each set of individuals for the overall household social standing determined by their occupations. The sum of b's for occupations for the husband and wife is .723, whereas for their parents the comparable figure is .138. This difference points to the vast difference in importance in the two sets of occupational achievements. Note, however, that parental occupations are not insignificant in this regard. They are simply far less important than are the occupations of the nuclear couple.

As other studies have found (see Rossi et al., 1974; Nock and Rossi, 1978; Sampson and Rossi, 1975), even within the nuclear family there is no equality in terms of the contribution made to family standing via occupations. A wife's occupation counts slightly less than half as much as does her husband's (ratio of b's=.496). Husband's and wife's occupations count slightly more than five times that of their parents (ratio of $(b_h+b_w)/b_{hf}+b_{wf})=5.24$). Stated differently, the husband's occupation is twice as important as is the wife's, and the wife's is slightly more than twice as important as is the combined importance of parents' occupations.

Similarly, the husband's education counts considerably more than does his wife's. The ratio of wife's to husband's education coefficients is .534—almost exactly that found for the relationship of occupational slopes (.496). At the highest value for education (college graduate=16 years) the wife's contribution to an estimated HPRES score would be quite noticeable, amounting to about 10 points (16 * .623=9.96). Parental educational attainments were found to be irrelevant to the reckoning of family social status.

To summarize results thus far, three general statements are warranted. First, it appears that information about social origins is of some importance. Ethnicity and race are not important for the social standing of a household, but parents' occupations are. An attempt to suggest some kind of spatial context within which such achievements occurred apparently failed. Migration patterns are not independent status effects for households. Thus, of all items considered, four were found to be unrelated to household prestige: ethnicity, husband's father's educational attainment, and wife's father's educational attainment, as well as migration status. This speaks directly to the guiding question of this research. Can we say anything about the relative importance of ascribed and achieved characteristics? We can say that there is a strain toward ascription to the extent that parents' *achievements* are taken to be ascribed characteristics. In the sense that they are characteristics over which an individual has no control and which serve to affect his or her family's social standing, they are properly considered ascriptive characteristics.

Second, while there is considerable variation in the importance of any single trait one person to another, male members consistently outweigh females in their importance to the family's social standing. Females contribute significantly to the family's social standing, but they contribute less than do males. Our findings in this regard are similar to those of Rossi et al. (1974), Sampson and Rossi (1975), and Nock and Rossi (1978).

Third, to the extent that educational attainment is important (which it is, generally), it is less important than is occupational prestige for any one person's individual contribution to family social standing. That is, looking at the contribution made by any single member of either generation, we find that the contribution is disproportionately affected by the occupational prestige of the person.

Parental achievements do play a role in determining household prestige. High-achieving parents provide some honor to their children. How much? Comparing two families where husband and wife have average scores on all characteristics but where parental occupations are at minimums or maximums, we find that parental achievements could change HPRES by almost ten points (9.50).

Each parent contributes about five points to this change. This example has used extreme values for parental characteristics, and usually the values for parental occupations would not be so large or so small. However, the point of this example was to illustrate the possible effect of father's occupation—an effect that we believe justifies our claim that there exists a significant ascriptive element to our stratification system.

The second equation in Table 3.2, regressing ZPRES on family characteristics, presents quite similar results as does the equation with HPRES. The only change of note is the enchanced explanatory power of the second equation. This suggests that the ZPRES standardization did remove some interindividual differences in mean rating and amount of variance in ratings. These differences, however, did not alter the structure of the equations appreciably.

Interaction Terms

As we noted earlier, our conceptual model included some non-additive effects. Two types of multiplicative interactions were investigated: the interactions of vignette variables one with the other and the interaction of vignette variables with rater characteristics.

We do not present the results of this analysis, as it is easily summarized. First, we were surprised to find that *no* interaction of rater and vignette characteristic emerged as substantively important. When we examined the interaction of characteristics of the vignette members, we found that the raters responded to certain combinations of characteristics in a manner somewhat different than would be predicted from an additive model. Generally, we found that raters rewarded families in which there were certain combinations of high achievements but did not dock families in which similar combinations of low achievement occurred. The patterns which were rewarded are not surprising. Families in which *both* husband and wife did exceptionally well occupationally are rewarded for this. Such families received higher ratings (albeit only slightly higher) than would be predicted by adding the individual effects of husband's and wife's occupations. Similar patterns obtain for either husband or wife when there is exceptionally high educational attainment combined with occupational attainment. While combinations such as these are not at all uncommon empirically, raters recognize them as special by rewarding them some very slight extra prestige.

The actual amount of "extra" reward given to families for such achievements varies depending on the type of interaction, but when such terms are included in the equations reported in Table 3.1, the predicted score for families is not altered appreciably. This is because the components of the interaction term are affected by the inclusion of the interaction term in the equation. Thus, for example, while we found some interaction effects due to the interaction of husband's education and husband's occupation, the additional increment due to this was approximately compensated for by the lessened effect of both education and occupation independently.

Consensus

We now consider the issue of interrespondent agreement or consensus. This is an important issue both substantively and methodologically. Substantively, it makes little sense to argue that our model describes the status attribution process for households if there is considerable disagreement among respondents. We have only *assumed* that the model described in Table 3.1 is an accurate portrayal of the aggregate process it seeks to describe. Were we to find considerable disagreement among respondents in their models, this would discredit the whole process to this point.

The problem at this stage of the research is how one defines consensus or agreement. Clearly, had all respondents assigned similar ratings to similar households, this would suggest agreement. Would it, however, suggest consensus? It is possible (though unlikely) that each respondent employs a clearly defined and understood scheme to households in assigning prestige ratings. Even less likely, though still possible, each respondent's cognitive model for assigning prestige may differ in important ways from all other respondents' cognitive models. Should both situations be found (each respondent having a well-defined model which is peculiar to that respondent), it is still possible tht similar households would receive similar ratings. In short, consensus may best be thought of in this instance as implying agreement of at least three types. We ask:

(a) Do respondents agree on the ratings assigned to comparable households?
(b) Do respondents agree on the characteristics which matter in deciding the prestige score to be assigned a household?
(c) Do respondents agree on the relative weight to be applied to each relevant characteristic?

We know that there is not complete agreement among respondents in the ratings assigned to comparable vignettes due to the existance of the error variance in estimated HPRES or ZPRES ratings from regression equations. Were there complete agreement of this kind, it is quite likely that our R^2 would be appreciably higher (although this is not necessarily the case). This is so because if ratings varied as did certain household characteristics, covariances would increase. Of course, if all increased, R^2 would likely approach unity. Such an increase in R^2 depends on the simultaneous dependence of ratings on *all* family characteristics—a rather unlikely result. Alternatively, should all respondents rely on the same characteristics in the same way, R^2 would approach unity—even if some characteristics were

TABLE 3.2 Univariate Statistics for Parameter Estimates of Linear Models for 536 Respondents

Parameter	Mean	Median	Standard Deviation	Minimum	Maximum	C.R.V.
Education (Years)						
Husband	1.199	.944	1.543	−6.751	7.651	1.28
Husb. Father	.177	.137	.957	−4.006	6.146	5.41
Wife	.571	.510	1.188	−8.066	5.742	2.08
Wife Father	.087	.141	.045	−6.491	3.141	.517
Occupational Prestige[a]						
Husband	.477	.445	.373	−1.034	2.838	.782
Husb. Father	.071	.051	.257	−1.796	1.263	3.62
Wife	.241	.237	.314	−1.330	1.329	1.30
Wife Father	.070	.049	.226	−0.876	0.996	3.23
Ethnicity[b]	.082	.072	.312	−1.239	2.303	3.80
Migration Status[c]	1.140	.517	5.065	−9.597	50.280	4.42
Constant	−28.757	−10.951	201.123	−988.315	1065.494	
R^2	.503	.527	.176	0.000	.934	

a. Occupational prestige scores from Ornstein (1977).
b. Ethnicity scores derived by Hodge, Siegel, and Rossi.
c. Categorical variable scaled to continuous variable (see text).

totally ignored. Since R^2 captures so many other things (misspecification, measurement error, nonlinearities or other errors in functional form, and the like), it is wholly inappropriate as a measure of consensus by itself. Only if we were to presume that there is absolutely *no error* in specification would it suffice. This is not an assumption which is justified.

However, our equation (Table 3.1) indicates that there is significant average reduction of errors in predicting HPRES or ZPRES scores gained by knowing the values of the households being rated (both statistically and substantively). At a minimum, we may take this as weak evidence of agreement in the way differences among households are evaluated. However, this evidence is hardly sufficient for our purposes.

Since the question we are asking is whether the equations in Table 3.1 are appropriate to describe all members of society, evidence that ratings are affected by respondent characteristics would indicate lack of agreement. In other words, were we able to explain a portion of the variance in ratings with respondent characteristics, we would have discovered systematic differences in ratings *due* to respondent characteristics—in other words, systematic lack of agreement. We performed regression equations in which one randomly selected vignette rated by each respondent was considered. The rating given this vignette was regressed on respondent characteristics (sex, race, age, education, occupation, ethnicity). This procedure was repeated five times (each equation was based on a different randomly selected vignette rated by each respondent and there were five such equations produced). None of the equations produced R^2s sufficiently large to reject the hypothesis that $R=0.0$. In short, respondent characteristics did not capture any variance in ratings.

Even this evidence, however, is hardly convincing. For there is a tremendous difference between systematic differences associated with respondent characteristics and agreement among respondents. While we now have some rather weak evidence relevant to the first question asked (agreement on rankings of similar households) and similarly weak evidence indicating that disagreements are not due to measurable respondent characteristics, it is still entirely possible that each respondent was employing a scheme which differs from those used by other respondents. In fact, there has been some discussion in the literature that our approach simply *covers up* dissensus by averaging across respondents (Baker, 1977). We have been faulted for our inability to account completely for the ratings given households. In short, some would suggest that consensus would imply our ability to develop a deterministic model of household social standing (rather than a stochastic one; Baker, 1977). Thus, we turn now to a consideration of the second and third questions raised earlier about consensus: Do respondents agree on which characteristics matter, and do they agree on how much such characteristics matter?

Since each respondent rated a large number of households, it is possible to examine each respondent's judgment process. These processes can then be compared to determine whether they are similar. Whereas the equations in Table 3.1 are aggregated over all respondents *and* over all the households rated, it would be possible to produce a similar set of equations which are based on the individual models used by each respondent. Such equations would be based on individual models rather than individual households.

The logic of the procedure used is as follows: An equation estimated on all rated households will reflect average tendencies in attributing prestige as well as idiosyncratic differences among respondents. An average of individual models will minimize the within-individual source of variation while allowing the between-individual differences in weighting of characteristics to remain. A comparison of an aggregate equation (estimated over all rated households) with the model of individual averages will inform us about the extent of interindividual as opposed to interhousehold (that is, vignette) *and* interindividual disagreement or consensus.

Table 3.2 presents univariate statistics summarizing the equations run for every respondent in the sample. The HPRES formulation of the rating was regressed on the ten family characteristics represented on the vignettes sorted by each respondent. Since ZPRES standardizes HPRES to each respondent's mean and variance in ratings, the ZPRES formulation will always produce identical results as the HPRES formulation for any single respondent. For this reason, the ZPRES results are not presented.

We begin by noting that it is certainly not the case that all respondents employed some well-understood model of status attribution. For some respondents (a very few) the vignette characteristics are not linearly related to the ratings given the households (and hence $R^2=0.0$). On the other hand, some respondents were consistent in their application of whatever attribution rules they employed, as revealed by the maximum value of R^2 for respondents of

.934. In short, no respondent was completely consistent in the application of whatever rules were used. There was considerable within-respondent variance. This must be kept in mind when considering the larger question of consensus, for if respondents were not consistent in their use of the ratings, this inconsistency will contribute to the explanatory power of any aggregate equations. The results do indicate that prestige evaluations are related to characteristics of households as specified in this research. In fact, taking the average R^2 from Table 3.2 we find that, on average, over half of all variance in HPRES can be explained by the characteristics which appeared on the vignettes. In short, there is undoubtedly *some* mechanism by which most individuals combine household characteristics to arrive at a prestige evaluation. Further, we know that this mechanism involves the characteristics specified on our vignettes.

We may compare the R^2 values obtained in Table 3.1 (.26) with the average of individual model R^2s (.503) to find that approximately 24 percent of the variance in rating households is due to individual inconsistencies in the application of rating schemes. Stated differently, within-respondent differences account for about 24 percent of all differences in prestige evaluations. There still remains, however, about half of the variance to be explained. Undoubtedly much of this variance can not be explained, as it is due to sampling errors, misspecification, or other unknown factors. Some of this difference, however, may be due to the differences among (rather than within) respondents. We turn now to consider this issue.

Now we ask whether respondents agreed on *which* characteristics matter and on how much they matter. The standard deviation of the parameter estimates from the individual equations may be read as the average amount of disagreement about the weighting of any family characteristic in explaining prestige. Thus, a characteristic for which the regression coefficients have a large amount of variance is one over which respondents disagreed about its importance in regard to family prestige. We cannot compare standard deviations in their original form, since they reflect the scoring of the variables involved. Hence, we seek a measure which allows a comparison free of the units of measurement involved. The Coefficient of Relative Variation (CRV) serves this purpose. The CRV is simply the standard deviation divided by the mean. Such a measure norms the standard deviation at its origin.

The last column of Table 3.2 contains the CRVs. First consider those for the estimates of education effects. Respondents disagreed least on the effect of the wife's father's education (CRV=.517). This characteristic is also the one with the least impact on prestige (average b=.087). In a similar manner, respondents showed relatively little disagreement on the importance of the husband's education (CRV=1.28), which is seen to have the largest effect on prestige (average b=1.199). Wife's education evoked more disagreement over its importance than did husband's (CRV=2.08) but still considerably less than was true for the husband's father's education. In sum, respondents agreed that the husband's education was to be given the most weight (of all education variables) and that the wife's father's education should be given the least weight. There was less agreement over how much the wife's education should count, although not so much as to alter the relative importance of this variable to the other education variables on the average. There was considerable disagreement over the importance of the husband's father's education.

Now consider the coefficients for the four occupations. We see immediately that there was relative agreement over the weight to be given husbands' occupations. (CRV=.782). Similarly, respondents agreed generally on the importance to be given the wife's occupation, although less so than for the husband's. There was much less agreement on the occupations of parents as reflected by the CRVs for husband's and wife's father's occupations of 3.62 and 3.23, respectively. We may summarize these findings by noting that respondents agreed that husband's occupation should count, and count most, and that wife's occupation should count, and count about half that of the husband. The respondents disagreed over the importance to be attached to the occupations of parents. Still, there is no evidence to suggest that large numbers of respondents assigned great importance to either parent's occupations. In short, there was considerable agreement on how family members' occupations should be evaluated.

On the remaining issues (migration status and ethnicity) we find considerable disagreement among respondents. In sum, we find the following characteristics evoking the most consistent effects among the respondents: wife's father's education, husband's occupation, husband's education, wife's occupation, and wife's education. There was more disagreement over how important the following are to family prestige: wife's father's occupation, husband's father's occupation, husband's father's education, ethnicity, and migration status.

We take these results to indicate that there is a stable scheme of allocating prestige to families which combines and weights educational and occupational characteristics of the nuclear couple. Other characteristics do not evoke such consensual responses. We are convinced that virtually all agree that the wife's father's education is irrelevant to family prestige. We are less sure of the importance of ethnicity, husband's father's education, migration status, and occupations of fathers. These latter characteristics do not conform to a consensually agreed-upon model of status attribution.

Finally, we ask whether respondents agree on the relative importance of the various characteristics which matter to family prestige. Taking the mean as the best indicator of central tendency in this case, the first column in Table 3.2 can be taken to represent a model which is an average of individual equations to be compared with the comparable HPRES equation in Table 3.1. How similar are these results? Since the results of Table 3.2 are not truly an equation (but rather the average of equations), there is no available criterion of structural similarity. We treat both as equations, however, for the present purposes.

Those effects which are most important to household prestige are virtually identical one equation to the other. For example, the slope on husband's occupation from Table 3.1 is .483, whereas the average of individual b's is .477. At most, such a difference in weighting of husband's occupation could produce different HPRES estimates of only .48 HPRES points. In fact, no two estimates differ by amounts sufficient to produce as much as five point differences in estimated HPRES. The same results are found if we use medican rather than mean values. The difference between the values for migration status are the only ones which differ appreciably. However, as this "variable" is actually a composite of b's from dummy variable regressions, we cannot conclude from these results whether respondents did or did not disagree on the importance of these statements. We suspect that they did disagree. All in all, the two "equations" are identical. They are so close that we may conclude that respondents agreed on the relative importance of the family characteristics.

We have presented what we consider a forceful argument for ways to measure the amount of consensus among raters. We found that respondent characteristics do not explain the variance in ratings. Further, interindividual differences in rating principles (that is, in the size of regression coefficients) are small. We did discover that considerable disagreement exists over which characteristics should count in the reckoning of prestige. Specifically, respondents differed considerably in how much weight they gave to parents' characteristics, as well as to ethnicity and migration status. Very little disagreement of any kind was found for the basic educational and occupational characteristics of the nuclear couple. In short, we assert that these latter characteristics are evaluated similarly from one respondent to another. Further, we assert that respondents agree that these are the characteristics which matter in reckoning household social standing. On other characteristics we find much less agreement.

Conclusion

The substantive conclusions to be drawn from the research reported here are that members of our society agree on those things which are to be considered in evaluating households' prestige standing. There were few surprises here, as respondents generally considered the educational and occupational attainments of family members. We found that husbands' characteristics outweigh wives characteristics about two to one. Further, we found that occupations count about twice what educations count in the process. These results corroborate those found many times before in similar studies.

There was also evidence that some members of society (although certainly not all) would consider parental achievements in their evaluation of a family unit. For such individuals, the prestige standing of a couple could be altered by as many as ten points depending on the occupations of the couple's fathers. Generally we found that there was less agreement on whether parental characteristics would matter and on how much they would matter than there was characteristics of the nuclear couple. Still, our evidence suggests that there exists an ascriptive strain to status attribution in our system. The lack of clear consensus on this issue suggests, however, that achievement is the primary vehicle by which prestige is realized.

Taken with evidence from other studies of family prestige, these results indicate that there is a clearly defined mechanism attributing social status on the basis of occupational and educational achievements. Other characteristics, achievements, and entitlements may play some role in prestige evaluations, but that role is secondary at best. This appears true whether the issue be parental achievements or such things as ethnicity or race. In short, we now believe that family social standing depends first and foremost on these achievements.

NOTES

1. Migration status refers to statements concerning the residential history of the vignette families—for example, "The couple moved from the country to a large city."
2. We wish to thank Sol Dutkas of Audits and Surveys for his help in monitoring and managing this project.
3. Standardized coefficients (beta coefficients) are not presented in this table. As noted, the variance of vignette characteristics are set by *design* of the production technique and bear little resemblance to the real-world variances of these characteristics. Beta weights are not understandable except within a framework of a world in which the variables studied here are distributed rectangularly (as are ours).

REFERENCES

Abrahamson, Mark, Ephraim H. Mizruchi, and Charlton A. Hornung, 1976, Stratification and Mobility. New York: Macmillan.

Baker, Paul Morgan, 1977, "On the use of psychophysical methods in the study of social status." Social Forces 55 (June): 898-920.

Blau, Peter M. and Otis D. Duncan, 1967, The American Occupational Structure. New York: John Wiley.

Bogardus, Emory, 1925, "Measuring social distances." Journal of Applied Sociology 9: 299-308.

Jencks, Christopher et al., 1972, Inequality: A Reassessment of the Effects of Family and Schooling in America. New York: Basic Books.

Nock, Steven L. and Peter H. Rossi, 1979, "Household types and social standing." Social Forces 57 (June): 1325-1345.

———1978, "Ascription versus achievement in the attribution of family social status." American Journal of Sociology 84 (November): 565-590.

Rossi, Peter H., William A. Sampson, Christine E. Bose, Guillermina Jasso, and Jeff Passel, 1974, "Measuring household social standing." Social Science Research 3 (September): 169-190.

Sampson, W. A., 1973, "The relative important of ascribed and achieved variables as family social determinants." Ph.D. Dissertation, Johns Hopkins University.

Sampson, William and Peter H. Rossi, 1975, "Race and family social standing." American Sociological Review 40 (April): 201-214.

Sewell, William H. and Robert M. Hauser, 1975, Education, Occupation and Earnings: Acnievement in the Early Career. New York: Academic Press.

Triandis, Harry C. and Leigh M. Triandis, 1965, "Some studies of social distance," pp. 207-217 in I. Steiner and M. Fishbein (eds.) Current Studies in Social Psychology. New York: Holt, Rinehart & Winston.

4

FAMILY PRESTIGE JUDGMENTS
Bringing in Real-World Complexities

JEFFREY K. LIKER

The study of family prestige has come a long way since the pioneering community research of August Hollingshead. Hollingshead's (1949) research on high school students in Morris, Illinois was largely concerned with class variation; however, at the time there were no clear guidelines as to what socioeconomic attributes were salient for making class distinctions[1] or the amount contributed by each attribute to socioeconomic status. Noticing that local community residents often used class-related constructs to describe their friends, co-workers, and neighbors, Hollingshead asked some of the more knowledgeable residents to assign social standing rankings to each of the students' families.

The vignette technique designed by Peter Rossi is a way of generalizing Hollinshead's approach beyond the boundaries of the local community. The researcher controls the flow of information to the "informants" and does not require them to have expert knowledge about their own communities or the nation as a whole. Random assignment of vignette attributes produces many of the statistical properties of a laboratory experiment. This volume presents applications of the technique that illustrate the substantial benefits of the approach, but we should also consider the *costs* of moving into the abstract realm of brief descriptions. Like laboratory experiments, the vignette technique maximizes "internal" validity, but does so possibly at the expense of "external" validity.

This chapter attempts to assess the external validity of vignette analysis by comparing the results from the family prestige *vignette*

Author's Note: The study these analyses were based on was designed by Peter H. Rossi. I gratefully acknowledge the editorial and substantive advice of Anne Shlay, Glen Elder, Jr., and Steven Nock. Peter Rossi and Alice Rossi provided important feedback on an earlier version of this work.

studies to results based on prestige judgments of *actual* households. This study goes beyond the local community to look at judgments made within a nationwide survey. As part of a larger study of family social standing designed by Peter H. Rossi, about 1500 respondents were asked to rate the social standing of families whom they knew— that is, families in their social worlds. They were asked to assign status rankings to families of their friends, relatives, neighbors, and co-workers and then to describe various socioeconomic characteristics of the families they judged. Analysis proceeded along the same lines as vignette studies of family social standing.

This study returns to the experiential worlds the respondents face on a day-to-day basis. This meant losing some valuable statistical properties of vignette analysis. In this real-world survey, the socioeconomic achievements of the families being rated were not orthogonal to the characteristics of the respondents. Thus, multicollinearily is a problem. In addition, we did not have the power to introduce variance into the characteristics of the families being judged. Unlike the nondiscriminatory vignette world, for example, this real-world study found many blacks who did not have access to persons in the upper range of occupations. Also, real-world families are not likely to have wives and mothers in the role of a doctor or lawyer.

The chapter begins with a review of the methods used in the study of real-world judgment processes. Second, we examine the association between respondent characteristics and the characteristics of families they selected from their networks of social ties. Third, we examine the determinants of these real-world judgments compared to the vignette results. Finally, we look at several subgroup analyses which illustrate the difficulties in interpreting social judgments made within the complexity of the discriminatory real world.

A Method for Studying
Real-World Judgments

Status evaluations of actual households were included as part of each of the family prestige substudies described in this volume. In the course of vignette evaluations, each respondent was given the following instructions (or cards) on what actual households to evaluate:

(1) The family that is your *closest neighbor.*

(2) The family of the person that you (or whoever is the main breadwinner in this house) work most closely with (i.e., *closest worker*).

(3) The family of the brother or sister that is closest to you in age (i.e., *closest sibling*).
(4) The family of the most successful among your friends and acquaintances (i.e., *most successful friend*).
(5) The family of the least successful among your friends and acquaintances (i.e., *least successful relative*).
(6) The family of the most successful among your relatives or those of your spouse (i.e., *most successful relative*).

These "designated households" were evaluated along a nine-point scale of "social standing" just as the vignettes were. In a subsequent interview, respondents were asked to think back to the families they chose to evaluate and to characterize them as follows:

(1) Occupation (including non-labor-force statuses) of all household members over 18 (up to four adults)—coded as NORC prestige score.
(2) Educational attainment of each member in years completed.
(3) Household size (number of adults).
(4) National origins of the family—coded as NORC ethnic prestige score.

In addition to these designated household characteristics, a variety of standard socioeconomic and demographic information about the respondent was solicited. Information on the "designated family" was solicited in an interview after the prestige rating task, eliminating the danger that these questions would suggest to respondents the salient status attributes. On the other hand, concrete evaluations were made in the midst of vignette ratings. This context may have influenced the respondent's prestige judgments in ways unknown.

The terms "closest," "most successful," and "least successful" were included to ensure some heterogeneity in the families respondents chose to evaluate. This procedure, it was hoped, would encourage the respondents to evaluate a sampling of their social ties across the socioeconomic status hierarchy. Recall that the vignette studies relied on a rectangular distribution of status characteristics covering the entire range of occupations and educational levels.

Since these real-world designators were included in each of the three subprojects, we began in theory with 9168 evaluations (1528 respondents rating six designated households each). In practice, however, there were many missing observations in the prestige ratings and in the characteristics of the designated families. There are several possible reasons for these missing data. Respondents may not have had a family to rate (for example, no siblings), may

TABLE 4.1   Percent Designated Household Information Missing for
             Intact Families Only
             (N = 6101)

Husband's Occupation[a]	Wife's Occupation	Husband's Education	Wife's Education	Family Ethnicity
0%	5%	16%	22%	25%

a. With few exceptions (less than one percent) missing information on the husband's occupation
meant no information was available about any of the other designated household characteristics.
Cases with no information on the household are not shown.

have forgotten whom they had rated by the time of the interview, or
may not have known specific items of information about the designated household. After eliminating all cases with missing prestige
ratings or missing data on all the requested attributes, 7497 remained.

This pool of rated households was reduced further to include only
intact (husband and wife present) households. This was done to
maximize comparability with the vignette studies which focused on
married couples. This left 6101 cases for analysis; however, these
cases were not always complete. In some cases one or more items of
information about the designated households were unknown to our
informants. These missing data are summarized in Table 4.1.

Missing information was not random with respect to designated
household characteristics or respondent characteristics. Clearly,
respondents knew more about the occupations of their associates
than they did about their educational achievements. Education is
generally a past achievement for married adults and is often not
visible in present lifestyle. Analyses suggest that occupations were
often used by respondents as clues to educational attainments. For
example, educational information was more often missing when
husbands were unemployed or when wives worked in the home.
Educational information was most often available when the husband
or wife in the designated household worked in high-status occupations where specific educational credentials are often prerequisite to
jobs (for example, a medical or law degree).

Respondents knew more about the husband's achievements than
about the occupational and educational accomplishments of the
wives, suggesting that husbands' achievements are more prominent
status features of the family. Indeed, the relative amounts of missing
information across designated family characteristics mirror the
relative contributions these characteristics make to prestige ratings
in other vignette studies. (Note that ethnicity is not predictive of
family prestige in such studies and this was least often known.) In

these outcomes, we see indications of a relationship between knowledge and status relevance; the best known attributes are those most relevant to status in American society.

Other correlates of missing information were as expected. Respondents knew the least about their neighbors and the most about their relatives. Better-educated respondents working in high-status occupations were more knowledgeable than lower-status respondents, and blacks were less knowledgeable than whites *ceteris paribus*. A total of 19 characteristics were examined. In a regression equation predicting whether an item was missing, they explained a modest 12 percent of the variance in missing educational achievements and less than 7 percent of the variance in missing occupational characteristics.[2]

It is not clear how this missing information affected the equations predicting the real-world status judgments. We know that judgments made by lower-status persons, particularly blacks, were disproportionately missing; however, this would affect the results only to the extent that such subgroups used different evaluative criteria than higher-status whites. (We address this issue in a later section.)

Several strategies were employed to investigate possible bias due to the missing data. All suggested that estimates were not significantly biased.

This missing data problem raises an important issue in status attribution processes: *Family attributes can be important status evoking qualities only if they are known to the observer.* These findings further highlight the importance of occupational achievements as status-evoking attributes, particularly for husbands, because they are most likely to be known to persons within our society. Other analyses show that the raters knew the least about the socioeconomic achievements of their neighbors and hence could not always rely on occupation and education as status cues. Perhaps among neighbors visible signs such as housing tenure and upkeep and the types of cars parked out front are more important for judgments of social standing. Although these data are not appropriate for a full investigation of the role of social knowledge in status judgments, this relationship is clearly a problem worthy of further investigation.

Structural Constraints on "Designated Households"

Characteristics of rated families in the vignette world are uncorrelated with characteristics of the raters. However, when respondents

TABLE 4.2   Correlations among Respondent and Designated Household
             Characteristics (Intact Designated Households)

Respondent's Status With:[a]	Closest Worker	Closest Neighbor	Closest Sibling	Unsucc. Friend	Success. Friend	Success. Relative
Designated Head's Occupation:						
r =	.61	.34	.34	.34	.38	.27
N =	(945)	(943)	(825)	(767)	(1130)	(1104)
Designated Head's Education:						
r =	.55	.45	.40	.42	.40	.31
N =	(777)	(665)	(796)	(667)	(1008)	(1058)
Designated Head's Ethnicity:						
r =	.69	.73	1.00	.77	.79	1.00
N =	(649)	(602)	(810)	(514)	(793)	(1091)

a. Respondent's status was computed as an index of family prestige, taking into account
occupation and education of the primary and secondary earners in the respondent's family.
Weights derived from vignette research on family social standing were used to compute the index.

rate the families of people they know, it is possible that they choose
people similar to themselves according to the options of a stratified
society. Neighborhood segregation (Duncan and Duncan, 1955;
Farley, 1977; Guest and Weed, 1976); workplace segregation, and
intergenerational transmission of socioeconomic status (Duncan
et al., 1972) all place constraints on social options and interactions
from day to day.

Studies that look at structural constraints on friendship networks
(Fischer et al., 1977; Curtis and Jackson, 1977; Laumann, 1966)
reveal that friends tend to be similar in terms of occupation,
education, and age (although these correlations seldom exceed .40).
The data on designated households provide an interesting picture of
the associational boundaries faced by the national sample studied
(see Table 4.2).

The most "constrained" relationships in terms of occupation and
education are in the work place. These correlations between the
respondents' characteristics and the characteristics of the designated
families (.61 and .55 for occupation and education) are moderate but
well above zero. The choices of most and least successful friends and
relatives are less constrained (correlations below .45). Yet, even
these correlations indicate substantial segregation when we consider
that the respondents could choose from all the people they knew or
were related to.

The most striking levels of segregation involve ethnicity. Ethnicity was coded by ethnic prestige scores that were generated in a study similar to occupational prestige studies (Hodge et al., 1964). Among nonrelatives, the correlations ranged from .69 to .79, an indication of considerable similarity in ethnic prestige between respondents and the friends, neighbors, and co-workers they chose to evaluate. Those of Western European origin tended to designate others of like origin, while blacks and Spanish-speaking Americans were generally embedded in networks of other minority group members. Indeed, *86 percent of the families evaluated by black respondents were also black, while 99 percent of the families nonblacks rated were also nonblack.*[3] Hence, blacks and whites evaluated social worlds with almost no overlap.

These results underscore an important difference between this real-world study and the vignette analyses, a difference which highlights the advantages of vignette research. The randomization technique used in the vignette studies ensured almost perfect orthogonality between the vignette characteristics and characteristics of the raters. By contrast, the households actually chosen by our respondents were similar to their own positions in the stratification system. The occupational and educational similarities are modest, but we find a remarkable correspondence between the ethnic/racial characteristics of the respondents and their social ties. In leaving the abstract world of vignettes and entering the interpersonal worlds of real people, status judgments are restricted by social, economic, and cultural position of the rater. How do these structural constraints affect status attribution processes?

Modeling Real-World Judgments

Several differences between the vignette world of families and the actual social worlds of respondents inform a comparison of the two sets of results. First, in the artificial vignette world, husband and wife characteristics were only weakly correlated, while in the real-world designated households spouses' characteristics tended to be more highly correlated (see Table 4.3). Marital homogamy is most striking for education; husbands' and wives' educational levels correlate at .69. Second, and perhaps more pertinent, in the vignette world 75 percent of wives participated in the occupational sphere and did so at *all* levels of occupational prestige. In this real-world study, the occupational and educational achievements of husbands tended to surpass those of their wives.

TABLE 4.3 Correlations Among Designated Family Characteristics (Intact Families)

Designated Family:	Husb. Occ.	Wife Occ.	Husb. Educ.	Wife Educ.	Husb. Unemp.	House-Wife	Black[b]
Husband Occ. (NORC)		.26	.66	.48	-.14	.01	-.15
Wife Occ. (NORC)[a]			.25	.32	-.06	.43	-.06
Husband Educ. (years)				.69	-.20	-.05	-.12
Wife Educ. (years)					-.17	-.21	-.04
Husband Unemployed						.04	.00
Housewife							-.07
X̄ =	45.9	45.6	13.3	12.7	12%	51%	8%
SD =	16.1	12.6	3.4	2.6	32%	50%	27%
N =	(5884)	(5730)	(5108)	(4741)	(6091)	(5730)	(6101)

a. Housewives were coded with an occupational prestige score of 51.0 (Bose, 1973).
b. There were many missing values on the designated family's ethnicity. Under the assumption that respondents could distinguish between blacks and nonblacks, missing cases on ethnicity were assumed to be nonblack.

The average occupational prestige of wives shown in Table 4.3 is somewhat misleading, since this score is dominated by the prestige score assigned to housewives (51.0; see Bose, 1973), who make up 51 percent of the sample. When housewives were removed from the sample, the average prestige score for wife's occupation dropped from 46.3 to 41.6, four points below the average score for husbands. Most of the differences between the occupational attainments of husbands and wives were found in the upper range of occupations where wives tended to be excluded from participation: Less than 2 percent of the wives in designated households worked in jobs with NORC prestige scores above 62 (on a 100-point scale), while 14 percent of the husbands worked in occupations higher than that level. Hence, wives were rarely found in such professional occupations as doctor (prestige scores=81.5), architect (prestige=70.5), or school-teacher (prestige=63.1).

These differences between the vignette worlds and the world of actual households complicate the task of interpreting the way real family attributes contribute to an overall family social status. Should vignette and real families be found to be evaluated by different processes, one does not know if this is due to differences in the types of families evaluated or because different evaluative processes are involved. That is, when processing information from the vignette world versus the real world, individuals might invoke differing cognitive processes for evaluating abstract versus concrete, personally specific information. Alternatively, any differences found in "judgment processes" may be due to *objective* differences between the families described in the nondiscriminatory vignette world and actual families coming out of the structural constraints within the real world. In short, the distribution of family attributes might influence the judgment processes.

The social judgment process underlying the prestige ratings of designated households is represented by the regression equation in Table 4.4. As in the vignette research, the nine-point rating of social standing was transformed to a range of 0 to 100, with 100 the highest rating. Considering first the role of the designated family attributes in the judgment process, these results look very much like the vignette results—with one important exception. *Wife's occupation appears to have been ignored by the raters judging the prestige of their designated households.* This clearly contradicts the vignette results, which consistently showed that wife's occupation was very important to the status attribution process, second only to husband's occupation.

TABLE 4.4   Regression of Family Social Standing Rating on Designated
             Household and Respondent Characteristics (Intact Families)[a]

Independent Variables	Raw Regression Coefficient	SE	Standardized Coefficient
Designated Household:			
Husband's Occupation (NORC)	0.34*	(0.03)	.20
Wife's Occupation (NORC)[b]	0.03	(0.04)	.02
Husband's Education (years)	0.91*	(0.18)	.11
Wife's Education (years)	1.24*	(0.22)	.12
Husband Unemployed (dummy)	-4.28*	(1.21)	-.05
Housewife (dummy)	1.07	(0.90)	.02
Race (0 = nonblack, 1 = black)	-3.46	(2.23)	-.03
Respondent:			
Age (Years)	0.12*	(0.02)	.07
Sex (0 = female, 1 = male)	-0.47	(0.75)	.01
Race (0 = nonblack, 1 = black)	5.93*	(1.96)	.07
Family Prestige Score (0-100)[c]	-0.10*	(0.03)	-.04
Constant	13.35*	(3.97)	
R^2 = .14*			
(N = 4578 Evaluations)[d]			

*$P < .05$
a. The dependent variable was the respondent's prestige ranking of the family transformed so that
100 was the highest and 0 was the lowest social standing.
b. Housewives were assigned a score of 51.0 (Bose, 1973).
c. This was based on occupation and education of the primary and secondary earners in the
respondent's own household.
d. Pairwise deletion was used. Shown is the minimum N in the covariance matrix this regression
equation was based on. This practice is followed throughout the chapter.

Other findings are consistent with those from abstract vignette
research. The occupational achievements of husbands are the single
most important determinant of family social standing (b=.34). Next,
educational attainments of husbands and wives were secondary in
importance. Educational attainments of wives were slightly more
important than husbands' for the family's social standing (b=1.24
and .91 respectively). The relative ranking of the importance of
husband's and wife's education is puzzling. Most vignette results
from other studies indicate that husband's educational attainment is
more important, although Meudell (Chapter 2) found that education
for husbands and wives were given equal consideration by raters.

Third, families with unemployed husbands lost status as a result.
An unemployed husband cost a family 4.3 points.[4]

Finally, black designated families were seen as 3.5 points lower in prestige than white families with comparable socioeconomic achievements. Again, this finding is consistent with abstract vignette research (Sampson and Rossi, 1975).

All the vignette studies described in this volume have shown that characteristics of respondents play only a minor role in the judgment process. Agreement on the ranking of specific families appears to be widespread across socioeconomic groups. Yet, in this real-world study, three of the four respondent characteristics examined were significant sources of variation in family social standing judgments. Respondents appear to have been more or less generous in their prestige attributions depending on their age, race, and their own family social status. However, these results are not easily interpreted, since characteristics of the families being judged depended on the respondent's characteristics.

Older persons were more generous than younger persons in judging the prestige of their friends, neighbors, and co-workers, a finding unanticipated by vignette results. It appears that two individuals differing in age by 25 years and evaluating comparable families would differ in their evaluations by 3 points (on a 100-point scale). These age differences may reflect differential values placed on "making it" in our competitive society. That is, older persons may have been more generous in their prestige ratings because they have either "made it" or haven't and feel less critical of social "marginals" or the upwardly mobile. The more critical evaluations made by younger respondents may reflect their own competitiveness and, perhaps, status insecurities.

An alternative explanation accounts for both the vignette results and the real-world results by shifting attention from the judgment criteria to the different social worlds accessible to younger and older respondents. *That is, the families evaluated by older and younger respondents may not be comparable.* Prior research shows that age is an important basis of association (see Fischer et al., 1977), so that older respondents in this study were probably evaluating friends, co-workers, and relatives who were older and hence in a more advanced career stage than the younger associates of younger respondents.[5] Occupational prestige scores do not take career stage into account. For example, an engineer is an engineer whether working at the junior level in a small company or as a top consultant in a prestigious engineering firm. Hence, we may be seeing this misspecification of occupational prestige absorbed by the age variable. This was not problematic in vignette studies, since the same abstract occupational titles were available to older and younger raters.

Race, the second important respondent characteristic, was found to have some influence on average prestige ratings in prior vignette research. Both Meudell (1977) and Sampson and Rossi (1975) reported that blacks were somewhat more generous in their prestige attributions compared to whites. Similarly, blacks in this study assigned families 6 additional points, on average, compared to whites. Nonetheless, black generosity did not apply to *all* designated households. Other results (see Table 4.8) showed that blacks were more generous only when evaluating families in which wives were gainfully employed.[6]

Finally, while the respondent's own family prestige appears to play a role in how he or she regards other families ($b=-.09$, $p<.05$), this was found to be an artifact of the study design which called for ratings of extremely "successful" and "unsuccessful" social ties (see Table 4.5). A family of one respondent's unsuccessful friend might well be a family of the successful friend of another respondent, yet both respondents were working with the same nine-point scale. Hence, floor and ceiling effects appear to explain the role of the respondent's prestige in the status attribution process.

Taken together, the respondent and designated household characteristics explained 14 percent of the variance in the prestige ratings, slightly lower than R^2 in most vignette studies. Clearly, other characteristics besides occupation, education, and race contributed to these family prestige judgments. For example, spouses' personality characteristics, housing tenure, and characteristics of children are some potentially relevant status attributes.

Methodological Artifacts and Contextual Effects

This section examines artifacts that may have been created by the method used to force heterogeneity into the respondents' choices of designated households. For example, the finding that wife's occupation played no role in the household's composite social ranking contradicts all previous vignette research. The reasons respondents may not have considered the wives' occupational contributions may have been, in part, a function of the study's design. In this study, respondents were asked to think of the *person* (not family) who is the most or least successful. The respondent was then asked to rate the family of *that* person. It is possible that the characteristics of this criterion person dominated the respondents' perceptions of the families they evaluated. If these criterion persons were predominately male, the status of these men may have dominated the respondents' judgments of their families. This type of judgment bias, however, does not appear to have occurred.

Results presented in Table 4.5 compared models for "closest" designated households with "successful/unsuccessful" households. The enhanced contribution of husbands' occupations in "successful/ unsuccessful" households (for prestige and employment status) compared to "closest" households ($p<.05$) is consistent with the perspective that respondents selected families on the basis of the *head's* characteristics thereby diminishing the importance of other family members' characteristics. However, education of the household heads in the successful/unsuccessful families was not regarded as more important, calling into question this interpretation.

Another way of testing for biasing effects is to look at the way households were judged by male compared to female raters. Assuming that women raters were more likely to select other women as their most/least successful friends, while men selected other men, the biases should lead women to emphasize wives' characteristics, while men might focus on husbands in their assessments of successful and unsuccessful families. There was no evidence of this. Separate equations were estimated for male and female respondents and there were no significant differences in rating criteria by sex (as indicated by tests of differences of b's (see column 5 in Table 4.6).

These results suggest that the methodology did not bias the judgment process; however, they do not explain why husbands' occupational achievements were so much more salient in the "successful/ unsuccessful" families than in the "closest" families.[7] One way of explaining these results is to consider the social contexts implied by the instructions to respondents. Instructions to think of most and least successful persons opened up the respondent's entire range of social ties as the context of evaluations. This is comparable in some ways to vignette studies where the social context is removed from people's familiar personal lives. In contrast, the contexts implied by

TABLE 4.5   Family Social Standing Regressions by Relationship to Respondent

Independent Variables	"Closest" Families[a]		"Success/Unsuccess" Families[b]		
	b	SE	b	SE	$t$difference[c]
Designated Household:					
Husband Occ. (NORC)	0.14*	(0.04)	0.49*	(0.04)	-6.19*
Wife Occ. (NORC)	-0.03	(0.05)	0.09	(0.05)	1.70
Husband Educ. (years)	0.75*	(0.26)	0.80*	(0.24)	0.14
Wife Educ. (years)	1.04*	(0.32)	1.37*	(0.30)	0.75
Husband Unemployed	-0.57	(1.79)	-6.47*	(1.63)	-2.44*
Housewife	0.81	(1.25)	0.98	(1.26)	-0.10
Black	-6.64	(2.98)	-1.81	(3.26)	-1.09
Respondent:					
Age (years)	0.15*	(0.03)	0.10*	(0.03)	1.18
Male	-0.26	(1.04)	1.09	(1.07)	0.90
Black	7.52*	(2.60)	4.73	(2.89)	0.72
Family Prestige	0.04	(0.05)	-0.13*	(0.05)	2.40*
Constant	19.56*	(5.38)	7.68	(5.75)	
$R^2 =$	.07*		.20*		
N =	(2055)		(2513)		

*P<.05
a. Model based on the "closest" neighbors, co-workers, and siblings.
b. Model based on the "successful" and "unsuccessful" friends and relatives.
c. This is a t-test of the difference between regression coefficients across designated household types. This was computed as the difference in the b-coefficients divided by the square root of the sum of the two squared standard errors.

each of the "closest" designators were more socioeconomically restrictive—that is, the immediate work environment, the immediate family, and the neighborhood.

For the head's occupation, the most restrictive context was the work place (see Table 4.2). Within a work place many co-workers will enjoy occupational prestige comparable to the respondent. Thus, we might expect the head's occupation to be the least important. For example, if faculty members were asked to evaluate the prestige of colleagues, their status as college professors may not be a distinguishing feature. Other characteristics, such as publications, rank, and graduate school attended, may take precedence over the occupational title "college professor" in the context of an academic department. Results show that husband's occupation was not an important status attribute when only "closest worker" households were examined (b=-.02, SE=.09), while the head's occupation

TABLE 4.6   Family Social Standing by Sex of Respondent

Independent Variables	Male Raters[a]		Female Raters[b]		
	b	SE	b	SE	$t_{difference}$
Designated Household:					
Husband Occ. (NORC)	0.32*	(0.04)	0.36*	(0.05)	0.62
Wife Occ. (NORC)	0.02	(0.05)	0.04	(0.05)	0.28
Husband Educ. (years)	0.59*	(0.25)	1.19*	(0.26)	1.66
Wife Educ. (years)	1.65*	(0.31)	0.93*	(0.31)	1.64
Husband Unemployed	-5.34*	(1.86)	-3.13	(1.79)	1.01
Housewife	2.08	(1.29)	0.22	(1.25)	1.03
Black	-0.63	(3.03)	-6.31	(3.35)	1.26
Respondent:					
Age (years)	0.11*	(0.03)	0.14*	(0.04)	0.60
Black	3.48	(2.67)	8.37*	(2.92)	1.24
Family Prestige	-0.09	(0.05)	-0.11*	(0.05)	0.28
Constant	16.50*	(5.19)	10.72*	(5.45)	
$R^2 =$	.13*		.15*		
$N =$	(2257)		(2288)		

*P<.05
a. Model based only on household prestige judgments by women respondents.
b. Model based only on household prestige judgments by men respondents.

was taken into account when evaluating neighbors (b=.21, SE=.08) and siblings (b=.20, SE=.08).

These results suggest that social context is relevant in the judgment process. Social rankings are made within a comparative framework, and this framework seems to depend on the situational context in which the families are judged.

In short, the only "artifactual" consequences of the specific instructions to respondents are as follows: First, the instructions supplied the raters with specific social contexts. Second, the instructions built in the floor and ceiling effects discussed above. Note that the respondent's own family prestige played a role in the evaluations of successful/unsuccessful households (see Table 4.5) but was unimportant in the evaluations of closest workers, neighbors, and siblings.

Race and Real-World Evaluations

Vignette studies of family social standing have consistently found that rating criteria appear to be shared by most major subgroups in

American society, with one exception. Analyses by Meudell (1977), Nock and Rossi (1977), and Sampson and Rossi (1975) provide hints that blacks placed greater emphasis than whites on the labor force participation of women. Most striking are Meudell's findings that blacks placed greater emphasis on wives' occupations than on those of husbands.

Surveys of black-white differences in sex-role ideology have discovered more favorable attitudes toward wives' labor force participation among black husbands than white husbands (Mason and Bumpass, 1975; Alexson, 1970). Black tolerance or the valuing of working wives may be due to the higher rates of labor force participation of black compared to white women. The importance of black women as key contributors to family income in America is traceable at least to the beginning of this century. According to Elisabeth Pleck (1978: 490):

> A far higher proportion of black wives were earning wages than any other group of married women: even with her husband at work, a black wife continued to earn a living. In 1900 the rate of wage earning was 26 percent for married black women and 3.2 percent for married white women. Nor does the contrast of black and immigrant wives narrow this difference. In nearly all American cities in 1900, the rate of employment for black married women was anywhere from four to fifteen times higher than for immigrant wives.

Pleck compares black families and Italian immigrant families of similar socioeconomic status, generally living in dire poverty, and finds a much greater prevalence of female wage earners in black families. She concludes (p. 491) that black women "found cultural support for working."

What does this have to do with family status? First, Rossi et al. (1974) found evidence of a relationship between attitudes toward female employment and the emphasis placed on wife's occupation in prestige ratings; greater support for female employment meant greater emphasis on women's occupations. Second, the greater economic importance of black women as wage earners may enhance their contributions to family social standing.

The comparison of black and white status attribution models (Table 4.7) reveals that only one attribute is clearly evaluated differently by blacks and whites—the labor force status of wives. Whites evaluated families more favorably when women were house-

TABLE 4.7 Family Social Standing by Race of Respondent

Independent Variables	Black Raters[a]		Nonblack Raters[b]		
	b	SE	b	SE	$t_{difference}$
Designated Household:					
Husband Occ. (NORC)	0.25*	(0.11)	0.36*	(0.03)	-0.96
Wife Occ. (NORC)	0.04	(0.13)	0.03	(0.04)	0.07
Husband Educ. (years)	1.14	(0.71)	0.83*	(0.18)	0.42
Wife Educ. (years)	1.87*	(0.92)	1.22*	(0.23)	0.69
Husband Unemployed	-8.38*	(4.02)	-3.61*	(1.27)	-1.13
Housewife	-6.00	(3.73)	1.99*	(0.92)	2.08*
Black	-2.82	(2.91)	-13.67*	(5.18)	1.83
Respondent:					
Age (years)	0.20*	(0.09)	0.12*	(0.03)	0.84
Male	-1.86	(2.72)	-0.54	(0.79)	0.47
Family Prestige	0.10	(0.14)	-0.11*	(0.04)	1.44
Constant	5.50	(12.02)	20.57*	(3.27)	
$R^2 =$	.18*		.14*		
N =	(439)		(4099)		

*P<.05
a. Model based only on households evaluated by black respondents.
b. Model based only on households evaluated by nonblack respondents.

wives (by 2 points, p<.05), but blacks did not attribute higher status to families with housewives. Indeed, there is a hint in these data that blacks regarded families substantially lower in prestige when wives did not work (6 points lower, t=1.61). While we cannot be confident in the reliability of this estimate for blacks, the real issue is the difference in the way whites and blacks view working versus non-working wives. These results indicate that *whites regard families in which the wife is employed 8 points lower in prestige compared to the way these families are viewed by blacks.* This black-white *difference* is statistically reliable at the .05 significance level (see also Table 4.8).

Do cultural differences between black and white attitudes toward female labor force participation account for these race differences in social standing judgments? Are blacks less likely to value female abstention from labor force participation because of the material necessity of female economic support of the family? There is no clear way of distinguishing *ideological* explanations from the *material* reasons in these real-world judgments, since black families were

TABLE 4.8   Family Social Standing Models for Designated Households with
             Working Wives Compared to Housewives

| Independent Variables | Designated Households With: | | | | |
| | Working Wives[a] | | Housewives[b] | | |
	b	SE	b	SE	$t_{difference}$
Designated Household:					
Husband Occ. (NORC)	0.28*	(0.04)	0.40*	(0.05)	1.87
Wife Occ. (NORC)	0.08*	(0.04)	no variation		—
Husband Educ. (years)	1.28*	(0.25)	0.52*	(0.25)	2.15*
Wife Educ. (years)	0.78*	(0.31)	1.67*	(0.32)	2.00*
Husband Unemployed	-6.25*	(1.69)	-2.11	(1.73)	1.71
Black	-5.46*	(2.79)	-1.46	(3.60)	0.88
Respondent:					
Age (years)	0.14*	(0.03)	0.10*	(0.04)	0.80
Male	-1.04	(1.04)	0.79	(1.09)	1.29
Black	10.55*	(2.48)	-0.54	(3.11)	2.79*
Family Prestige	-0.13*	(0.05)	-0.06	(0.05)	0.99
Constant	11.40*	(5.18)	12.30	(7.60)	
R^2 =	.15*		.15*		
N =	(2280)		(2287)		

*P<.05
a. Model based on designated households in which the wife worked.
b. Model based on designated households in which the wife was a housewife.

generally evaluating more economically deprived families than were
whites:[8] Families accessible to blacks differ in many ways from those
accessible to whites, and these *objective* differences may account for
apparent differences in black compared to white judgment processes.

Working Wives, Housewives, and
Family Social Standing

To this point the results support the idea that for wives, the
decision to work makes some difference in the social standing of their
families. In the white world, wives can raise the prestige of their
households by remaining in the home. In the black world, working
wives bring their families at least as much prestige as housewives and
possibly more.

Can we conclude from this real-world study that family prestige is unaffected by the specific jobs (that is, prestige) wives hold? This question is not easily answered in this study. One difference between the real world and the vignette world is the large number of house-wives in real families. Half of the women in this study were house-wives, and all received the same prestige score of 51.0. By assigning the same score to all housewives we assume that they make equal status contributions to their families. This may not be true.

To test for possible differences in the way respondents evaluated families with and without working wives, separate models were estimated for designated households containing working wives and housewives. The results (see Table 4.8) indicate that designated households with working wives were given some credit for the prestige of the wife's occupation. However, the contribution of wives' occupational prestige to the overall social standing of the family (b=.08, p=.05) is quite small and hovers on the margins of statistical reliability. Two families different only in the prestige of the wife's occupation by 40 points (more than 2 standard deviations) would differ in their social standing by 3.2 points.

Several unanticipated differences are apparent in the way working wife versus housewife households are evaluated. There appears to be an interaction between wife's labor force status and the importance of her and her husband's education. For some unknown reason, when wives work, their education appears to be less relevant to the social standing of the household and their husband's education appears to take on greater importance.

To elaborate further the difference associated with the wife's labor force behavior, we consider the issue of respondent race. Blacks and whites did not differ in the overall score they assigned to families with housewives, yet blacks rated households with *working* wives 10.5 points higher than did whites—further evidence of the black-white difference in the valuation of working wives in families. As we saw, whites penalized families when wives worked, while there was some evidence that blacks rewarded families with higher status when wives were working.

This race difference in the way working wives are viewed becomes more complex when we consider black-white differences in the valuation of working versus housewife households. Table 4.9 presents separate models by race and by wife's labor force status. Here we focus on the way the effect of husband's employment is modified by the employment status of the wife. For families rated by black

TABLE 4.9 Race Differences in Attribution of Status to Working Wife- Versus Housewife-Designated Households

Independent Variables	Black Raters[a]						Nonblack Raters[b]					
	Working Wives		Housewives		t diff.		Working Wives		Housewives		t diff.	
	b	SE	b	SE			b	SE	b	SE		
Designated Household:												
Husband Occ. (NORC)	0.03	(0.13)	0.53*	(0.20)	2.10*		0.33*	(0.05)	0.39*	(0.05)	0.85	
Wife Occ. (NORC)	0.22	(0.14)	—		—		0.05	(0.04)	—		—	
Husband Educ. (years)	1.88*	(0.86)	0.30	(1.25)	1.04		1.13	(0.26)	0.50	(0.26)	1.71	
Wife Educ. (years)	1.31	(1.08)	2.46	(1.64)	0.59		0.74*	(0.32)	1.71*	(0.32)	2.14*	
Husband Unemployed	−1.88	(5.00)	−14.93*	(6.93)	1.53		−7.04*	(1.81)	−0.51	(1.74)	2.60*	
Black	−4.53	(3.47)	−0.32	(5.42)	0.65		−21.27*	(6.91)	−5.73	(7.72)	1.50	
Respondent:												
Age (years)	0.22*	(0.11)	0.14	(0.17)	0.40		0.14*	(0.04)	0.10	(0.04)	0.71	
Male	−3.11	(3.19)	−0.61	(5.11)	0.42		−1.04	(1.11)	−0.05	(1.11)	0.63	
Family Prestige	−0.02	(0.16)	0.26	(0.27)	0.89		−0.15*	(0.05)	−0.08	(0.05)	1.00	
Constant	9.08	(13.61)	3.88	(34.32)			23.41*	(4.42)	11.18	(6.74)		
R^2 =	.18*		.19*				.15*		.14*			
N =	(285)		(148)				(1967)		(2131)			

*Significant at .05 level
a. Model based only on households evaluated by black respondents (for designated households with and without working wives.)
b. Model based only on households evaluated by nonblack respondents (for designated households with and without working wives.)

138

respondents, the occupational prestige of the husband affects the family's prestige only when the wife is not working. Other differences in equations for black raters, while suggestive, are not statistically significant.

These results are consistent with a material necessity interpretation of the role of employment in black families. What may matter the most to blacks evaluating their primarily black social ties is family income, regardless of whether the money is being brought in by the husband, the wife, or both. What is most devastating to family status is when both partners are unemployed and hence not bringing home any paychecks. Note that this interpretation does not apply to the results for white respondents.

For whites, the husband's occupation is the most important status attribute regardless of his wife's labor force status. Note that in families with unemployed husbands and employed wives there is considerable loss of status (b=-7.04). However, an unemployed husband has practically no effect (less than one point reduction in status) on family status as long as his wife remains in the home. Hence, for whites it is probably not income per se, but role performance that appears to be most pertinent to family status. When roles are reversed and when wives become the sole bread-winners, the family loses considerable status in the eyes of their friends, relatives, neighbors, and co-workers.[10]

In sum, there is some evidence that the types of jobs wives hold make a difference to family social status in real-world judgments, although not as much as was evident in the abstract vignette studies. These results also showed that the valuation of other family attributes were modified depending on whether or not wives in the families were employed, a finding not anticipated from abstract vignette research.

Are Family Prestige
Vignette Studies Valid?

Analysis of real-world evaluations indicates that *vignette analysis does not bias the mechanisms underlying judgment processes. Vignette analysis provides an accurate portrayal of normative judgment criteria without real-world constraints.*

This real-world study validated most of the findings from vignette studies of family social status. In intact families, husbands' occupational achievements dominated the perceived status, a finding common to vignette results. As in vignette research, educational attainments of both husbands and wives are given about half as much weight as are occupations in family prestige judgments. In addition, black families are regarded as lower in status than whites, independent of socioeconomic achievements. Finally, as in vignette studies, blacks and whites used different criteria in their valuations of families with working versus nonworking wives.

Considering the abundance of information available to our respondents about their designated social contacts, it is remarkable that these same characteristics surfaced as pertinent to family social standing as in the vignette judgments where relatively little information was made available to the raters. Nonetheless, real-world and vignette results are not *totally* comparable; contradictory evidence cannot be ignored. Although vignette analysis appears to uncover abstract normative guidelines accurately, the real-world results suggest that these guidelines do not always apply within specific social contexts. Unlike the world of hypothetical vignettes, real-world phenomena are tied to structural constraints.

The most outstanding difference between the vignette and real-world results was the weight attached to wives' occupational achievements. Working women may have received some credit for working in high rather than low prestige jobs—however, not as much as discovered in the vignette studies.

How can we explain this apparent contradiction? One plausible interpretation is that raters were unrealistically egalitarian when judging the vignette descriptions of families. After all, the vignette world eliminated sex discrimination in the work roles of men and women, and perhaps within this ideal world raters used ideal judgment criteria. However, even in the nondiscriminatory vignette world, raters discriminated and gave wives only half the credit they gave husbands in comparable occupations.

Alternative explanations for this apparent failure to take the occupational prestige of wives' work into account in the real-world judgments focus on the characteristics of women's work and family roles in the real world. In general, in the real discriminatory world, married women are expected to invest most of their energies in family life. Jobs for women have relatively low status, and in white middle-class families working wives usually provide supplementary income to the husband's contributions. Indeed, half of the women in the designated households were housewives, and the estimated prestige score for housewives of 51.0 was higher than 78 percent of the jobs working wives held.

Many of the wives in the designated households were undoubtedly also mothers, and their roles as mothers, homemakers (working wives also do most of the housework), and participants in community activities may have been more salient to respondents than what they did to earn supplementary income for their families. For example, wives appeared to be given more credit for educational accomplishments in this real-world study than in the vignette world. Education may be related to their performance as mothers, hostesses, and participants in community activities.

Unfortunately, no information was available about whether these women were working full-time or part-time or whether they had young children at home. Indeed, women working full-time who also had young children to take care of may have been viewed critically by white respondents who felt that a mother's place is in the home.

The vignette descriptions of families took husbands and wives outside of the family context and did not describe how families distributed household tasks. Perhaps wives' occupations would be given less weight in a vignette study that described family roles. For example, a family vignette might include the number of children at home and the age of the youngest child. Vignettes describing husbands and wives working full-time while their children are in day care might also be included. Descriptions of the wife's performance as a homemaker might be included to see if this interacts with labor force participation in the prestige judgments. Poor homemakers who worked might not be viewed kindly by raters.

Another way vignettes could be designed to portray the real world more accurately would be to approximate actual distributions of labor force participation. Half of the wives would be assigned to the housewife category, and full- and part-time jobs could be assigned in the same proportion as in the real world. Relative salaries of husbands and wives would indicate who are the primary and secondary wage earners. Raters with more restricted and more realistic descriptions of wives' jobs might reduce their reliance on this characteristic as a basis for their prestige judgments.

These real-world results suggest the importance of social context in family prestige judgments, but they do not undermine the value of vignette research as a method for discovering normative, judgment criteria. Clearly, this research shows that we face interpretation difficulties in examining the real world when characteristics being judged are confounded by characteristics of the judges and variation in relevant attributes is often seriously restricted by societal constraints. Indeed, these interpretation difficulties prompted Rossi to develop the vignette methodology and underscore the significance of the technique.

NOTES

1. For Hollingshead, class and status were treated as equivalent constructs. Obviously many sociologists would disagree with this practice.

2. Dummy dependent variables were created equal to one if the item of information was missing and equal to zero otherwise. By regressing these dummy variables on 19 characteristics of the respondents and their designated families, net contributions of each characteristic to missing knowledge were estimated. The modest R^2 for these equations suggests that lack of knowledge was largely idiosyncratic.

3. Less than 3 percent of these "nonblacks" were Puerto Rican or Latin-American, while 97 percent were Caucasian. Hence, "nonblack" and "white" are used interchangeably to describe the race of nonblacks.

4. Other analyses (not shown here) demonstrated that the husband's occupational prestige and employment status interacted to influence social standing. That is, unemployment was particularly devastating to social status when the head was working in a low-status occupation prior to becoming unemployed. Note that this is consistent with the actual effects of unemployment on high- and low-status persons. For high-status persons, unemployment often means that they are between jobs and have the resources to maintain their living standard, while unemployment can be devastating to a low-status family that is highly dependent on every paycheck coming in on time. An interaction term multiplying occupational prestige by the unemployment dummy produced a positive and significant effect. Inclusion of the interaction enhanced the additive effect of unemployment to -11 points, a level consistent with the vignette results.

5. Unfortunately, respondents were never asked to describe the ages of members of their designated households. Of course, in the case of closest siblings the instructions requested that respondents choose siblings closest to them in age.

6. Separate regression analyses for designated households with working wives and families with housewives showed that black respondents rated working wife households 10.6 points higher in prestige than did whites ($p<.05$), other things being equal; however, there were no black-white differences in the way families with housewives were rated.

7. An early interpretation of the particularly strong emphasis placed on occupation in the successful/unsuccessful families focused on the variance in occupation. Theoretically, the only reason a regression coefficient would be sensitive to the range of values would be if the relationship was nonlinear—that is, if respondents were evaluating occupations in the middle range as the same in prestige and focusing on the large differences between, say, doctors and janitors for making status distinctions. To test this, vignette analyses were done within specified ranges of husbands' and wives' occupations (below 40, 40-60, and greater than 60). The results did not support the

nonlinear hypothesis; the regression coefficients did not depend on the range of occupational prestige.

8. An attempt was made to test this material necessity hypothesis by dividing the designated households into two groups according to the husband's occupational prestige (NORC greater or less than 37 points), assuming a greater need for women to work when their husbands had low-status jobs. As expected, white raters rewarded families with housewives only when husbands worked in high-status occupations (by 2.4 points, $p<.05$ compared to a coefficient for housewives of -0.3 for white raters judging low-status families). Moreover, blacks devalued families with housewives only when husbands worked in low-status occupations (by 10.7 points, $t=1.55$ compared to a housewife coefficient of -3.1 for high-status families). These differences in the valuations of wives' labor force status depending on the prestige of their husbands' jobs were consistent with the hypothesis, but they were not statistically significant.

9. As described in note 4, husband unemployment was particularly costly to the family's social standing when he normally worked in a low-status job.

10. This same kind of phenomena surfaced in another type of analysis. A model for only those families in which the wife was working in an occupation equal to or higher in status than her husband's was estimated. The results showed that as the gap between the wife's occupational prestige and her husband's occupational prestige widened (that is, she worked in a significantly higher-status job than him), the family's prestige was significantly reduced. It seems that there is social disdain for families in which wives are the "household heads," at least in white society.

REFERENCES

Axelson, Leland J., 1970, "The working wife: differences in perception among negro and white males." Journal of Marriage and the Family 32: 457-464.

Bose, Christine E., 1973, Jobs and Gender: Sex and Occupational Prestige. Ph.D. dissertation, Johns Hopkins University.

Curtis, Richard and Elton F. Jackson, 1977, Inequality in American Communities. New York: Academic Press.

Duncan, Otis D. and Beverly Duncan, 1955, "Residential distribution and occupational stratification," American Journal of Sociology 60: 493-503.

Duncan, Otis D., David L. Featherman, and Beverly Duncan, 1972, Socioeconomic Background and Achievement. New York: Seminar Press.

Farley, Reynolds, 1977, "Residential segregation in urbanized areas of the United States in 1970: an analysis of social class and racial differences." Demography 14: 497-518.

Fischer, Claude S., Robert M. Jackson, C. Anne Stueve, Kathleen Gerson, Lynne M. Jones, and Mark Baldassare, 1977, Networks and Places. New York: Free Press.

Guest, Avery M. and James Weed, 1976, "Ethnic residential segregation: patterns of change." American Journal of Sociology 81: 1088-1111.

Hodge, Robert W., Paul M. Siegel, and Peter H. Rossi, 1964, "Occupational prestige in the United States, 1925-63." American Journal of Sociology 70: 268-292.

Laumann, Edward O., 1966, Prestige and Association in an Urban Community. Indianapolis: Bobbs-Merill.

Mason, Karen Oppenheim and Larry L. Bumpass, 1975, "U.S. women's sex role ideology 1970." American Journal of Sociology 80: 1212-1219.

Meudell, Marcia Bonner, 1977, Dynamic and Static Determinants of Household Social Standing. Ph.D. dissertation, University of Massachusetts.

Nock, Steven L. and Peter H. Rossi, 1977, "Ascription versus achievement in the attribution of family social status." American Journal of Sociology 84: 565-590.

Pleck, Elisabeth H., 1978, "A mother's wages: income earning among married Italian and black women, 1896-1911," pp. 490-510 in M. Gordon (ed.) The American Family in Social-Historical Perspective. New York: St. Martin's Press.

Rossi, Peter H., William A. Sampson, Christine E. Bose, Guillermina Jasso, and Jeff Passel, 1974, "Measuring household social standing." Social Science Research 3: 169-190.

Sampson, William and Peter H. Rossi, 1975, "Race and family social standing." American Sociological Review 40: 201-214.

5

PRISON REFORM AND STATE ELITES
A Retrospective

RICHARD A. BERK
PETER H. ROSSI

In barest outlines, a corrections system is an organizational device that takes persons who have been convicted of crimes, administers sentences ordered by the courts, and then discharges them into civilian life when the sentences have been completed. Depending upon the specific state criminal codes involved and upon the courts, a corrections system has some discretion in the treatment of convicted offenders, the exact amount varying widely from state to state and case to case. Offenders may be sent to a minimum security prison or a maximum security prison; parole may be granted as quickly as possible or the maximum sentence imposed. Prison regimes may be arbitrary, capricious, and cruel, or they may be just, predictable, and as humane as imprisonment can be. In some way the punishment is supposed to "fit the crime," prison treatments are to maximize the possibility of rehabilitation, and society is to be protected from the recurrence of antisocial behavior.

To change a corrections system in its functioning means to make changes in the ways sentences are made, in the sentences themselves, and in the criteria used for discharging persons from the system. The decisions made by the courts and the corrections system are necessarily complicated. Convicted offenders vary in a wide variety

Authors' Note: Reprinted and adapted from Prison Reform and State Elites *by Richard A. Berk and Peter H. Rossi (Cambridge, MA: Ballinger © 1977) with permission of the publisher.*

of ways: Offenses range in seriousness; extenuating circumstances may be present; an offender may have no previous record of convictions or he may have a considerable dossier; an offender may be a juvenile, a young adult, or mature. Changes in the corrections system may involve milder treatments for some types of offenders and not for others. In the criminal code some offenses may call for mandatory treatment provisions that involve the harshest possible treatment, while other offenses may carry a wide choice of tratments ranging from almost instant parole to lifetime incarceration. Two persons may agree on what changes ought to be made but disagree on which sorts of convicted offenders ought to be given the new treatments involved.

What we are trying to get at in this chapter is the meaning of reforms *in practice* to members of the elites in the three states (Florida, Illinois, and Washington) at the level of what should be done with specific convicted offenders. In some ideal sense, we would have liked to present to them concrete, possibly actual cases of convicted offenders and ask each respondent what kind of corrections treatment ought to be accorded to each of the cases. Thus, we might have proceeded to summarize a number of trial records in order to present to a respondent a record on which he could make a judgment regarding what he thought would be an appropriate treatment for that offender—whether he would grant an offender probation, assign him to a community treatment center, or sentence him to prison. It is not at all easy to put together a set of concrete cases that covers the full range of decisions the criminal justice system has to make. Each case tends to be somewhat idiosyncratic. It would be difficult to cover a wide variety of crimes and types of offenders in a set of cases tht could be given easily to respondents and that could be analyzed in a sensible fashion.

We chose to put together hypothetical cases of convicted offenders. In these hypothetical cases, the characteristics of the offenders and the crimes of which they were convicted were systematically varied. Each hypothetical offender was described in a short vignette containing a brief description of the offender in terms of the crime of which he was convicted, his age, and his previous criminal record.

There are several advantages of hypothetical vignettes as opposed to concrete cases. First, in hypothetical cases it is possible to choose characteristics of the offenders to accentuate the salience of those characteristics in which one is particularly interested. In the world of real offenders, most have been convicted of a narrow variety of crimes, cluster heavily in the early years of adulthood, and have a narrow band of previous convictions. In a hypothetical world it is possible to provide wider ranges of offenses, previous records, age, and any other characteristic that might be considered relevant.

Second, it is possible to produce sets of vignettes in which offender characteristics are unrelated to each other, so that the effects of differences in a particular characteristic can be separated from those with which it is ordinarily associated. For example, in the real world, young offenders tend to commit different crimes than older ones. Hence, it is difficult to separate out the effects of age from offenses in the sentences courts give to convicted offenders. In the fictitious world represented by our offender vignettes, older offenders and younger ones can be described as having been convicted of the same set of crimes. Because of this characteristic, we can separate the effects of offenders' ages and their offenses on the sentences deemed appropriate.

Finally, vignettes can be written so that certain detail can be omitted. The physical appearance of a specific offender, for instance, may be important in the judgment of his particular case, but since the effects of physical appearances are not likely to be directly affected by broad policy changes of the kind considered here, it may be best to ignore such factors. Consequently, two characteristics of possible relevance were deliberately omitted. We restricted ourselves to male offenders, mainly on the grounds that there are relatively few women in state prisons. Second, we did not specify the convicted offender's race, an individual characteristic that is also probably of considerable importance in the actual treatment of offenders. We were well aware of the criminal justice literature that makes the impact of race and class its central problem but were reluctant to raise this controversial issue and hence distract respondents from the assessment variables that, for our purposes, were more relevant to *manifest* corrections policy.

These advantages of vignettes argued strongly for their use in this study. We needed some measure of the ways our respondents would treat individual offenders, a way the effects of various offender characteristics on those judgments could be assessed, and some way of sampling the judgments of respondents in order to assess each respondent's "traditional" or "progressive" leanings with respect to types of offenders.

The vignettes used in this study were formed out of the cross-classification of the following characteristics:

(1) Age of offender: Five ages were permitted: 15, 19, 22, 35, and 50.

(2) Previous record: Seven types of previous records were permitted: no previous record, only misdemeanors, one felony involving property, several felonies involving property, one felony involving persons, several felonies involving persons, and several felonies involving both persons and property.

(3) Crime of which convicted: Forty crimes were chosen, varying in their seriousness and covering mainly offenses that are common. "Seriousness" was measured by a separate special survey conducted in Baltimore.

These three characteristics permit the writing of 1400 unique vignettes, each bearing a unique description of a hypothetical convicted offender.

In actuality, only 1160 of the 1400 possible combinations were used in the study, since there were some with unusual, odd, or impossible combinations (e.g., 35 and 50-year-old men convicted of "repeated running away from home," or 15-year-olds who were convicted of "selling worthless stocks and bonds"). These anomalous vignettes were deleted from the total vignette universe.

The remaining 1160 "sensible" vignettes were divided into 20 samples of 40 vignettes each. Each sample was chosen systematically from among the 1160 combinations in such a fashion as to ensure the statistical equivalence of the samples. Analysis of variance of the "seriousness scores" of the crimes included in the samples showed that the variations in such scores from sample to sample were consistent with the hypothesis that they differed only by sampling error.

Each respondent was given two of the vignette samples in his questionnaire or interview, one sample to be rated by him according to the "treatment" he thought *desirable* and *appropriate* to the offender described in each vignette and the other sample (a different sample than the first) to be rated according to what were his impressions of the *typical* treatments accorded to such offenders in his state. The samples were administered to respondents randomly—that is, each respondent had the same probability of receiving each of the samples.

The respondent was asked to designate one of the nine treatments listed below as appropriate to each offender vignette (or as typical treatment accorded in his state):

(1) Release under supervision to his local community for a period of up to one year.

(2) Release under supervision to his local community for a period of one to five years.

(3) Part-time confinement (nights and/or weekends) in a residential center in a local community for a period of up to one year.

(4) Part-time confinement (nights and/or weekends) in a residential center in a local community for a period of up to one year.

(5) Incarceration full time in a prison for up to one year.

(6) Incarceration full time in a prison for one to five years.

(7) Incarceration full time in a prison for more than five years.

(8) Confinement in a mental hospital for treatment.

(9) Referral to a medical facility for treatment.

The first seven "treatments" are designed to form a scale ranging from the least restraint on personal freedom to a maximum degree of restraint. At the outset we could not be sure whether the seven treatments did form such an ordinal scale, much less whether they could be treated as having equal intervals. Subsequent analysis indicated that respondents treated the response categories as if they formed an equal interval scale, and hence responses 1 through 7 are treated in the analysis as if they had equal interval properties.[1]

Obviously, treatments 8 and 9 cannot be treated as falling somewhere among the first seven. They will have to be treated separately. Because so few respondents used these ratings, we will simply ignore them, discarding the few responses of this kind that the respondents gave. In a larger sample, it may be possible to make a special analysis of these ratings and of the crimes to which they are considered appropriate.

The vignettes and their ratings can be handled in three ways. First, since each vignette in the total set of 1160 was rated by from three to twelve respondents, the modal number of respondents being between seven and nine, an *average* treatment rating can be computed for each vignette constituting an unbiased estimate of the average for the entire set of respondents. Since each respondent had an equal chance of rating each of the vignettes, the respondents who rated any one vignette may be considered a random subsample of the total sample, and hence, the average rating is an unbiased estimate of the average rating that the total sample would have given. These average vignette ratings (1160 in all) can be used to uncover the rating principles used collectively by the respondents in allocating offenders to desired (or typical) treatments.

Second, each respondent can be characterized by the *average* of the ratings he gave to the 40 vignettes that appeared in his sample.

This individual average rating can then be used as an indicator of the respondent's stringency-leniency in handling convicted offenders (in the case of the ratings of what he would consider to be desired treatments) and of his perceptions of the stringency-leniency of the corrections system in his state (in the case of his ratings of what he perceived to be the typical treatment in his state). These individual *average* ratings (266 in all) can then be analyzed to uncover the ways different respondents varied in their leniency-stringency toward the treatment of convicted offenders.

A third mode of analysis regards each separate rating as the basic unit, a procedure that makes it possible to relate characteristics of individual respondents to ratings. Under this procedure there are 10,640 observations, each consisting of a vignette that has been rated by an individual. This analysis provides much the same information as the first described above but also provides additional data on how differences among individual respondents affect their ratings.

All three modes of analysis are presented in this chapter to illustrate how these ratings can be handled. It should be noted that the first two modes are based on rather small numbers and expected to be somewhat fragile and, hence, likely to change in a larger sample of states from sampling fluctuations alone.

The Structure of Collective Judgments About Convicted Offenders

To each respondent the sample of vignettes he was given to rate must have seemed a hodgepodge collection of somewhat arbitrarily put together descriptions. Indeed, some of the respondents interviewed by the senior authors kept looking over the set of vignettes in an attempt to understand the principles underlying the selection of the particular combinations of offender characteristics that appeared. Of course, that is exactly what we wanted the respondents to experience so that it would be difficult for them to develop a set of self-conscious principles that would guide their selection of treatments for the vignettes. That is, if we systematically varied the combinations that appeared in each respondent's samples, it might have been possible for them to decide consciously to vary treatments according to a weighting system that, for example, counted previous records half as much as the crime of which the offender was convicted.

The fact that each sample was a chance combination of vignettes made it difficult for respondents to develop biasing response sets of this kind.

Yet, there is an underlying rationale to the judgments made by elite members concerning the convicted offenders described in the vignettes. The rationale can be uncovered by examining the mean ratings given to the vignettes and the regression of those averages on offender characteristics. The mean ratings may be taken as representing the total sample's collective judgments concerning either the treatment considered appropriate by the respondents or their perception of the typical treatment accorded to such offenders in their corrections system. The term "collective judgment" is used in this connection to express the fact that it is the *average rating* given to a vignette that is being predicted by the regression equation. Thus, the analysis does *not* tell us directly how individuals varied their judgments of vignettes according to the characteristics that went into the vignettes' construction. It does tell us how the vignette characteristics affected the average (or collective) judgments of the sample of elite members interviewed.

The average rating given to vignettes in the "appropriate treatment" rating task was 4.08, a value corresponding to "part-time confinement in a residential center for a period of from one to five years." The standard deviation of the average ratings was 1.7, indicating that about two-thirds of all the appropriate treatment collective judgments fell between 2 and 6. When we consider that the crimes involved are deliberately chosen to range across a wide band of seriousness, and hence represent more crimes on the less serious side than would ordinarily be found among prison inmates, this relatively lenient average sentence is to be expected.

In contrast, the collective perception of "typical treatment" accorded to convicted offenders in their states is an average rating of 4.59, a half-point higher on the scale than what was considered appropriate treatment collectively by the respondents, a point somewhere between a sentence of part-time confinement for one to five years and incarceration for up to one year. The standard deviation of collective perceptions of typical treatment is 1.6, not appreciably different from that computed for desired treatments.

Collectively, our respondents were more lenient in the treatments they deemed *appropriate* and desired than they saw being *typically* accorded in their states' corrections system. The pattern of differ-

TABLE 5.1   Regression Analysis of Average Typical Treatment Ratings for
            Convicted Offender Vignettes
            (N = 1160 Vignettes)

A. *Zero Order Correlations, Means and Standard Deviations:*

	Average Typical Ratings	Offender Age[a]	Previous Record[b]	Crime Seriousness[c]
Average Typical Ratings		.12	.36	.73
Offender Age			.07	.00
Previous Record				.00
Crime Seriousness				
Means =	4.59	30.5	2.05	6.5
SD =	1.58	12.66	1.24	1.15

B. *Regression Statistics: Dependent Variable = Average Typical Treatment Ratings*

Vignette Characteristic	Unstandardized Regression Coefficients	Standardized Regression Coefficients	Significance
Crime Serious Score	.991	.725	p < .01
Previous Record	.450	.355	p < .01
Age	.012	.095	p < .01
Intercept =	-3.176		
R =	.815		
R² =	.665		p < .01

a. Age entered as shown in vignettes (i.e., 15, 19, 22, 34 or 50).
b. Previous Record coded as follows:

Record = 0
Misdemeanor = 1
One Property or
Person Felony = 2
Several Property or
Person Felonies = 3
Several Property *and*
Person Felonies = 4

c. Crime Seriousness Score obtained from Baltimore Survey (see Berk and Rossi, 1977).

ences is, of course, very much in line with the findings of previous chapters. Our elite respondents were more "progressive" in their views than they perceived their states' corrections practices to be.

Although there is considerable risk in making such comparisons, it does *not* appear that the gap between the collective judgments of "appropriate" and "typical treatments" is as big as some of the differences respondents reported between themselves and their perceptions of groups in their states, such as the general public and the police. Perhaps what the respondents are reporting is that the

TABLE 5.2   Regression Analysis of Average Desired Treatment Ratings for
Convicted Offender Vignettes
(N = 1160 Vignettes)

A. *Zero Order Correlations, Means and Standard Deviations:*

	Average Typical Ratings	Offender Age	Previous Record	Crime Seriousness
Average Desired Ratings		.12	.40	.73
Offender Age			.07	.00
Previous Record				.00
Crime Seriousness				
Mean =	4.08	30.5	2.05	6.5
SD =	1.66	12.66	1.24	1.15

B. *Regression Statistics: Dependent Variable = Average Desired Treatment Ratings*

Vignette Characteristic	Unstandardized Regression Coefficients	Standardized Regression Coefficients	Significance
Crime Seriousness Score	1.05	.728	$p < .01$
Previous Record	.523	.391	$p < .01$
Age	.013	.096	$p < .01$
Intercept =	-4.249		
R =	.835		
R^2 =	.697		$p < .01$

NOTE: See Table 5.1 for definitions of variables.

corrections system in its working is more progressive than one might
have expected on the basis of the climate of state public opinion.

The multiple regression analysis of collective *typical* ratings is
shown in Table 5.1. In the upper panel of the table are zero-order
correlation coefficients showing the pairwise interrelationships of
average typical treatment ratings and the three vignette characteristics. The first row of correlations are findings, but the remaining
correlation coefficients reflect the design of the vignettes. Thus, the
coefficients of .00 between offender age and crime seriousness and
previous record and crime seriousness merely reflect the fact that
every age category used was associated equally often with almost
every crime used in the vignettes. The fact that the second- and third-
row correlations are either zero or very small shows that the design of
the study was successfully carried out.

Table 5.2 presents the same analysis for desired treatments. The
zero-order correlation coefficients in the second and third rows are

identical to those in Table 5.1, since they reflect the same design elements.

The bottom parts of Tables 5.1 and 5.2 contain the regression statistics for typical and desired treatments. Note that the multiple correlation coefficients are quite high—.82 and .84, respectively—indicating that there is considerable structure to the collective judgments made by our respondents. Indeed, almost two-thirds of the variation in the average ratings can be accounted for by the characteristics that go into the construction of the vignettes. This result is hardly unanticipated. Since the only information we gave to the respondents are the characteristics that go into the construction of the vignettes, it is to be expected that this information should count very heavily in the ratings. We can also expect that the amount of unexplained variation will decline as the sample size is increased and as the numbers of respondents who contribute to each average increase correspondingly. At least some of the unexplained variance is due to sampling error incorporated into the average ratings, an error that can be anticipated to be relatively large, since samples that contribute to these ratings range in size from 2 to 8.

Since we are dealing with 1160 cases, the multiple correlation coefficients are statistically significant at astoundingly low probabilities. (We were not able to find a published table of the sampling distribution of F that contained probability values for the F values involved.)

The unstandardized regression coefficients shown in Tables 5.1 and 5.2 indicate the weights to be applied to each of the characteristics that would produce the best estimate of the average rating based on the linear regression model. Thus, the equations for "typical" and "desired" collective judgments are:

$$\hat{Y}_{Typ} = -3.176 + .991X_1 + .450X_2 + .012X_3$$

$$\hat{Y}_{Des} = -4.249 + 1.05X_1 + .523X_2 + .013X_3$$

$\hat{Y}_{Typ}$ = estimated average score for "typical treatment"

$\hat{Y}_{Des}$ = estimated average score for "desired treatment"

where X_1 = Crime Seriousness Scores

X_2 = Previous Record (see Table 5.1 for code used)

$$X_3 = \text{Age of Offender (years)}$$

For example, the estimated "typical" treatment score for a 35-year-old offender who has been convicted of "beating up a spouse" (crime seriousness score of 5.8) and who has a record of one previous felony is 3.89 and the estimated "desired" treatment score is 3.34. The collective judgment of desired appropriate treatment would place the convicted offender in short-term (up to one year) part-time confinement arrangement, while the "typical" treatment would place the offender closer to longer-term part-time confinement (one to five years).

A similar calculation for a convicted offender whose crime was rape (and who was also 35 and had a previous conviction record of one felony) yields an estimated incarceration score of 6.3 for the *typical* treatment in the three states and 5.9 for the *desired* treatment. The difference between these two estimated scores is primarily a matter of how many years of incarceration the sentence should be. The estimated typical treatment in a state puts the convicted offender away in a sentence that is close to five or more years in prison, while the desired treatment is from one to five years in prison.

The main difference between the two equations lies in the values computed for the intercepts. The typical ratings have a higher intercept than the desired ratings, indicating that by and large our respondents saw that the corrections systems of their states were treating convicted offenders correctly according to their crimes, ages, and previous records, but the respondents would like to see a more lenient treatment given to all offenders. The leniency is shown in the fact that the intercept value for the desired ratings is almost one scale value lower than the typical treatment.

The standardized regression coefficients provide a measure of the relative strengths of the three characteristics and indicate that for both "typical" and "desired" collective judgments, the "seriousness score" of the crime is clearly the most important characteristic, followed by previous record and age.[2] The last variable, age, is given a relatively minor role in both analyses. In short, collective judgments about treatment stress the seriousness of the crime most heavily and use characteristics of the offender as secondary criteria.

It is not easy to reconcile these findings with the approval our respondents have given in previous chapters to rehabilitation and community-based treatment "futures." However, both futures are vague on exactly how specific types of offenders are to be treated. The rehabilitation orientation stresses that offenders are to be retrained and subjected to therapeutic measures, but the specific retraining and rehabilitation measures to be applied to specific types of offenders certainly were not spelled out in our description of this future. The community-based corrections future also has the same vagueness concerning which offenders were to be incarcerated, released, or held in part-time confinement. Because of these ambiguities, it is impossible to judge confidently whether our respondents are collectively sentencing hypothetical offenders consistent with their overwhelming endorsement of either the rehabilitation or the community-based "futures." While at face value liberal pretensions appear to have been abandoned, it is difficult to be certain.

These analyses demonstrate that the collective judgments of the elite respondents are quite lawful. The average scores given to the vignettes by extremely small subsamples of respondents can be well accounted for by the characteristics that went into the construction of vignettes. Furthermore, we saw that the structure of judgments was similar for both "appropriate" treatments and perceived "typical" treatments, although the respondents on the average were more lenient in their treatments than they saw their corrections system typically behaving.

Respondent Differences in the Treatment of Convicted Offenders

The vignette ratings can also be used to characterize individual respondents. Since each of the 29 samples administered to the respondents is a fair sample of the total set of vignettes (and, hence, statistically equivalent to each other), we can compute the average scores given by each respondent to the vignettes in his sample and use that score to characterize the respondent's leniency-stringency in treating convicted offenders. We can also compute the same average over the vignette sample rated according to his perception of the typical treatment accorded to convicted offenders in his state and use that average to measure his perceptions of the leniency-stringency of his state's corrections system.

These individual average scores can then be subjected to the same analytic technique employed in the first section of this chapter in order to uncover the sources of variation from individual to individual.

TABLE 5.3   Regression of Respondent Mean Desired and Mean Typical
Ratings on Respondent Characteristics
(N = 256)[a]

Respondent Characteristic	Desired Ratings		Typical Ratings	
	b	T-value	b	T-value
I: Positions[b]				
Prosecutors	1.15[d]	9.20	.84	.24
State Elected Officials	.78[d]	6.64	.08	.32
Local Elected Officials	.77[d]	4.60	.88[d]	2.89
Judges of Criminal Courts	1.09[d]	10.72	.12	.58
Police	.57[d]	2.95	-.50	-1.09
Bar Assoc. and Public Defenders	.60[d]	2.88	.41	.63
Corrections Officials	.28	.89	-.23	-.30
Corrections Rank and File	.32	.92	0.06	.14
II: State[c]				
Washington	-.24[d]	-2.06	-.09	-.16
Illinois	-.08	-.21	-.43[d]	-3.24
III: Biography and Experience				
Age	-.008	-1.11	-.009	-.74
Education	-.09	-1.52	-.04	-.16
Visited Prisons	.23	1.11	-.06	-.44
Met with Prisoners	-.01	-.50	.23	1.06
Talked with Prisoner Rep.	.68	.93	-.29	-.79
Intercept	4.10		5.27	
$R^2 =$	.10[d]		.06	

a. Individual means are computed over the ratings of each respondent and hence represent the average of the treatments accorded by each respondent to typical and desired vignettes.
b. Omitted category is "Other Partisans."
c. Omitted state is Florida.
d. $p < .05$.

Table 5.3 contains the results of regressing the individual mean ratings for desired and typical treatments on a variety of individual respondent characteristics. Note that because "positions" and "states" are dummy variables, the resulting b-coefficients are relative to respondents in the omitted categories of "Other Partisans" and the state of Florida, respectively. Thus the b-coefficient of 1.15 for prosecutors should be interpreted as a net increment of 1.15 points in treatment scores for prosecutors as compared to "Other Partisans" (that is, state and other variables held constant). Since "Other Partisans" have been shown in previous analyses to be quite a liberal group on corrections issues, most of the coefficients for other positions are positive, indicating that, *ceteris paribus,* the latter are more punitive in the kinds of treatments they want meted out to convicted offenders. Since our dependent variable is a 5-point scale, this increment cannot be easily dismissed.

Despite a few such coefficients, all the individual respondent characteristics used do not account for much of the variation from individual to individual in the mean treatment ratings given in either the desired or typical ratings. Only 10 percent of the variance in individual means could be accounted for in the desired ratings, an amount that just barely reaches the conventional .05 statistical significance level. Even less variance in the individual means for typical ratings is accounted for (6 percent), an amount that does not succeed in getting over the .30 threshold.

Looking now at all the b-coefficients for desired ratings, we see that only the positions of the respondents make much difference. Prosecutors and judges would like to see convicted offenders have slightly more than a one-point increment in severity of treatment. State and local elected officials are almost as punitive, adding about three-quarters of a point. Recall that these coefficients are all in comparison to "Other Partisans," ordinarily a very liberal group, which helps to explain why, along with police, public defenders and influential members of the bar also have positive coefficients of about half a unit.

Only state elected officials and Illinois residents have regression coefficients that reach conventional levels of statistical significance in the regressions on typical treatment averages. The former believe that typical sentences are more severe, the latter believe they are less severe. Of course, since respondents were asked to report on what typically occurs within their states, we should expect to find a good deal of consensus among respondents and therefore little in the way of explained variance and few (if any) important b-coefficients.

In short, we find that respondents from a variety of positions, biographies, and experiences agree on what is going on within their present corrections system. There is a bit less agreement on the desired state of affairs, however. Compared to the liberal "Other Partisans," judges, prosecutors, elected officials on both the state and local levels, police, and parts of the legal profession more generally, would want to see more stringent treatment of criminals in their systems. All agree, nevertheless, that the desired state of affairs would be one in which less punitive sentences were routinely handed out to convicted offenders.

TABLE 5.4   Regressions of Typical Vignette Ratings Within Each State on
                    Vignette Characteristics

| | | *b-coefficents* | | | | |
State	Age	Crime Seriousness Score	Previous Record	Intercept	R^2	N
Florida	.007	.945[a]	.452[a]	-2.62	.35[a]	3754
Illinois	.017[a]	1.02[a]	.431[a]	-3.77	.38[a]	2484
Washington	.012[a]	1.02[a]	.467[a]	-3.88	.40[a]	3117

a. .05 significance for the null hypothesis that b-coefficient equals zero.

Interaction Effects Between
Respondent and Vignette Characteristics

We have now considered in some depth the ways characteristics of vignettes affect mean ratings and the ways respondent biography affects mean ratings. The next logical question is how, if at all, these two clusters of independent variables interact in the production of respondent assessments.

We will look at the typical treatment ratings first. Table 5.4 presents regression analyses computed separately within each of the three states. Note that the regressions were computed on the ratings received by individual vignettes, since the number of respondents who rated each of the vignettes within each state was too small to compute average ratings within a state. The effect of using individual vignette ratings is to lower considerably the amount of variance explained. The regression coefficients, however, are unaffected; they are identical, except for rounding error, to those obtainable by using average ratings received by vignettes. (Also note that a somewhat more statistically efficient procedure which would have also routinely permitted the equivalence of significance tests *across* equations could have been employed through the use of single equation models with interaction terms by state. However, this was discarded as unnecessarily cumbersome, given the low priority we have given statistical inference. See Johnston, 1972: Section 6.3.)

The differences among the three states are far less than the overall similarities. Consistent with the overall patterns in Table 5.1, elite respondents in each of the states report that their particular criminal justice system most emphasizes the seriousness of the crimes involved; next, the previous record of the convicted offenders; and

TABLE 5.5   Regression of Vignette Desired Ratings on Vignette Characteristics
Within Each Position

		b-coefficients				
Position	Age	Crime Serious-ness Score	Previous Record	Intercept	R^2	N
State Elected Officials	.014[a]	1.07[a]	.524[a]	-4.52	.45[a]	1501
Corrections Officials	.014[a]	1.03[a]	.534[a]	-4.68	.43[a]	1728
Corrections Rank and File	.016[a]	1.11[a]	.427[a]	-4.70	.44[a]	1245
Police	.007	1.14[a]	.429[a]	-4.68	.44[a]	1077
Criminal Court Judges	.010	1.10[a]	.538[a]	-4.38	.48[a]	1291
Prosecutors	.010	1.12[a]	.532[a]	-4.38	.49[a]	616
Bar and Public Defenders	.009	.97[a]	.544[a]	-3.97	.39[a]	764
Local Elected Officials	.009	1.06[a]	.398[a]	-4.08	.43[a]	835
Other Partisans	.012	.91[a]	.426[a]	-3.93	.36[a]	664

a. .05 significance.

least, the age of the offender. Within this overall similarity however,
some small differences do appear. In Florida, the intercept value is
shifted toward heavier sentencing, indicating that Florida respondents,
as we could anticipate from earlier findings, report that their criminal
justice system metes out tougher penalties. Floridians also report
that the age of the offender is given a bit less attention in sentencing,
as suggested by the fact that the b-coefficient for age is smaller by
about one-half. Illinois and Washington may resemble each other
more closely than any other pair, but even in this case, Washington
respondents report that their system weighs previous records more
heavily and age less heavily in giving out sentences. In short, there is
little evidence for important interaction effects by state for the
typical ratings, and other types of interactions for the typical ratings
(not reported here) were even less interesting.

Interaction effects for desired ratings were also very small, with
differences by respondent position the only findings worth reporting
in any detail. For Table 5.5, we computed separate regressions of
desired vignette ratings on vignette characteristics for each of the
nine different positions. First, the amount of variance explained
ranges from 36 percent (in the case of other partisans) to 49 percent
in the case of prosecutors. Indeed, the two most heterogeneous
groups, the other partisans and the bar association officials and
public defenders, are the ones in which the smallest amounts of
variance are explained. (We combined these two possibly quite dis-

similar types of respondents mainly in order to get a large enough N to sustain separate analyses, reasoning that lawyers were more similar to each other regardless of their occupations than each would be to other groups. Apparently that may not be the case.)

Other differences among the groups center on the role age of respondent plays in judgments, with the first three groups in Table 5.5 stressing that role slightly more than the last six groups. On the role played by criminal records, there appears to be similar disagreement, with state elected officials, corrections officials, criminal court judges, prosecutors, and bar association and public defenders putting a bit more emphasis on previous records than the other groups.

In summary, there is little evidence of important interaction effects between respondent characteristics and vignette characteristics for either the typical or desired treatments. This conclusion survived a variety of different analytical procedures both in the variables considered and various weighting schemes for measures whose scales could not simply be assumed to possess equal interval properties. For example, we regressed previous record on mean vignette rating and then used the resulting regression coefficients to construct a new scale for previous record. In later analyses, this refinement yielded trivial improvements and was thus discarded.

Summary

This chapter has attempted to take the study of desired prison reform from the level of abstractly phrased programs and specific prison reforms to the level of what should be done with specific convicted offenders. Our respondents by and large endorsed a system of sentencing that was less harsh than they saw their present criminal justice system pursuing. In that sense, our elite respondents—including those in the criminal justice sytem as well as outside—were for more lenience in the treatment of criminal offenders and more likely to endorse the use of means other than incarceration in conventional prisons.

The elites were also in favor of a system of allocating sentences that weighted most heavily the seriousness of the crime for which an offender was convicted and then the previous record of the offender. The weight attached to an offender's age favored the young slightly, although some would not put any weight on this factor at all.

In contrast to the powerful effects of vignette characteristics, respondent biography played a very small role. While differences consistent with earlier chapters did in fact appear, by and large they reflected surprising homogeneity. In other words, earlier differences among respondents at a more abstract level in part dissolved in the face of actual sentencing options. While prosecutors, for example, were still more punitive than high-level corrections officials, the practical implications of this disparity are not nearly as striking as disputes over more theoretical issues. Hence, the rhetoric surrounding corrections reform may typically be very misleading.

In short, the analysis presented in this chapter broadly supports the results of previous chapters. Generally, the elite would like to see less harsh treatment meted out to convicted offenders than they believe the present system provides. However, a liberalization of the criminal justice system receives far more than lip service on the level of abstractly presented reforms. Actual sentencing decisions reveal a more traditional posture, perhaps because of strictures existing within current corrections systems. In other words, liberals and conservatives may have had their ideal preferences constrained by a reality in which many desirable options were simply not available. There were, for example, very few community-based corrections facilities in 1973. Alternatively, questions about more abstract principles and hypothetical reforms may encourage respondents to reveal their more ideological side and thus produce a more polarized picture. In any case, were political compromises to be attempted at a more concrete, specific level of discourse, there would seem considerable consensus on which to build modest reforms.

A RETROSPECTIVE

With the 20-20 hindsight of five years, the vignette procedures used in *Prison Reform and State Elites* do not appear to be greviously in error. The underlying vignette dimensions (that is, age, offense, and prior record), the sampling strategy and statistical analysis still seem reasonably sound. On the other hand, while we may not have been guilty of gross incompetence, our efforts were significantly handicapped by the relatively primitive sampling technology popular at that time. In particular, the state elites study was undertaken with a stratified sampling procedure for the vignettes that guaranteed a fully crossed design (with "impossible" combinations eliminated). More recent studies have used simple random sampling (with replacement) that does not guarantee that each cell in the design matrix be covered.[3] The implications of the older technology will be discussed shortly. In addition, were we to analyze the vignette data today, we would supplement the ordinary least squares procedures with techniques that are more sensitive to the bounded nature of the vignette rating variables (that is, sentence) and that are better able to capitalize on any information contained in the residuals. We will see shortly that questions of bias and efficiency are involved. These and other considerations suggest that given a second chance, there are three major enhancements that might well be introduced.

More Elaborate Vignettes

Since we designed the vignettes used in *Prison Reform and State Elites,* a host of studies have addressed the question of whether the sentences given to convicted offenders reflect factors of doubtful legal validity (see Hagan, 1974; Chiricos and Waldo, 1975; Bernstein et al., 1977; Swigert and Farrell, 1977; Lizotte, 1978; Hagen et al., 1980). While the evidence is hardly compelling, some have claimed that the courts discriminate against minorities and the poor. Other things being equal, blacks and Hispanics, for instance, receive longer sentences. Sometimes critics charge that the courts consciously use minority status as a factor in sentencing, and sometimes other variables such as employment are used that inadvertently single out minorities for unusually harsh treatment.

Prison Reform and State Elites was not a study of sentencing practices or sentencing inequities. The basic question addressed through the vignettes was what sentences in principle *should be* given to offenders varying in age, prior record, and the instant offense. We hoped that the vignette analysis, coupled with other information, would help us understand the possibilities for reform in corrections policy. Yet it now seems that we could have undertaken a richer analysis had we incorporated some of the variables that have surfaced in recent studies of sentencing. We did consider including race but felt that little would be learned. The obvious inappropriateness of race as a sentencing factor was assumed to be insulting to respondents and might produce little more than the "proper" reaction; race would prove unimportant in predicting the "desired" sentence. And while race might affect respondent perceptions of the "typical" sentence, the risks of alienating respondents seemed too high. In addition, staff members of LEAA, the project's sponsor, voiced opposition to including race, on the grounds that injecting racial discrimination into prison reform issues would muddy the waters.

In retrospect, the decision to exclude race from the vignettes was probably correct. However, it might have been instructive to include some indicator of employment and perhaps marital status and education. Much like age and previous record, employment, marital status, and education are sometimes taken as measures of an offender's rehabilitation potential and/or likelihood of committing new crimes (see Coffee, 1978). Moreover, these attributes are not distributed equally across different ethnic groups and social classes. Had they affected the desired sentence selected by respondents, we might well have been able to contribute to the literature on sentencing inequities. Indeed, it might even have made sense to reduce the number of levels included for age and instant offense in order to incorporate additional biographical characteristics of offenders.

With these issues in mind, gender becomes another candidate for inclusion. Like race, the major obstacle was that respondents would perhaps be offended, although our hunch now is that they probably would not have been. While there is almost certainly a consensus that ethnic background should not affect one's sentence, there may be considerable difference of opinion about gender. In *Prison Reform and State Elites,* we decided to exclude gender in part because the vast majority of people sentenced in 1976 were men. While this is still true, the absolute number of women being sentenced has certainly increased. In 1982 one might well want to include gender.

Note also that if the objective is to simulate actual sentencing decisions, then one might include the kinds of information typically available from the trial record and/or probation reports. For example, in crimes for which there are specific victims, it might be appropriate to add victim characteristics such as age, sex, socioeconomic level, and race. The consequences for the victim might also be introduced to capture something of the retributive dimensions of sentencing.

Many of the elements described above were discussed at the time we designed the research. One important reason for not including them was that the resulting vignette sampling space would have outstripped the number of vignettes that could have been rated. In other words, since our sampling procedures forced a fully crossed design (with "impossible" combinations eliminated), large chunks of the sampling space would be neglected. Under current vignette technology in which there is no requirement that the sampling space be fully covered, we could have employed more complicated vignettes.

In summary, we suspect that a far richer story could have been extracted if some additional biographical characteristics had been included in the vignettes. On the other hand, our earlier shortsightedness probably did not produce serious biases in the estimated regression coefficients. Given the orthogonal design, any new additive effects would have left the original estimates unchanged (within sampling error). Only the presence of interaction effects would have had an impact on the causal parameters reported. While it is certainly possible that conditional relationships might have surfaced, there is no a priori reason to believe (and no evidence in the available data) that important interactions were neglected.

Adjustments for Truncation

By and large, the multivariate analyses undertaken in *Prison Reform and State Elites* were garden-variety ordinary least squares. Given the statistical technology readily available in that period, ordinary least squares was probably the best procedure available. However, building on the work of Tobin (1958), a number of econometricians (for example, Amemiya, 1973; Heckman, 1979; Olsen, 1980; Goldberger, 1981) have pointed out that ordinary least squares will yield biased and inconsistent estimates of the regression parameters when the endogenous variable is truncated. And in *Prison Reform and State Elites,* the outcome variables for the vignettes were truncated.

A truncated endogenous variable is characterized in part by a floor (and/or a ceiling) beneath (above) which no observations can be obtained. Measures of earnings provide a good illustration. Since it is impossible to earn negative wages, there is a lower boundary to the wage distribution. In addition, a relatively large number of observations usually will "clump" at the boundary of zero, because in a typical sample of working-age individuals many will be unemployed. A random sample of female adults in the United States, for instance, would find that perhaps 40 percent were not in the labor force.[4]

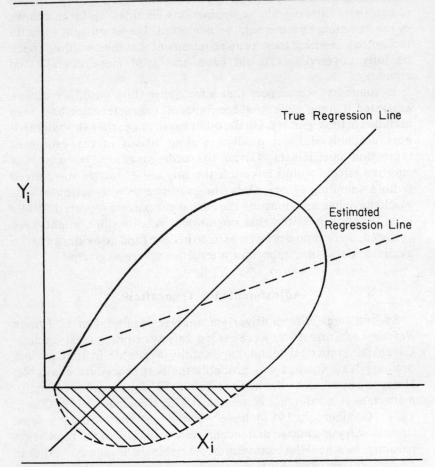

Figure 5.1   The Impact of a Truncated Endogenous Variable

There are now several useful didactic discussions of the truncation problem in the literature (see Stromsdorfer and Farkus, 1980: 32-41; Berk, 1980: 70-76), and readers who do not wish to wrestle with the material in the primary sources are strongly urged to consult these references. What follows, then, is a brief summary of the issues that is the absolute minimum necessary to evaluate the analyses undertaken in *Prison Reform and State Elites*.

Figure 5.1 shows the consequences of having an endogenous variable that is seriously truncated at zero. The usual scatter plot between two variables is assumed to be elliptical and roughly symmetrical around the regression line. When this holds and one meets the usual ordinary least squares assumptions (see, for example, Hanushek and Jackson, 1977: 45-74), one obtains an unbiased estimate of the regression coefficient(s). The result is represented by the "True Regression Line" in Figure 5.1. However, when the endogenous variable is truncated, any part of the regression ellipse that would have fallen below the lower boundary is lopped off. Thus, the shaded area in Figure 5.1 is lost, and one is, in effect, working with a flattened ellipse. When one then tries to estimate the regression parameters, bias and inconsistency necessarily follow. Note that the "Estimated Regression Line" in Figure 5.1 is too flat.

In principle, an enormous number of endogenous variables commonly used in the social sciences are vulnerable to truncation. Indeed, it is difficult to think of variables that are not potential candidates. However, whether or not the bias is important depends fundamentally on the proportion of observations clumping at the boundary and, therefore, where the scatter plot falls within the X-Y coordinates (Greene, 1981a, 1981b). If a relatively small proportion of the cases falls at the lower boundary, the scatter plot is not significantly flattened. Looking at Figure 5.1, this would mean that the entire ellipse is shifted upward so that it barely touches the X axis; the shaded area virtually disappears. Thus, while the endogenous variable is still truncated, the impact of the truncation can, for all practical purposes, be ignored. (The same logic applies when the truncation is from above.) In short, the severity of the problem depends on the degree of clumping at the boundary.

In the vignette analyses undertaken in *Prison Reform and State Elites,* it is clear that our regression results were vulnerable to two kinds of truncation bias: There was a lower limit ("release under supervision to his local community for a period of up to one year") and an upper limit ("incarceration full time in a prison for more than five years"). The likely consequence was biased estimates of the regression coefficients that were almost certainly *underestimates* of the true causal effects.[5]

What could have been done? One solution would have been to define the problem away by asserting that the upper and lower bounds were real and truly captured the full range of sentiment. Even if more severe sentences had been included, they would not have been selected. In a like manner, were it possible to represent "negative sentences" (for example, cash reward for a "crime" that "needed" to be committed),[6] these sentences would not have been used. Thus, there was really no truncation of respondent preferences.

While it might have been possible to eliminate the truncation problem through some kind of conceptual gymnastics, no doubt new difficulties would have been introduced. Firm upper and lower bounds almost certainly would have meant abandoning the linear functional form for an S-shaped relationship (for instance, the logistic) with asymptotes at the minimum and maximum sentences. In other words, if the responses were really restricted between the upper and lower bounds, this information should be represented in the functional form applied. However, in addition to substantially complicating the interpretations of causal effects (which are no longer constant),[7] estimation procedures for intrinsically nonlinear equations are quite costly to use. In short, although we recently had some success with logistic models for bounded vignette rating scales,[8] we hesitate to recommend such approaches as part of a routine "solution" to the truncation problem.

A better solution would have relied on statistical procedures that directly model and therefore correct for any truncation bias. Truncation bias of the kind relevant to *Prison Reform and State Elites* falls within a Tobit formulation (Tobin, 1958), and Tobit estimation techniques existed at the time we were analyzing the data. However, we were in principle faced with a two-sided Tobit problem which had yet to be formally addressed. Moreover, even if the one-sided approach would have sufficed in practice, Tobit estimation software was not widely available. In other words, even if we had been aware of Tobin's work, it is not clear that we would have proceeded any differently.

The important issue, however, is whether our results were seriously in error through the failure to adjust for truncation. Fortunately, only about 20 percent of our observations for both the "desired" and the "typical" sentences fell on the upper and lower boundaries. On intuitive grounds, therefore, the scatter plots were not especially flattened, and the biases in our OLS regression coefficients were not serious. More specifically, it is probable that each of our regression coefficients were attenuated by the *same* proportion so that all of the causal effects were about 80 percent of what they should have been.[9] In other words, the *relative* magnitudes of the regression coefficients were unaffected, and the modest overall attenuation is probably unimportant, partly because of the somewhat arbitrary nature of the sentencing scale. This is not to argue, of course, that our OLS procedures were appropriate. We are only saying that in this instance, the distortions were probably not serious. Analyses done today should capitalize on appropriate statistical techniques for truncated endogenous variables.

Capitalizing on the Pooled Design

A few moments' thought will suggest that the vignette data collected for *Prison Reform and State Elites* can be conceptualized as a pooled cross-sectional and time-series design. It is readily apparent that each respondent represented a cross-section in the usual sense that one defines cross-sectional units. However, it is also true that the sequence of ratings was a time series. At the very least, one can conceptualize the rating processes as an ordinal pattern: the first vignette rated, the second vignette rated, and so on. Yet since the ratings unfolded over time, a temporal pattern was also involved. To the degree that respondents proceeded through the vignettes at a steady pace, the temporal pattern approximated the usual discrete time series. Alternatively, psychological time may have been more important than real time (since we were measuring a psychological process). Respondents may have felt that they were spending about the same interval on each vignette, and in "psychological time" this may have been correct.

The existence of variation over respondents and over the rating sequence provides an organizational and statistical framework that was not fully exploited in *Prison Reform and State Elites*. To begin, it would have been possible in principle to estimate separate regression equations for each respondent. Recall that for both the "desired" and the "actual" rating exercises, 40 vignettes were sampled. That is, for each respondent we had two samples of 40 observations from which each respondent's rating structure could have been extracted. In other words, we could have proceeded as if there were interaction effects for each vignette variable by each respondent.

Had there been no evidence of serial correlation in the residuals of each respondent's equation, ordinary least squares would have been appropriate.[10] If we had found serially correlated residuals, however, generalized least squares would have been a better choice. Had we

failed to apply generalized least squares in the face of serially
correlated residuals, we would have produced inefficient estimates
of the regression coefficients and biased estimates of their standard
errors. We suspect that given the relatively short interval in which
the rating was accomplished during the interviews, the usual kinds of
serially correlated residuals would *not* have materialized; random
perturbations affecting any one rating would have affected *all* ratings
in a similar manner. We will have more to say about the consequences
shortly.[11]

The obvious problem with separate regression equations for each
respondent is that generalization becomes difficult. Therefore, it
makes sense to "collapse" the data across respondents (that is, pool
them) with similar biographical characteristics. In particular, we
estimated separate equations by state and respondent "position."
The interaction effects we found, however, were small and often
attributable to sampling error. In other words, we found little
systematic variation in rating structures for the biographical factors
we considered.[12]

A failure to find important interaction effects as a function of
biography implies that a single regression equation will suffice to
represent for all respondents any systematic variation in the vignette
ratings. Recall that much of the substantive discussion in fact
revolved around just such an equation. However, the absence of
interaction effects does not mean there were no individual differences.
Rather, it implies that any individual differences must be found in the
error processes all too easily summarized in the usual regression
error term. It is here that we failed to exploit the data fully.

First, it is entirely possible that the residual variances for different
respondents were not equal. For example, there might have been
greater consensus among prosecutors than judges, and this might
have been reflected by less variation in the residuals. Second, to the
degree that the vignette ratings were sensitive overall to random
forces such as the respondent's mood, recent press coverage of crime
in the local media, or especially heavy involvement in criminal
justice matters, each respondent would have been subject to *random
variation in the average ratings given.* In other words, for each
respondent there would have been an implicit regression equation
with a random intercept drawn from some probability distribution.
Third, just as the overall level of each respondent's rating may have
been sensitive to chance forces, the marginal impact of each vignette

characteristic may also have been sensitive to chance forces. For example, if a particularly serious crime by a teenager had made front-page headlines, it is quite possible that vignettes including younger offenders would have received harsher sentences than would ordinarily be the case.

If such processes were operating, our ordinary least squares coefficients would have been unbiased. However, since the errors no longer would meet the full array of OLS assumptions (with the exception that the expected values of the errors for each observation are still zero),[13] our estimates of the regression coefficients would have been inefficient, and the estimates of their standard errors would have been biased. Then it would have been better to apply statistical procedures designed for models with random coefficients and heteroskedastic residuals (see Judge et al., 1980: 347-353). Briefly, these techniques are variants on the theme of generalized least squares where information contained in the residuals and in the regression coefficients (and intercepts) across respondents is used to reweight the data.

At the time the vignette analyses were undertaken, software for random coefficient models was not readily available, and that is still true today.[14] An important question, therefore, is what differences would have surfaced had a random coefficients model been estimated. First, since our OLS coefficients were unbiased and the sample size was large, it is unlikely that the GLS and OLS regression coefficients would have differed substantially. Moreover, the added efficiency provided by the GLS technique was in some sense irrelevant given samples in the thousands; important causal effects would have been estimated with sufficient accuracy under both approaches. Finally, given the large samples, the bias in the estimated standard errors under OLS almost certainly would have been too small to produce misleading false positives or false negatives.

It is important to stress that these conclusions rest on the assumption that the OLS equations were properly specified. Misspecification not only would have produced the usual biases in the estimated regression coefficients, but also would have introduced structure in the residuals for which GLS is *not* appropriate. For example, if vignette ratings had affected each other in a serial fashion (the first affecting the second, the second affecting the third, and so on), and this "contagion" effect was not represented formally in the model, estimates of the regression coefficients for the included variables would be biased. It is almost certain that the residuals would be serially correlated as well. Alternatively, if there were systematic differences in rating structure for individuals not captured with appropriate product variables, the error structure would look a lot like the error structure in the random coefficients model, but would clearly stem from other sources.

Finally, it might have proved instructive to examine the distribution of residuals for certain vignettes and respondents. Given the large sample size, the sampling distributions of the estimators can be assumed to be normal regardless of how the error term is distributed (ignoring the truncation issues). That is, statistical inference is unaffected. However, it would have been substantively useful to determine whether the residuals were typically distributed in a symmetric manner and/or with the kind of clustering one expects with normality.

Consider, for example, drug-related crimes. We might have found a bimodal distribution in the residuals, indicating that while one group of respondents sought much harsher sentences, another group sought much more lenient sentences; the residuals would cluster at either large positive or large negative values. Such a pattern would be evidence for a very special kind of dissensus in which, over and above the effects of the regressors, opinions were polarized. To take another example, suppose that for prosecutors the residual distribution was skewed in a negative direction. While the bulk of the residuals were small and positive, there were a few individuals for whom the residuals were large and negative. Thus the "mavericks" among prosecutors would be those who were "soft on crime." In contrast, one might have found exactly the opposite tendencies among public defenders. Most of the residuals would have been small and negative, while for a few individuals, large positive residuals would have been found. Hence, the "mavericks" among public defenders would be the "hardliners." None of these possibilities were considered in *Prison Reform and State Elites.*

Conclusions

In the six years that have passed since the analyses undertaken in *Prison Reform and State Elites,* we have certainly aged and perhaps grown wiser. In retrospect, we did not fully exploit the potential in the design of the vignettes or the possibilities for richer and more powerful statistical analyses. Were we to do the study again today, we would no doubt pursue many of the ideas described above. However, it is important to stress that the primary result of such efforts would be to extend the findings reported. There is no reason to assume that the findings discussed are seriously in error.

NOTES

1. The tests involved transforming the scores into a variety of forms (logarithms, power functions, etc.) and testing whether each transformation yielded in analysis better fitting results than the assumption of equal intervals. In no case did any transformation produce closer fittings than the equal interval assumption.

2. Since the variances of the characteristics are unequal and quite unlike the variances of such characteristics in the real world of convicted offenders, the standardized regression coefficients to some degree are dependent on the particularities of the way the vignettes were constructed. We had planned to run multiple regression analyses in the larger study in which these characteristics would be given distributions (by weighting) which would correspond more closely to the distributions of such characteristics in the "real world" of convicted offenders.

3. To be more specific, in *Prison Reform and State Elites* the sampling space was laid out, and then a stratified sample was chosen so that each cell in the fully crossed design (with "impossible" cells eliminated) contained some minimum number of observations. On later reflection, it was apparent that one could "unconstrain" the selection process through simple random sampling with replacement. While one risked that some cells would be thinly covered or even neglected altogether, the likelihood of any analysis needing to focus on single cells (or even a very small number of cells) was remote. In other words, unless very high-order interaction effects were contemplated, there was no need to guarantee that the full sample space was thoroughly covered. In turn this meant that, in principle, a far larger number of vignette characteristics and levels could be included.

4. Limiting one's analysis to employed women will typically not solve the problem. All one will usually accomplish is transforming a truncated variable into a censored variable (Goldberger, 1981: 361), and censored variables cause virtually the same kind of problem as truncated variables.

5. Looking at Figure 5.1, the upper bound would flatten the scatter plot from above just as the lower bound flattens it from below. The result is still greater attenuation of the estimated regression line.

6. The idea "negative sentences" is not totally crazy. For example, might there not be some sentiment (in retrospect, perhaps) for civil rights activists who committed property offenses while overturning Jim Crow ordinances?

7. In linear models, the slope by definition is a constant. In nonlinear models, by definition the slope is not constant, and therefore causal effects vary. For S-shaped curves such as the logistic, the causal effects of regressors are largest for regressor values near their means (that is, not at the extremes). An excellent discussion of nonlinear models can be found in Draper and Smith (1981: 458-517).

8. In this work vignettes were designed to characterize interactions between students and faculty that might be defined as sexual harassment. The rating scales ranged from 1 to 9 for "no, this is not sexual harassment" to "yes, this is sexual harassment."

9. These estimates are based on very recent work (for example, Goldberger, 1981; Greene, 1981a, 1981b) addressing one-sided truncation and assuming that the regressors are drawn from a multivariate normal distribution. The first premise is false for our data, but since no formal distinction is made between truncation from above and from below, we see no reason why their effects alone cannot be added when both are present. Moreover, with the help of David Rauma we undertook Monte Carlo simulations of this assertion and of the estimator that it implies. The simulations were fully consistent with the assumption that two-sided truncation could be treated as the sum of two one-sided truncations. The second premise is also false for our data, but Greene (1981b) has Monte Carlo simulation evidence indicating that the normality assumption with respect to the regressors is robust.

10. While the residuals across respondents might have been correlated, procedures for seemingly unrelated equations (see Judge et al., 1980: 243-257) would not have improved efficiency because each equation would have included the same set of regressors.

11. We will not discuss the possibility of estimating separate regression equations for each "time period" because there seems little reason to suspect that rating structures would have differed depending on where in the order a vignette was rated (first, second, third, etc.). However, should that have been a possibility, in principle there would have been no obstacles.

12. This is not to say that there were absolutely no interaction effects by biography in the data. However, we tried a large number of possible interaction effects and came up empty.

13. The residuals within respondents would have been correlated with one another and there would have been heteroskedasticity across respondents.

14. With a little creativity and a lot of effort, it would be possible today to use statistical packages such as SAS to produced estimates for random coefficient models.

REFERENCES

Amemiya, T., 1973, "Regression analysis when the dependent variable is truncated normal." Econometrica 41: 997-1017.
Berk, R. A., 1980, "Recent statistical developments: implications for criminal justice evaluations," in M. W. Klein and K. S. Teilman (eds.) Handbook of Criminal Justice Evaluation. Beverly Hills, CA: Sage.

Berk, R. A., D. M. Hoffman, J. E. Maki, D. Rauma, and H. Wong, 1979, "Estimation procedures for pooled cross-sectional and time series data." Evaluation Review 3: 385-410.

Bernstein, I. N., W. R. Kelly, and P. A. Doyle, 1977, "Societal reaction to deviants: the case of criminal dependents." American Sociological Review 42: 743-755.

Chiricos, T. G. and G. P. Waldo, 1975, "Socioeconomic status and criminal sentencing: an empirical assessment of a conflict proposition." American Sociological Review 40: 753-772.

Coffee, J., 1978, "The repressive issues of sentencing accountability, predictability and equality in the era of sentencing commissions." Georgetown Law Journal 66: 975-1107.

Draper, N. and A. Smith, 1981, Applied Regression Analysis. New York: John Wiley.

Goldberger, A. S., 1981, "Linear regression after selection." Journal of Econometrics 15: 357-366.

Greene, W. H., 1981a, "On asymptotic bias of the ordinary least squares estimator of the tobit model." Econometrica 49, 2: 505-514.

1981b, "Estimation of some limited dependent variable models using least squares and the method of moments." New York: Department of Economics, Cornell University. (mimeo)

Hagan, J. I., H. Nagel, and C. Albonetti, 1980, "The differential sentencing of white-collar offenders in ten federal counts." American Sociological Review 45: 802-841.

Hagen, J., 1974, "Extra-legal attributes and criminal sentencing: an assessment of sociological viewpoint." Law and Review 8: 357-383.

Hanushek, E. A. and J. E. Jackson, 1977, Statistical Methods for Social Scientists. New York: Academic Press.

Heckman, J., 1979, "Sample bias as specification error." Econometrica 47: 153-162.

Johnson, J. J., 1972, Econometric Methods. New York: McGraw-Hill.

Judge, G. G., W. E. Griffiths, R. C. Hill, and T. Lee, 1980, The Theory and Practice of Econometrics. New York: John Wiley.

Kmenta, J., 1971, Elements of Econometrics. New York: Macmillan.

Lizotte, A. J., 1978, "Extra-legal factors in Chicago's criminal counts: testing the conflict model of criminal justice." Social Problems 25: 564-580.

Olsen, R. J., 1980, "A least squares correction for selectivity bias." Econometrica 48: 1815-1820.

Stromsdorfer, E. W. and G. Farcus (eds.), 1980, Evaluation Studies Review Annual, Volume 5. Beverly Hills, CA: Sage.

Swigert, V. L. and R. A. Farrell, 1977, "Normal homicides and the law." American Sociological Review 42: 16-32.

Tobin, J. (1958) "Estimation of relationships for limited dependent variables." Econometrica 26, 1: 24-36.

6

CHILD ABUSE
Problems of Definition

KAREN GARRETT

Child abuse or, more generally, domestic violence, has come to be regarded as one of the major social problems of the modern era. Horror stories of abuse, as reported in newspapers and portrayed on television, have sensitized the general public to the violent home. Police, judges, attorneys, doctors, and social workers—those legally responsible for the protection of children—are plagued by questions of causes, cures, and the prevention of child abuse and neglect. The growing recognition of and concern with domestic violence has been paralleled by a proliferation of research projects intended to provide some idea of the actual number of families involved and to get at the underlying causes of this phenomenon.

We are by now well aware of the fact that brutal beatings resulting in broken bones or death are in clear violation of the law and that children whose lives are in danger may be temporarily or permanently separated from their parents. But what can we say about a parent who

Authors' Note: The research reported here is part of a larger study of child abuse conducted at UCLA, Dr. Jeanne Giovannoni, Principal Investigator. The data were collected in 1976 as part of a Los Angeles Metropolitan Area Study administered by the Institute for Social Science Research at UCLA. The generous help of ISSR and Dr. Giovannoni is gratefully acknowledged.

"accidentally" breaks a child's arm in the course of a mild spanking? Or, as is more common, the parent who relies on spankings as a means of discipline? Even more problematic are those cases of neglect: Which types of parental omissions are harmful to a child's well-being and which are within the boundaries of acceptable child rearing? Beyond the most obvious, there is considerable confusion about the definition of child abuse and neglect. Moreover, this confusion does not reside solely at the level of the general public; it is a major problem for all professionals who come into contact with parents and children.

Unlike most criminal legislation (which is often more exact in the definition of criminal behavior) child abuse codes lack specificity. This lack of specific guidelines is reflected in policy manuals used by social workers. The Massachusetts Department of Public Welfare, for example, defines "abuse" as

(a) a physical injury by other than accidental means which causes or creates a substantial risk of death or protracted impairment or physical or emotional loss of impairment of the function of any bodily organ; and

(b) the commission of a sex offense against a child as defined in the criminal laws of Massachusetts.

"Neglect" is defined as

the impairment of a child's physical, mental or emotional conditions as a result of the failure of the child's parent or other persons responsible for his care to exercise a minimum degree of care:

(a) in supplying the child with adequate food, clothing, shelter, or education, or medical care, though financially able to do so or offered financial or other reasonable means to do so; or

(b) in providing the child with proper supervision or guardianship.

Such vague definitions rely on the caseworker's discretion. He or she must determine the point at which acceptable child-rearing practices have been violated, whether a particular action taken by a parent is actually "abuse," "neglect," or neither.

While researchers have devoted a great deal of effort to constructing typologies of neglectful and abusive families (see Zalba, 1967; Terr, 1970) and discussions of causes, cures, and preventions

(Helfer, 1973; Steele and Pollock, 1968; Morris et al., 1964; Delsordo, 1963), they have yet to come tc terms with the problem of definition. Indeed, researchers differ with regard to their conceptions of the relevant features of an abuse incident. Gil (1970), for example, stresses the motivations of perpetrators in potential abuse incidents as the criteria for making assessments. Nurse (1964), on the other hand, emphasizes the consequences of abuse and neglect. Young (1964) focuses on the interactions between adults and children, recognizing that there are gradations of seriousness—moderate and severe—dependent on the features of an act. Boehm (1964) includes an emotional dimension suggesting that those acts endangering the mental health of a child should be included in the definitions of abuse.

The ambiguity of existing definitions of abuse and neglect has several noteworthy consequences. On the one hand, successful treatment and preventive strategies depend on some degree of consensus among those involved: To be effective, social service agencies and other professionals must be sensitive to community standards of appropriate and inappropriate child-rearing. The issue of consensus is equally important for researchers. The extent to which their findings are helpful in solving abuse problems depends on a more precise and consistent formulation of what this phenomenon actually is. As long as the problem of definition is not addressed, attempts to prevent or intervene in violent homes will fall short of their goals.

The research reported here addresses three major issues relevant to the problem of defining child abuse and neglect. First, a major objective of our research is to clarify the types of acts toward children which are considered to be serious transgressions of acceptable child-rearing practices.

Second, and of greater sociological interest, we are concerned with the way the more specific features of an abuse incident influence assessments of the seriousness of that incident. Do certain characteristics of perpetrator and victim affect judgments of the incident? Evidence from research concerned with crime seriousness suggests that ratings for individual crimes are partly related to the social and personal characteristics of the individuals involved (see Rose and Prell, 1955; Landry and Aronson, 1968). Our research incorporates this concern by examining the way the characteristics of children and adults involved in abuse incidents affect the seriousness judgments pertaining to those incidents. For example, are incidents involving older children generally seen as less serious than those involving younger children? Or are judgments made solely on the basis of the act reported?

Finally, this research considers the way the characteristics of those involved in making judgments come to bear on their assessments of abuse and neglect.[1] The central question here is that of consensus: Do observers in the general population agree on the relative seriousness of abuse incidents or are there significant subgroup differences? Again, with regard to assessments of crime seriousness, there is evidence to suggest that different groups of the population vary in their responses to the same crime (Rossi et al., 1974). Boehm's (1964) study of community and social agency responses to child abuse and neglect showed differences between the two groups. However, the possibility of intracommunity differences was unexplored. These differences are explored in our research.

The overall intent of this research is to provide a model of how various components of an incident combine to influence a seriousness rating of that event. More specifically, this model of seriousness should reflect the relative influences of the particular *act,* the characteristics *of those involved* in the incident, and the characteristics *of those making seriousness judgments.*

Research Design

The Vignettes

To measure responses of individuals to incidents which may constitute abuse or neglect, our research uses brief descriptions of incidents as objects to be rated on a seriousness continuum. These descriptions (vignettes) consist of a set of characteristics considered to be most readily observable in the first contact with a possible child abuse or neglect incident. Thus the variables in each vignette include an act involving a guardian and a child, a description of the child and guardian, the occupation of the main breadwinner, and the ethnic composition of the hypothetical household.

The act. The first variable listed in each vignette is a description of an act involving a guardian and a child. These acts by no means exhaust the realm of abusive acts, although we believe that they represent a "reasonable" sample of those events that may be construed as "abuse" or "neglect." We have tried to include acts of emotional as well as physical abuse and neglect. Because we are interested in the definition process, we have included acts ranging from those we consider extremely serious to those we consider within the limits of acceptable child rearing.

In addition, and in light of suggestions by several researchers that the seriousness of an incident may depend on the consequences of that incident (Nurse, 1964; Morris et al., 1964), half of the acts include descriptions of a consequence. These consequences apply to the child described in the vignette. For example, for the act describing an occasion when the guardian and the child engaged in sexual intercourse, the consequence is "the child suffers recurring nightmares." In most cases, consequences are specific to individual acts.[2] In sum, there are two conditions in which each act of abuse appears, one without a consequence and the other with a consequence. Appendix A includes all acts and consequences which might follow.

Description of the child. The second set of variables in the vignette comprise a sex and age description of the child involved in the reported incident. Because child protection laws are concerned with children up to the age of sixteen, the age variable in the vignettes ranges from six months to fifteen years.[3]

An additional child characteristic in the form of a desriptive statement is included in half of the vignettes. For example, the child may be described as "happy," "healthy," or "above average mentally." On the other hand, he or she may be characterized as "emotionally immature," "unhealthy," or "extremely nervous." These descriptions are not intended as consequences of the act reported in the vignette, merely as additional information about the child. In all, we have included sixteen descriptions, eight of which may be seen as positive characteristics and eight which may be interpreted as negative. Obviously, we cannot include all possible descriptions of children. Our intent in including these characteristics is primarily to assess the influence of more qualitative descriptions on seriousness ratings. (See Appendix B for the complete set of descriptive statements for the child.)

Description of the guardian. The next set of variables in the vignettes describes the guardian involved in the incident. While recognizing that the perpetrators of child abuse and neglect may include a wide range of individuals who come into contact with a child, this research is restricted to guardians. The guardian relationship may be that of natural parents, adoptive parents, foster parents, or relatives with guardianship.

In half of the vignettes, the description of the guardian also includes a descriptive statement. Eight of the possible sixteen descriptions may be seen as positive (for example, "appears cooperative") and eight as negative (such as "appears belligerent"). Again, our intent here is to assess the influence of more qualitative descriptions of the guardian on seriousness ratings. (See Appendix C for the complete set of descriptive statements for the guardian.)

Description of the household. The final vignette component is a description of the household and is intended to measure the impact of social status and ethnicity on seriousness ratings. Social status is measured by main breadwinner's occupation (using NORC prestige score values for occupations). While this measure may be simpler than some of the more complex models of household status, it represents a feature most easily observed in everyday life.

The "ethnicities" used in the vignettes include Caucasian, Mexican-American, black, Jewish, Native American, and Asian—categories selected because we believe that finer distinctions among ethnic groups (British, French, French-Canadian, and so on) are not likely to be meaningful categories to respondents in the Los Angeles area.

Vignette production. The vignettes were constructed using a computer program to write each vignette by selecting randomly the specific characteristics as listed above. Thus, vignette components are systematically varied, and each vignette represents an almost unique combination. (The probability of any vignette appearing more than once is extremely slight.) Not all possible combinations were allowed to be written: We excluded those describing inconceivable or extremely unlikely combinations. For example, we consider it extremely unlikely that a six-month-old child would smoke marijuana; thus, this combination was excluded.

The random assignment of vignette characteristics is an important feature of our design; thus, we have kept restrictions to a minimum. The expected value of correlations between most vignette characteristics is zero (except in those cases where we have imposed restrictions), assuring us that these characteristics have been randomly assigned and are statistically independent. Table 6.1 shows that the intercorrelations among most independent variables are minimal. (The correlations between positive and negative child

TABLE 6.1 Correlations Among Vignette Characteristics and Seriousness Ratings

		(1)	(2)	(3)	(4)	(5)	(6)	(7)	(8)	(9)
Child's age	(1)		.00	.00	-.02	.00	.01	.00	.00	.00
Occupation of main breadwinner	(2)			.00	.00	.01	.00	.01	.00	.01
Child's sex	(3)				.01	.01	.00	.00	-.01	.00
Seriousness rating	(4)					.13	.03	-.02	.02	-.02
Consequence dummy	(5)						.01	-.01	-.01	.01
Negative child description	(6)							-.33	.00	.00
Positive child description	(7)								.00	-.01
Negative adult description	(8)									-.33
Positive adult description	(9)									

descriptions and positive and negative guardian descriptions are merely a product of our design: Vignettes including a positive description cannot include a negative description for the same participant.) From the correlation matrix for vignette characteristics and seriousness ratings we can anticipate that descriptions of acts will be the most important vignette component, while consequences of acts will also be influential.

From the very large set of all possible vignettes, random samples of 60 vignettes each were selected. Each respondent received one such sample of the total possible vignettes, with each vignette printed on a blank IBM card.

In addition, each vignette packet was prefaced by four vignettes which were identical for all respondents. These vignettes (which we have labeled "give-away" vignettes to avoid confusion) were included to guard against any bias created by the first vignette presented to the respondent. The characteristics of these vignettes were fixed for all respondents and, in our judgment, ranged from very serious (forcing the child into mutual masturbation) to not serious (leaving the child alone at a supermarket). The ratings for these vignettes were averaged for each respondent, and the average was used as an indication of a respondent's overall tendency to rate high or low on a seriousness continuum. This average allowed us to control for individual variations in respondent ratings in our final analysis. The average "give-away" scores act to standardize ratings across respondents on the basis of their individual rating tendencies.

Each respondent was asked to rate each of the 64 vignettes on a seriousness scale ranging from one to nine (least to most serious). Respondents were given a board with nine envelopes, numbered one through nine, attached to it. The sorting task consisted of placing each vignette into an envelope according to its perceived seriousness.[4] Of 19,264 possible ratings, we received 17,345 usable vignettes (90 percent). (Respondents were given the option to lay aside vignettes they felt they were unable to rate.)

In addition to vignette ratings, we used a brief interview to gain an idea of the background characteristics of our respondents—for example, sex, race, age, and occupation. This information was used to measure the differences between respondents with regard to their seriousness judgments. Thus, from our data we were able to discuss the ways both the constituent features of the vignettes and the characteristics of the respondents affect seriousness ratings.

Description of the Sample

Respondents for this research were selected as a subsample of a larger household sample participating in a Los Angeles Metropolitan Area Study (LAMAS) conducted by the Institute for Social Science Research at the University of California at Los Angeles. While the LAMAS sample is a probability sample of Los Angeles residents, we excluded Spanish-speaking households from the subsample used in our research. In addition, we specified that our sample included equal portions of males and females. In total, we obtained vignette ratings and interviews from 301 adults living in the Los Angeles area.

The average respondent was 45.3 years of age and had completed high school. While the number of children in respondents' households ranged from none to six, the average number of children was close to one. The mean household income level for our sample was $14,000 per year. Seventy percent of our respondents were white, 14 percent were black, 9 percent were Mexican-American or other Latin American, and 4 percent were Asian. Close to 54 percent of our respondents were Protestant, 25 percent were Catholic, 6 percent were Jewish, and 11 percent expressed no religious preference.

Research Findings

Analysis of Vignette Components

We obtained a total of 17,345 rated vignettes from the 301 respondents in our sample. The overall average rating for all vignettes was 6.7, indicating that respondents tended to rate vignettes on the high seriousness end of the scale. The average score for the "give-away" vignettes, rated by all respondents, was 6.3.

To measure the extent to which vignette components influence seriousness ratings, we regressed the ratings assigned to the vignettes on the vignette characteristics themselves, the unit of analysis being the individual vignette. The relevance of each vignette component to the seriousness ratings is discussed below.

The act. An index of seriousness scores attributed to child abuse and neglect acts was constructed by calculating an average of all ratings received by vignettes with the same acts.[5] (see Appendix A for the wording of the acts, the consequences, and mean ratings). Those acts involving physical harm to the child received ratings higher than those involving parental neglect. For example, burning a child on the buttocks with a cigarette was generally regarded as more serious (receiving an average rating of 8.3) than failing to see that the child brushes his or her teeth (receiving an average rating of only 4.1). This finding is consistent with Boehm's (1964) observation that the community expresses more concern over events that might be physically harmful to the child. However, it is of some interest to note that vignettes reporting some physical acts against a child for disciplinary purposes were not considered as serious as acts which appear to have no apparent justification. In fact, the act receiving the lowest average rating was that which stated "the guardian usually punishes the child by spanking with the hand."

Acts describing some type of sexual contact were generally regarded as very serious by respondents. The highest average score (8.6) was received by the act of sexual intercourse between the guardian and the child.

The degree of consensus with regard to the seriousness of an act is reflected in the standard deviation associated with that act. As we might expect, there is greater agreement for those acts which fall in the high seriousness end of the seriousness continuum, while there is more disagreement for those acts considered less serious. Thus, for the act receiving the highest average seriousness rating ("On one occasion, the guardian and child engaged in sexual intercourse"), we find a standard deviation of 1.1, whereas for the act receiving the lowest average rating ("The guardian usually punishes the child by spanking with the hand"), the standard deviation is 2.6.

To measure the influence of acts themselves on seriousness ratings, we used the average ratings of acts without consequences as

TABLE 6.2   Regression of Seriousness on Vignette Characteristics

SUMMARY		
R^2 = .15255	F = 222	Intercept = .0419
	14/17345	
	N = 17345	
	EQUATION	

Vignette Characteristics	b	T
Mean act rating (without consequence)	1.004	45.551
Consequence (0 = no, 1 = yes)	3.288	16.129
Sex of child (0 = male, 1 = female)	.025	.770
Age of child	-.012	-3.379
Positive description of child (0 = no, 1 = yes)	-.141	-2.473
Negative description of child (0 = no, 1 = yes)	.096	1.687
Positive description of guardian (0 = no, 1 = yes)	-.154	-2.711
Negative description of guardian (0 = no, 1 = yes)	.104	1.819
Occupation of main breadwinner	.001	1.253
Interaction Term: Mean act rating X Consequence	-.420	-13.347
Interaction Term: Negative description of child X Negative description of guardian	-.055	-.548
Interaction Term: Positive description of child X Positive description of guardian	.230	2.302
Interaction Term: Negative description of child X Positive description of guardian	.143	1.438
Interaction Term: Positive description of child X Negative description of guardian	.047	.475

an independent variable in our regression equation. (Using these average ratings allowed us to treat acts as interval variables.) From the regression equation for vignette characteristics (Table 6.2), we can see that the description of the act is an important feature of an incident in determining seriousness. The unstandardized regression coefficient for the act description is roughly 1.0.

Consequences. To assess the influence of a reported consequence, a dummy variable was constructed by assigning a value of one to all vignettes including a consequence and a value of zero to those vignettes without consequences. Knowledge of a consequence tended to increase the seriousness ratings assigned to vignettes by 3.2 points. This increase might be explained by our selection of consequences, since they were generally specific to a given act and tended to be serious (by our own judgment). It may be that randomized consequences including *both* positive and negative results would affect seriousness in a different way.

When we examined average ratings for acts without consequences, we found that at the high seriousness end of the continuum ratings were not significantly affected by the addition of a consequence, while ratings for less serious acts were increased when consequences were included in the vignettes (see Appendix A). To elaborate on this observation, an interaction term was included in the final regression (mean rating for an act times presence/absence of a consequence). The significant coefficient for this term b=-.42; T=13.4) suggests that as the seriousness of an act increases, the additional knowledge of a consequence has less of an effect on the rating assigned to the vignette than is the case for vignettes including less serious acts. Conversely, knowledge of a consequence has a greater effect on the seriousness rating assigned to vignettes reporting a less serious act than those reporting more serious acts.

Child characteristics. Surprisingly, the sex of the child described in the vignette made no significant difference in the seriousness rating assigned to the vignette. The child's age, however, had a significant effect on the ratings. As we might expect, incidents involving older children tended to be rated less serious than those involving younger children.

A separate regression analysis of the behavioral descriptions of the child (Appendix B) revealed them to be of only small significance in accounting for variation in seriousness ratings. Six attributes were statistically significant: "appears emotionally immature," "appears to cry a lot," "seems difficult to communicate with," "appears unhealthy," "appears cooperative," "appears healthy." However, the total equation explained less than one percent of rating variability. For our final regression equation, all the behavior descriptions were coded into "positive" or "negative" categories. Positive child attributes are those describing the child as happy, healthy, cooperative, and so on and which we would expect to decrease seriousness ratings. Negative child attributes, portraying the child as unhappy, unhealthy, nervous, and the like, we would expect to increase seriousness ratings. The statistical significance of these variables suggests that while many individual attributes may not be significant, qualitative descriptions of the child have some influence on seriousness considerations in the expected directions. When respondents were presented with a vignette including a positive description of the child, they tended to rate the vignette .09 points more serious than those vignettes not including such descriptions. On the other hand, vignettes including a negative description of the child were rated .14 points less serious than those vignettes not including child descriptions.

The regression equation for the vignette components includes two general categories of positive and negative characteristics (Table 6.2). Positive guardian characteristics were expected to decrease seriousness ratings, while negative characteristics were expected to increase ratings. These expectations were confirmed. When a vignette included a positive description of a guardian, it was rated .15 points less serious than a vignette which did not include a statement describing the guardian. If a vignette included a negative guardian description, it was generally rated .10 points more serious than it would have been if no description was provided. The statistical significance of the descriptive variables for both adults and children suggest that qualitative descriptions of the individuals involved in a potential abuse incident are of some importance in seriousness judgments—although the influence of these descriptions is minor in comparison to other more significant vignette characteristics.

Interaction effects between child and adult descriptions. Several interaction terms were constructed to assess the possible interrelationships between child and adult descriptions included in the vignettes. We suspected that these descriptions, when occurring in a single vignette, would have a multiplicative effect on seriousness over and above that contributed by each characteristic alone. For example, those vignettes describing a male guardian and a female child may have been rated as more serious than those involving a male guardian and a male child. Many interactions were computed, only some of which proved statistically significant, as indicated in Table 6.2.

We observed significant interaction effects between the descriptive statements for the adult and those describing the child. Those vignettes including positive descriptions of both the child and adult were rated as more serious than vignettes that did not include any type of description or only a description of either the child or adult. This result is difficult to interpret in light of the negative relationship between positive adult characteristics and seriousness. It suggests that when a description of an abuse incident includes a positive assessment of an adult and any assessment of a child, it is considered as more serious than those vignettes which do not include such descriptions. Although these interactions do not significantly increase the explanatory power of our model, we recommend further investigation in this area. (Including interactions in the regression equation for vignette components increases the explained variance from 15.221 percent to 15.255 percent.)

Household characteristics. Our measure of household prestige, the occupational prestige of the main breadwinner in the hypothetical household, is of little relevance to the seriousness assessments made by our respondents. The NORC score assigned to the main breadwinner was not significant, suggesting that our respondents did not use socioeconomic status distinctions when ranking the vignettes.

Guardian characteristics. In a separate regression analysis, seriousness scores were regressed on the categories of guardianship. The R^2 for this analysis was .00034; thus we conclude that our respondents did not make distinctions among types of guardianship when considering the seriousness of an incident. However, further analysis should take into account the distinctions respondents may make between guardians and other adults who come into contact with children.

A separate regression analysis of seriousness ratings on the behavioral descriptions of the guardians in the vignettes showed only three categories to be significant: "appears emotionally immature," "appears cooperative," and "appears to be a kind person." This equation did not achieve statistical significance.

Summary of the vignette analysis. The vignette components by themselves explain roughly 15 percent of the variation in seriousness ratings. Of greatest significance in determining seriousness judgments is the act itself and its consequences. However, ratings are also affected by the age of the child described in the vignette and the statements describing both the child and the adult involved in the incident. Furthermore, assessments are independent of considerations of participants' sex and social status of the household in which the event is said to occur.

TABLE 6.3   Regression of Seriousness on Selected Respondent Characteristics

	SUMMARY	
$R^2 = .05301$	$F = 55.5$	Intercept $= 7.8034$
	$15/14895$	
	$N = 14895$	
	EQUATION	

Respondent Characteristics	b	T
Respondent's sex	.182	3.925
(0 = male, 1 = female)		
White respondents	-.595	-10.529
(0 = no, 1 = yes)		
Black respondents	-.028	-.365
(0 = no, 1 = yes)		
Married respondents	.451	9.401
(0 = no, 1 = yes)		
Protestant respondents	.323	6.091
(0 = no, 1 = yes)		
Catholic respondents	.590	9.654
(0 = no, 1 = yes)		
Respondent's education	-.090	-10.824
Respondent spent most of childhood in a medium-	-.232	-4.267
sized city (50,000-250,000)		
(0 = no, 1 = yes)		
Respondent spent most of childhood in a suburb	-.105	-1.396
near a large city		
(0 = no, 1 = yes)		
Respondent spent most of childhood in a large	-.016	-.340
city (over 250,000)		
(0 = no, 1 = yes)		
Respondent owns home	.070	1.661
(0 = no, 1 = yes)		
Duncan Score for head of household	-.004	-4.005
Female-headed household (0 = no, 1 = yes)	.072	1.278
Number of children in household	-.053	-3.375

Analysis of Respondent Characteristics

We now turn to an analysis of the effect of respondent characteristics on seriousness ratings and the question of consensus. Our first concern is the extent to which seriousness ratings can be attributed to the characteristics of respondents involved in the rating task. If respondent characteristics account for a considerable portion of the variation in seriousness ratings, we might conclude that seriousness ratings are largely dependent on the particular characteristics of respondents. On the other hand, if our model based on respondent characteristics is a poor predictor of seriousness ratings, we can conclude that there is some consensus as to the seriousness of potential child abuse incidents, and that our model of seriousness based on the constituent features of the vignette is a good indicator of seriousness.

To the extent that respondent characteristics may explain seriousness ratings, we are then concerned with the possibility of differences among respondents. That is, what are the significant subgroups of respondents who differ in their assessments of incidents as more or less serious, and how do these differences affect serious ratings?

To investigate this issue, we first regressed the seriousness scores assigned to individual vignettes on respondent characteristics (Table 6.3). The resulting model accounts for only 5 percent of the variation in seriousness scores, suggesting that respondent characteristics play a significantly smaller role in predicting seriousness values than do the component features of the incident. Nevertheless, many of the characteristics in this model are statistically significant (although the regression coefficients are quite small). These significant variables include the respondents' sex, race, education, religious preference, marital status, occupation of the head of household, and number of children living in the household.

In general, female respondents tended to rate incidents described in the vignettes .2 points more serious than did their male counterparts. Along the lines of religious preference, as we might expect, Protestant and Catholic respondents tended to rate incidents as more serious than did respondents of other religions or those declaring no religious preference.

Marital status was also a salient feature differentiating respondents, with married respondents rating incidents .5 points higher than single, divorced, or widowed respondents. At the same time, however, our findings indicate that the presence of children in the respondents' households has a significant negative effect on seriousness judgments. Those with more children tend to rate incidents as less serious than those with fewer children, suggesting that greater contact with children in the household leads to a more generous interpretation of the incidents.

The most interesting findings to emerge from this part of the analysis are those related to racial, ethnic, and social class characteristics of respondents. Earlier research has indicated that nonwhite and lower-class families are overrepresented in cases of abuse and neglect (Gil, 1970). Similarly, studies of child-rearing practices (Swanson and Miller, 1960; Kohn, 1964) have indicated that these groups are more likely to use physical means (as opposed to the more psychological techniques of the middle classes) to discipline children. Findings like these have perpetuated the myth that nonwhite and lower-class families are more tolerant of parental violence or mistreatment. In fact, our findings suggest that the opposite is closer to the truth. White respondents rated the vignettes close to .6 points less serious than did Latin Americans, Native Americans, Asians, and "others." Blacks did not rate incidents significantly different than other nonwhites. Of those variables intended to measure socioeconomic status, (income level, home ownership, and occupational prestige) only the occupational prestige of the head of the respondents' household had a significant effect on seriousness ratings. Those at the higher ends of the Duncan prestige scale tended to rate incidents as less serious than those at the lower end of the scale. Similarly, our findings indicate a negative relationship between educational attainment of the respondent and his or her seriousness ratings. As educational level increases, respondents tend to rate incidents as less serious.

A second regression equation was calculated to include the "give-away" score for respondents (Table 6.4). Again, this score was derived from an average of the four "give-away" vignettes rated by all respondents and is interpreted as a measure of respondents' rating tendencies. Respondents with high average scores were considered to have tendencies to rank incidents toward the high seriousness end of the scale, whereas those with low averages were seen as having tendencies to rank incidents toward the low end of the scale. These averages, when included in the regression equation for respondent characteristics, act to standardize the respondents according to their individual rating tendencies. As Table 6.4 indicates, when the rating tendencies of the respondents are included in the regression equation, the explanatory power of our model is greatly increased. Thus, a respondent's rating tendency, coupled with his or her demographic profile, explains close to 14 percent of the variance in seriousness ratings.

This latter equation, including an average score for "give-away" vignettes as an independent variable, suggests that the rating

TABLE 6.4   Regression of Seriousness on Respondent Characteristics and
Average Rating Tendencies

SUMMARY
$R^2 = .13757$ N = 14895   Intercept = 4.5785
EQUATION

Respondent Characteristics	*b*	*T*
Respondent's sex	.046	1.050
(0 = male, 1 = female)		
White respondents	-.395	-7.289
(0 = no, 1 = yes)		
Black respondents	-.095	-1.294
(0 = no, 1 = yes)		
Married respondents	.335	7.284
(0 = no, 1 = yes)		
Protestant respondents	.275	5.427
(0 = no, 1 = yes)		
Catholic respondents	.413	7.064
(0 = no, 1 = yes)		
Respondent's education	-.068	-8.589
Respondent spent most of childhood in a medium-sized city (50,000-250,000) (0 = no, 1 = yes)	.044	.832
Respondent spent most of childhood in a suburb near a large city (0 = no, 1 = yes)	.020	.277
Respondent spent most of childhood in a large city (over 250,000) (0 = no, 1 = yes)	.097	2.107
Respondent owns home (0 = no, 1 = yes)	-.060	-1.479
Duncan Score for head of household	-.003	-3.375
Total household income	-.000	-1.028
Female-headed household (0 = no, 1 = yes)	.141	2.640
Number of children in household	-.093	-6.183
Average rating tendency (mean "give-away" score)	.471	38.194

tendencies may themselves be linked to respondent characteristics, since this score absorbs several of the significant variables in the original equation (Table 6.3). To measure the relationship between the demographic characteristics of our respondents and their rating tendencies, we regressed the average score for the "give-away" vignettes on all respondent characteristics. All of the respondent characteristics save total income were significant. The R^2 was .10.

This suggests that respondents differ in their *average* rating tendencies according to background characteristics but agree on the principles used to evaluate vignettes.

Summary of the analysis of respondent characteristics. Our findings indicate that respondent characteristics account for close to 14 percent of the variance in seriousness rankings. Of greatest significance are the respondents' tendencies to rank high or low on a seriousness continuum, which are themselves reflections of the more demographic characteristics of our respondents. Respondents who tend to rank incidents as less serious are generally male, white, better educated, and living in households where the main breadwinner enjoys higher occupational prestige and where there are more children. On the other hand, those respondents ranking the vignettes toward the high seriousness end of the scale are typically female, married and/or Protestant. We conclude that there are indeed significant subgroup differences which influence judgments of seriousness. More important, however, these differences are especially prominent with regard to individual tendencies to rate incidents as high or low seriousness. Given such tendencies, however, little in our research suggests subgroup differences in terms of *which* things are considered in making seriousness judgments.

Summary and Discussion

To determine the combined effect of vignette components and respondent characteristics, we have calculated a regression equation which includes all significant vignette components and the average rating tendency of respondents (since it reflects demographic characteristics) (Table 6.5).

These results suggest that assessments of potential child abuse incidents are made on the basis of the constituent features of the incident and the characteristics, particularly the rating tendencies, of those involved in the assessment process. More specifically, seriousness considerations are based on knowledge of the act itself, the consequence of that act, the age of the child involved, and the qualitative attributes of both the child and the guardian. These judgments are further delimited by personal characteristics and overall rating tendencies of those making the judgments. Thus, seriousness scores for child abuse incidents reflect a complex network of situa-

TABLE 6.5   Regression of Seriousness on Vignette Characteristics and
             Mean "Give-Away" Score

SUMMARY		
$R^2 = .2645$	F = 585.5	Intercept = -3.0274
	9/14895	
	N = 14895	
	EQUATION	

	b	T
Mean act rating (without consequence)	.991	44.639
Consequence	3.185	15.512
(0 = no, 1 = yes)		
Age of child	-.014	-3.809
Positive description of child	-.078	-1.923
Negative description of child	.114	2.788
Positive description of guardian	-.059	-1.437
Negative description of guardian	.077	1.880
Interaction Term: Mean act rating X	-.405	-12.791
Consequence		
Average rating tendency (mean "give-away" score)	.508	46.946

tional and individual-specific factors. To the extent that we can
predict the level of seriousness from the compositional features of an
incident alone, there is some degree of consensus as to what types of
events might be classified as child abuse. On the other hand, this
consensus is mediated, to a limited extent, by the characteristics of
the assessors and, to a greater extent, by their overall rating
tendencies.

The analysis presented here has both theoretical and practical
implications. On the theoretical side, the analysis demonstrates the
existence of a normative order in this domain of deviant behavior.
Ratings of the seriousness of child abuse incidents are neither ideo-
syncratic nor highly dependent on the personality or social coordinates of the beholder. While ratings of the incidents to some degree
are modified by the characteristics of victims and perpetrators, the
incidents themselves vary considerably in seriousness.

On the practical side, the findings indicate that there may be a
sufficient normative structure to serve as a guideline in the formation
of more specific legal codes and accompanying administrative
regulations. For human service agencies, the results of our analysis
indicate the areas in which they could achieve widespread public

support for intervention activities and those in which public support is at best ambiguous. Because the effectiveness of intervention ultimately rests on a certain degree of consensus between agencies and families, it is important that the criteria by which abuse is defined among the general public be taken into account.

Appendix A

Abuse Acts and Their Consequences

	Mean* Seriousness Rating	S.D.
The guardian has not taken the child to the dentist. The child has difficulty eating.	5.090	2.574
The guardian ignored the child's complaint of an earache and chronic ear drainage. The child was found to have a serious infection and damage to the inner ear.	7.387	1.825
The guardian ignored the fact that the child was obviously ill, crying constantly, and not eating. When finally taken to the hospital, the child was found to be dehydrated.	7.342	1.875
The guardian has not given the child medication prescribed by a physician. The child has a throat infection.	6.826	1.753
The guardian has failed to obtain an eye examination for the child. The child complains of not being able to see things at a distance.	5.447	2.429
The guardian, who is divorced, has a steady boy (girl) friend with whom he has intercourse often. The child knows this.	4.887	2.957
The guardian, who is divorced, is a homosexual. The child knows this.	5.581	2.850
The guardian and spouse have intercourse where the child can see them. The child suffers recurring nightmares.	6.908	2.520
The guardian makes the child steal small articles out of the supermarket. The child was caught stealing.	7.926	1.396

The guardian regularly fails to feed the child for periods of at least 24 hours. The child was hospitalized for six weeks for being seriously underweight.	7.439	1.804
Over the past year, the guardian failed to prepare regular meals for the child. The child often had to fix supper. The child has an iron deficiency.	5.229	2.625
The guardian always insists that the child clean his/her plate, which is heaped full of food. Doctors have warned that the child's health will suffer if he/she continues to eat so much.	4.940	2.550
The guardian makes no effort to keep the child clean. The child's hair is matted with bits of old food.	5.522	2.305
The guardian does not see to it that the child brushes teeth. The child's teeth have a green film around the gums.	4.072	2.294
The guardian does not wash the child's hair or bathe the child for weeks at a time. The child has impetigo in several places.	6.141	2.391
The guardian does not see to it that the child has clean clothing. Food stains and dirt are splattered all over the child's clothes.	4.981	2.582
The guardian banged the child against the wall while shaking him/her by the shoulders. The child suffered a concussion.	7.738	1.859
The guardian hit the child in the eye with a fist. The child suffered a black eye and a cut lip.	7.792	1.681
The guardian immersed the child in a tub of hot water. The child suffered second-degree burns.	8.134	1.500
The guardian usually punishes the child by spanking with the hand, leaving red marks on the child's skin.	4.033	2.586
The guardian usually punishes the child by spanking with a leather strap, leaving red marks on the child's skin.	6.397	2.548
The guardian repeatedly suggested to the child that they have sexual relations. The child suffers recurring nightmares.	8.108	1.635
The guardian repeatedly showed the child pornographic pictures. The child suffers recurring nightmares.	7.190	2.146

The guardian ignores the child most of the time, seldom talking or listening to the child. The child constantly fights with other children.	6.033	2.439
The guardian constantly screams at the child, using foul names. The child does not play with other children.	6.369	2.158
The child has severe behavior problems. The guardian has allowed the child to undergo treatment, but refuses to cooperate him/herself.	6.839	2.111
The guardian has kept the child locked in a room since birth. The guardian feeds and bathes the child, and provides basic physical care. The child is underdeveloped.	7.797	1.915
The guardian dresses the child in boy's clothing and keeps her hair cropped short like a boy's. The child fights with other children.	5.256	2.412
The guardian dresses the child in girl's clothing, sometimes putting makeup on him, and keeps his hair in long curls. The child fights with other children.	6.493	2.431
The guardian regularly left the child alone inside the house during the day, often not returning until amost dark. On one occasion, the child started a small fire.	6.294	2.412
The guardian regularly left the child alone inside the house after dark, often not returning until midnight. On one occasion, the child started a small fire.	6.931	2.323
The guardian regularly left the child alone outside the house during the day until almost dark. Neighbors have spotted the child wandering five blocks from home.	6.462	2.351
The guardian regularly left the child alone outside the house after dark, often as late as midnight. Neighbors have spotted the child wandering five blocks from home.	7.221	1.861
The guardian regularly left the child with neighbors without knowing who would assume responsibility and be in charge. The child wandered five blocks from home.	6.058	2.165
The guardian leaves bottles of whiskey around the house in places where the child can get to them. The child drank some and became intoxicated.	6.022	2.573

The guardian became very drunk while alone taking care of the child. The child drank some whiskey and became intoxicated.	6.687	2.139
The guardian always allows the child to stay around during drinking parties. The child has occasionally become intoxicated.	5.744	2.380
The guardian, when drinking whiskey, lets the child sip out of the glass. The child has become intoxicated.	5.626	2.450
The guardian got very high smoking marijuana while alone taking care of the child. The child took a drag of marijuana.	6.679	2.408
The guardian always allows the child to stay around when he/she has friends over to smoke marijuana. On one occasion, the child took a drag of marijuana.	6.559	2.546
The guardian always allows the child to stay around when he has friends over to experiment with cocaine. The child asks to take drugs.	7.602	1.721
The guardian lives with the child in an old house. Two windows in the room where the child plays are broken. The child's hands were cut and required three stitches.	5.563	2.603
The guardian lives with the child in a small rented house. No one ever straightens up the house. Rats, cockroaches, and decaying garbage are everywhere.	4.484	2.549
The guardian lives with the child in a skid row neighborhood. Derelicts sleep in the doorway of the building in which they live. One of the derelicts accosted the child.	6.000	2.508
The guardian knows that the child is often truant but does nothing about it. The child is failing in school.	6.063	2.196
The guardian never sees to it that the child does any homework, and allows the child to watch television all evening, even though the child is failing in school.	5.311	2.276
The guardian does not provide any health care for the child. The child complains of physical ailments.	6.339	2.382
The guardian has repeatedly failed to keep medical appointments for the child. The child has a congenital heart defect.	6.215	2.216
The guardian, who is divorced, brings home differ-	6.276	2.462

ent men/women often. The child knows about his/her sexual relations.

The guardian is a prostitute. The child knows this.	6.062	2.639
The guardian permits a relative who is a prostitute to bring customers to the house. The child knows this.	7.123	2.015
The guardian makes the child take stolen merchandise to a store that sells it illegally. The child knows that this is illegal.	7.562	2.032
The guardian allows an uncle to store stolen merchandise in the house. The child knows this.	6.097	2.524
The guardian feeds only milk to the child. The child has an iron deficiency.	6.969	2.159
The guardian brought the child to the hospital three times for being underweight. During each stay the child gained weight, but lost it upon returning home.	5.828	2.689
The guardian usually leaves the child on a filthy, sodden mattress. Infected sores cover the child's body.	6.457	2.223
The guardian always lets the child run around the house and yard without any clothes on. The child has a bad cold.	6.017	2.795
The guardian struck the child with a wooden stick. The child suffered a concussion.	6.300	2.606
The guardian burned the child on the buttocks and the chest with a cigarette. The child has second-degree burns.	8.331	1.336
On one occasion, the guardian and the child engaged in mutual masturbation. The child suffers recurring nightmares.	7.887	1.738
One on occasion, the guardian and the child engaged in sexual intercourse. The child suffers recurring nightmares.	8.546	1.136
The guardian is a moderate drinker, but an uncle who is an alcoholic visits the home often, drinking constantly in front of the child. He once allowed the child to become intoxicated.	5.597	2.559
The guardian uses marijuana occasionally, but an uncle who is an addict visits the home often and has used cocaine in front of the child. The child asks to take some of the drug.	7.235	2.062

The guardian is a drug addict. The child knows this.	7.503	1.808
The guardian lives with the child in a hotel apartment. There are no adequate cooking facilities. The child is malnourished.	5.101	2.609
The guardian frequently lets the child stay home from school for no good reason. The child is failing in school.	5.735	2.337
The guardian frequently keeps the child out of school. The child is failing in school.	5.142	2.379

*Average computed for acts when no consequence is specified.

Appendix B

Descriptive Statements of the Child

Negative Descriptions
Appears emotionally immature
Appears to cry a lot
Appears below average mentally
Appears shy
Appears very belligerent
Seems difficult to communicate with
Appears unhealthy
Appears very nervous

Positive Descriptions
Appears happy
Appears emotionally adjusted
Appears above average mentally
Seems easy to communicate with
Appears cooperative
Appears outgoing
Appears healthy
Seems to get along well with peers

Appendix C

Descriptive Statements of the Guardian

Negative Descriptions
Appears emotionally immature
Sees a psychiatrist regularly
Appears depressed
Has spent some time in prison
  for petty theft
Appears very egocentric
Appears below average mentally
Appears belligerent
Seems difficult to communicate with

Positive Descriptions
Seems easy to communicate with
Appears emotionally adjusted
Appears above average mentally
Appears happy
Appears cooperative
Is respected by friends
Appears to be a kind person
Appears ambitious

NOTES

1. Sociological studies of agencies and organizations—often rooted in a labeling perspective—suggest interagency differences in definitions of deviance which are related to the purposes of each agency (Cicourel, 1968; Piliavin and Briar, 1964). Using a modified form of the vignette analysis used in our research, Giovannoni and Becerra (1979) explored interagency differences among those involved in child abuse cases.

2. This research does not measure the influence of the severity of consequences. Our intent is to assess whether or not consequences are relevant to seriousness assessments.

3. The age variable is treated as continuous, although it is not incremented equally. We use only odd-numbered years but include six months as the youngest possible age.

4. The actual wording was as follows: "I would like to begin by asking you to rate a stack of cards that have a short statement about specific parent-child situations. As you can see there are a series of envelopes on this board. The envelopes are numbered from one (1) through nine (9). These numbers represent a nine-point scale of seriousness between least and most. For example, if you feel an act was only moderately serious, you might rate it a 4, 5, or 6. If you feel it is less serious, but not least, you might rate it 2 or 3 or if you feel it was more serious, but not most, you might rate it 7 or 8. Please rate the card you have just read on this scale according to how serious you feel the act is for the well-being of the child. Use 9 for the most serious acts and 1 for the least serious acts. Remember, this is only your opinion of the seriousness of the act, there are no right or wrong answers."

5. That each act was accompanied by a unique description of the child, guardian, and household does not prevent the use of mean act scores, since these latter characteristics were all randomly assigned to the acts and all characteristics are uncorrelated with one another. The random assignment of vignette characteristics to each act serves to neutralize any effect these characteristics may have on the average rating for the act. If an act is elaborated by a set of descriptions that might enhance its seriousness, it is equally likely that the act would appear elsewhere accompanied by desciptions which would lower its average rating.

REFERENCES

Boehm, B., 1964, "The community and the social agency define neglect." Child Welfare 43: 453-464.

Cicourel, A., 1968, The Social Organization of Juvenile Justice. New York: John Wiley.

Delsordo, J., 1963, "Protective casework for abused children." Children 10: 213-218.

Elmer, E., 1963, "Identification of abused children." Children 10, 5: 180-184.

Gil, D., 1970, Violence Against Children: Physical Abuse in the United States. Cambridge: Harvard University Press.

Giovannoni, J. M. and R. M. Becerra, 1979, Defining Child Abuse. New York: Free Press.

Helfer, R. M., 1973, "The etiology of child abuse." Pediatrics 51, 4: 777-779.

Kempe, C. H., 1962, "The battered child syndrome." Journal of the American Medical Association 191: 17-24.

Kohn, M., 1964, "Social class and parental values," in R. L. Coser (ed.) The Family: Its Structure and Function. New York: St. Martin's Press.

Landry, D. and E. Aronson, 1968, "Liking for an evaluator as a function of his discernment." Journal of Personality and Social Psychology 9: 133-141.

Massachusetts Department of Public Welfare, 1975, Services to Families and Children. Massachusetts Social Services Policy Manual.

Miller, D. and G. Swanson, 1958, The Changing American Parent. New York: John Wiley.

Morris, M., R. Gould, and P. Matthews, 1964, "Toward prevention of child abuse." Children 11: 55-60.

Nurse, S. M., 1964, "Familial patterns of parents who abuse their children." Smith College Studies in Social Work 35, 1: 11-25.

Piliavin, I. and S. Briar, 1964, "Police encounters with juveniles." American Journal of Sociology 69: 206-214.

Rossi, P. et al., 1974, "The seriousness of crimes: normative structure and individual differences." American Sociological Review 39: 224-237.

Rose, A. and A. Prell, 1955, "Does the punishment fit the crime? A study in social valuation." American Journal of Sociology 61, 3: 247-259.

Steele, D. and A. Pollock, 1968, "Psychiatric study of abusive parents," in R. Helfer (ed.). The Battered Child. Chicago: University of Chicago Press.

Terr, L. C., 1970, "A family study of child abuse." American Journal of Psychiatry 127, 5: 665-671.

Young, L., 1964, Wednesday's Child. New York: McGraw-Hill.

Zalba, S., 1967, "The abused child II: a typology for classification and treatment." Social Work 12: 70-79.

7

MODELING DISTRIBUTIVE JUSTICE JUDGMENTS

WAYNE M. ALVES

Studies of distributive justice exist in widely disparate literatures ranging from contributions to philosophical ethics (for example, Rescher, 1966; Rawls, 1971; Nozick, 1974) to a fairly large body of empirical research that focuses on the reactions of individuals to inequity sentiments (see Adams, 1965; Walster et al., 1978) and on conditions which give rise to equity processes (for example, Berger et al., 1972; Cook, 1975; Jasso, 1980). The research described in this chapter (Jasso and Rossi, 1977; Alves and Rossi, 1978) begins with the observation of widespread inequalities of social rewards (earnings) and asks how such inequalities are justified by members of American society. Simply put, the vignette analysis approach to modeling distributive justice judgments attempts to empirically answer the question, "What is fair?" In the first portion of this chapter we will describe the main findings of this research, relying mainly on Alves and Rossi's (1978) work, while in the second part we will examine some conceptual issues relating to empirical modeling of distributive justice judgments along with implications for additional research.

The Empirical Structure of Distributive Justice Judgments

In order to understand how unequal distributions of earnings are justified in American society, both Jasso and Rossi (1977) and Alves and Rossi (1978) described a large number of individuals and households using relevant social characteristics and their earnings.[1] In the Alves and Rossi study a national probability sample of over 500 persons responded to these "vignettes" by indicating to what extent the described individuals or households receive what they deserve, ranging from "extremely underpaid" to "extremely overpaid," with "fairly paid" being the midpoint between the extremes of inequitable payment. These evaluations then served as judgments to be explained. Specifically, Alves and Rossi were concerned with what norms were actually used in making fairness judgments about earnings, as well as the extent to which there was agreement or consensus regarding the criteria for making these evaluations.

Several main findings emerged from Alves and Rossi's research (described more fully below). First, there was considerable tolerance for variation in earnings, as reflected in the modal fairness judgment being "fairly paid." Second, people pay attention to a variety of criteria, reflecting both merit and need considerations, although it was clear that they do not give equal attention to those criteria. For example, husband's attainments were given more weight in determinations of both underpayment and overpayment. Third, there was evidence of clear and systematic variation in the structure of earnings judgments attributable to characteristics of respondents. Though one's location in the American social structure had some influence on evaluations of earnings fairness, the unique contribution of such effects (for example, education or occupation) to fairness ratings was so negligible that they presented little challenge to the other main findings. Finally, Alves and Rossi found considerable "tightness" in the implicit *fair earnings* distributions derived from respondent evaluations of the vignettes. That is, the range of fair earnings (those amounts fully justified by relevant individual or household characteristics) was much narrower than the empirical distribution of income. In the remainder of this section we examine these findings in considerably more detail, illustrating the usefulness of vignette analysis for unraveling macro-normative judgments regarding the distribution of social rewards and privileges. Though this discussion relies heavily on Alves and Rossi (1978), the Jasso and Rossi (1977) findings are entirely consistent.

Who Should Get What?

In our study, Rossi and I took as *problematic* the existence of a consensual normative framework for making judgments regarding fair distributions of earnings. Another way of putting this is to say we were empirically concerned with the principles which underlie popular judgments of earnings fairness. The essential distributive justice question can be posed as follows: How are inequalities in the distribution of social goods justified in a society? We saw this as a macro-sociological issue relating more to the question of just what criteria are to count in justifying unequal allocations of reward or privilege than to the question of whether or not rules for making such judgments exist. There seems to be considerable agreement that such rules do exist (for example, Rawls, 1971; Nozick, 1974; Homans, 1964; among others). It should also be noted that ours is a very different question from asking what are the sources of such judgments (that is, the conditions under which equity judgments arise; see Berger et al., 1972; Cook, 1975; Jasso, 1980; Walster et al., 1978).

Methods

To pursue the question of justifying inequality in the distribution of earnings, we posed the following operational questions:

—What *characteristics* of individuals and households enter into earnings fairness judgments?
—What *weights* are given those characteristics in arriving at judgments of earnings fairness?
—How much *consensus* exists in these criteria and the weights to be applied?

It was clear to us that the vignette analysis approach would best allow us to answer these questions. Our next task was one of crucial importance and substantive difficulty—specifying just what characteristics should go on the vignettes. We wished to have earnings and individual and household characteristics assigned at random, although theoretical substance had to dictate the relatively few substantive characteristics that were to be used in creating the vignettes. We believed that the choice of criteria most appropriate for specifying the vignettes should be guided by appropriate models of status and income attainment, as well as considerations gleaned from our examination of the concept "distributive justice." We chose to specify the vignettes using the following characteristics:

Merit Considerations:
Occupation   —51 occupational titles for which occupational prestige scores were available. Occupations were assigned roughly proportional to the probability

of their appearance in the civilian labor force. Scored in terms of unpublished NORC scores.

Education — In years for each adult member of the household. For example, 16=completed college; 10=completed tenth grade.

Need Considerations:

Marital Status — Used in one-person households only (single, widowed, and divorced).

Children — Number of children in the household, ranging from none to six. In one-person vignettes only widowed or divorced persons were assigned children.

Status Considerations:

Welfare — "being on welfare" was assigned to roughly 2 percent of the vignettes instead of an occupation. While some case could be made for considering "being on welfare" as an occupation, we thought it more appropriate to regard it as a status characteristic.

Sex — Needed only for one-person households since we specified information for both persons in husband-wife households.

Ethnicity — Scored in terms of prestige scores derived from NORC unpublished data.

The specification of the status characteristics was largely because of their importance in any theory of stratification.

Unique decks of vignettes (consisting of 50 vignettes each) were generated using a computer. Characteristics of vignette households were expected to affect the fairness ratings *in combination.* That is, we expected respondents to evaluate earnings fairness by *comparatively* weighing the various characteristics used to describe each household or individual. As such, to ensure a sensible distribution of combinations of characteristics, we decided on random allocation of characteristic values to each vignette, with some exceptions. Except for occupations (which were assigned proportional to their number in the civilian labor force), variables were rectangularly distributed in the total sample of vignettes, resulting in larger than real-world variances and minimal correlation among characteristics (in most cases almost zero).

Though random assignment of vignette characteristic values was used to construct vignette sample decks, we did build in other design features. We omitted all education-occupation anomolies (for example, physicians were constrained to have college educations). We also did not allow widely discrepant attainments between husbands and wives (husbands and wives' occupational attainments were not allowed to differ by more than 50 prestige points). The net result of these constraints on the vignette sample was to build a little correlation back into the sample, although not nearly as much as we would find empirically. In addition, besides 2 percent of all vignettes having "being on welfare" designated in place of an occupational title, 25 percent of the husband-wife vignettes specified the wife's occupation as "housewife," and 10 percent of all vignettes specified ethnicity as "Black-American." It should be pointed out here that the subset of vignettes for each "special" group (housewife, welfare, or blacks) have identical (within sampling error) distributions on remaining characteristics, including earnings. For example, variances among the vignettes concerning blacks are identical to those concerning other ethnic groups, except for the ethnicity specification. The virtue of this is to allow us to specify an effect that is attributable to the label "Black American."

The respondent sample. The vignettes were evaluated and rated by a national probability sample of 522 adults residing in private households, during interviews conducted by Audits and Surveys of New York. Sex quotas within households were set to ensure that roughly half of the interviews were conducted with adult men and half with adult women. Since respondents received *unbiased* samples of vignettes (differing only within random sampling error limits), we thought it unlikely that respondents might develop response sets. Particular values of each characteristic, as well as combinations of characteristics, appear with comparable frequencies. Judgments of relative earnings fairness were made on a scale from "extremely overpaid" (scored as "1") through "fairly paid" (scored as "5") to "extremely underpaid" (scored as "9"), which we chose to regard as an interval scale. We tried various transformations of the data (squaring, taking logs, and "stretching" the fairly paid category toward the extremes), but no sensible gains in interpretation resulted. Let us now turn to a more detailed consideration of the findings from this research.

Findings

Tolerance for inequality. One of the more important findings of our research is the tolerance for variation in earnings considered fair.

The modal rating of all vignettes was "fairly paid," 28 percent of the vignettes being so rated. As Panel A of Table 7.1 indicates, the mean rating for the vignettes evaluated by our respondents was 5.0, with the judgments symmetrically distributed around their average. This pattern in the distribution of earnings-fairness ratings held for both one-person households (27.8 percent rated "fairly paid") and husband-wife households (28.4 percent similarly judged). If we lump together the fairly paid category with the slightly overpaid and underpaid categories *half* of all vignettes evaluated by the respondents fell within that narrow range. Since any amount of earnings specified[2] on the vignettes appeared with roughly the same frequency as any other (within random sampling error limits), this tendency to cluster judgments around the fairly paid category indicates considerable tolerance for earnings differences. Another way of saying this is that earnings differences among households are justifiable. The question of critical importance is, *how* are these differences justified?

Justifying earnings differences. The distribution of earnings-fairness ratings presented in Table 7.1 are compatible with a variety of normative structures regarding fair distributions of earnings, except, of course, any which maintain that *all* earnings allocations are "fair." The zero-order correlations presented in Panel B indicate that various characteristics of households are related to the earnings-fairness rating that household receives. It should be pointed out that these correlations are the only empirical correlations of interest regarding the vignette characteristics. The remaining zero-order relationships among vignette characteristics are consequences of our *design.*

The findings of interest to us involve the ways in which the characteristics of households are *combined* to come up with the earnings-fairness ratings for each household. The descriptive statistics in Table 7.1 foreshadow the results of regression analyses, undertaken to unravel the earnings-fairness judgments, which are presented in Table 7.2. Several general findings are important. First, there is a "strain" in the earnings effects in which higher incomes per se push the judgments toward "extreme overpayment" (b=-.0352 for one-person households and -.0218 and -.0156 for husband's and wife's earnings, respectively, in husband-wife households). As such, lower income is likely to generate judgments of being underpaid. That the earnings coefficients are the most important coefficients in

TABLE 7.1   Distribution of Earnings-Fairness Ratings and Descriptive
Statistics for One-Person Vignettes

A. *Earnings-Fairness Ratings:*

Fairness Rating	Proportion Receiving Rating
1. Extremely overpaid	8.0
2. Much overpaid	7.6
3. Somewhat overpaid	9.5
4. Slightly overpaid	10.8
5. Fairly paid	28.4
6. Slightly underpaid	10.9
7. Somewhat underpaid	9.1
8. Much underpaid	7.3
9. Extremely underpaid	8.4
Mean Rating	5.00
Ratings (N)	26,081
% vignettes rated	97.72

B. *Descriptive Statistics for One-Person Vignette Characteristics:*

Characteristic	Mean	Standard Deviation	Zero-Order Correlation with Rating
1. Gross earnings ($ hundreds)	156.1	110.2	-.642
2. Occupation (NORC score)	43.0	16.1	.207
3. Education (years)	6.5	3.3	.127
4. Children (N)[a]	2.3	2.8	.124
5. Dummy for welfare status[b] (1 = welfare family, 0 = other)	.024	.152	-.135
6. Sex (1 = male, 2 = female)	1.5	.5	-.005
7. Ethnicity[c]	43.3	13.4	.011
8. Earnings squared[d]	36,511	266,633	.579
9. Earnings-occupation interaction	6,707	5,675	-.427
10. Tax rate[e]	.85	.12	-.027

a. "Children" is best conceived as "dependency" and is scored 0 = single person; 1 = married, no children; 2-7 = number of children.
b. Approximately 2% of the household vignettes described the families as "being on welfare."
c. Scored in terms of prestige scores derived from unpublished NORC data.
d. In subsequent analyses earnings squared are gross earnings squared multiplied by .01.
e. Tax rate is one minus net income shown in vignette as a ratio of gross income.

each equation presented in Table 7.2 simply means that the
respondents were perceptive of the fact that a household cannot be
"overpaid" unless it is characterized by high earnings. The coeffi-

TABLE 7.2   Regression of Earnings-Fairness Ratings on Vignette Characteristics[a]

A. *One-Person Households:*

	b	b*	t
1. Gross earnings ($ hundreds)	-.0352	-1.7241	-24.3
2. Earnings squared	.0045	.9516	15.5
3. Occupation (NORC score)	.0099	.0712	2.9
4. Earnings-occupation interaction	.0001	.1786	4.2
5. Education (years)	.0535	.0789	5.6
6. Children (N)	.1115	.1364	10.1
7. Dummy for welfare status (1 = welfare family, 0 = other)	-1.0765	-.0729	-5.1
8. Sex (1 = male, 2 = female)	-.1016	-.0226	-1.7
9. Ethnicity	.0046	.0273	2.0
10. Tax rate	.7854	.0403	2.9

Note: R^2 = .530, F = 293.9, N = 2,613, intercept = 7.6.

B. *Husband-Wife Households:*

	b	b*	t
1. Husband's gross earnings	-.0218	-.0832	-41.4
2. Wife's gross earnings	-.0156	-.8238	-41.5
3. Husband's earnings squared	.0021	.4471	20.1
4. Wife's earnings squared	.0011	.2105	11.9
5. Husband's occupation	.0109	.0799	9.0
6. Wife's occupation	.0162	.1114	12.8
7. Husband's education	.0286	.0434	8.3
8. Wife's education	.0172	.0256	5.0
9. Children (N, 0-6)	.0756	.0781	15.9
10. Dummy for welfare status	-.6958	-.0428	-8.3
11. Ethnicity	.0003	.0019	.4
12. Husband's-wife's earnings interaction	.00003	.2971	30.1
13. Husband's earnings-occupation interaction	.00002	.0486	3.1
14. Wife's earnings-occupation interaction	-.00001	-.0306	-1.8

Note: R^2 = .453, F = 1,350.3, N = 22,874, intercept = 6.85.

a. Unless otherwise noted, variables in husband-wife households analysis are specified the same as those for one-person households. See notes accompanying Table 7.1 for more detail.

cients for the earnings-squared variables all have positive signs indicating an attenuation in the amount of "overpayment" generated by additional increments of earnings as earnings grow large. To some extent this attenuation is artificially imposed, since we provided respondents with a scale to fit their evaluations into, though some attenuation may also be attributed to the relatively small marginal gains provided by \$100 increments in earnings once total earnings have become large.

Second, it is clear that merit, need, and status considerations enter into the judgments of earnings fairness, combining to produce a justification for locating households along the fairness continuum. While the merit (occupation and education attainments) and need (dependents or number of children) considerations are general and apply to both one-person and husband-wife households, the status characteristics enter differentially in judgments regarding one-person and husband-wife households' earnings fairness. For example, while "being on welfare" results in both one-person and couple households being judged more "overpaid" than their non-welfare counterparts, ethnicity only matters in the case of one-person households ($b=.0046$). One-person households with greater ethnicity prestige tend to be judged underpaid relative to their lower prestige counterparts. Sex does not significantly affect judgments of earnings fairness for one-person households but does in the case of husband-wife households where husbands' characteristics carry more weight than wives'. It should be noted that while husbands' attainments generate more "underpayment," it is also the case that husbands' earnings also generate more "overpayment" ($b=-.0218$ versus $-.0156$ for wives). Of course, these differences between husbands and wives also reflect the fact that while respondents combine several competing criteria when formulating earnings-fairness judgments, they do not pay *equal* attention to all criteria. In general, examination of the standardized regression coefficients in Table 7.2, (b^*s) indicates that occupational attainments carry the greatest weight (following earnings and earnings associated terms), followed by children, education, and status characteristics in respective order.

Finally, there are also some *compensatory* effects present in the findings; effects which serve to attentuate the main effects of a particular earnings attainment. For example, significant earnings-occupation interactions for both one-person ($b=.0001$) and husband-wife ($b=.00002$ for husband's) households indicate that unusually high occupational attainments serve to offset the earnings "strain" toward overpayment. Similarly, in households in which both the husband and wife have high earnings attainments, there is a tendency for respondents to resist the earnings strain, as reflected in

TABLE 7.3   Multiple Regression of Total Earnings in Dollars on Husband-Wife Household Vignette Characteristics[a]

Characteristic	b	t	Range	Equally Fair Earnings Range
1. Husband's occupation (NORC)	$ 62.00	11.6	8.2-81.5	$ 4,526.
2. Wife's occupation (NORC)	52.00	8.7	8.2-81.5	3,796.
3. Husband's education (years)	139.00	5.7	5-16	1,529.
4. Wife's education (years)	63.00	2.5	5-16	693.
5. Children (N)	325.00	9.6	0-6	1,950.
6. Welfare dummy (1 = welfare family, 0 = other)	-2,377.00	-3.9	0-1	-2,377.
7. Housewife dummy[b]	-9,954.00	-47.4	0-1	-9,954.
8. Vignette rating	-4,148.00	-113.1	1-9	-33,184.
9. Ethnicity score	-5.00	-1.0	22-65	-258.

Note: $R^2 = .471$, F = 2,259.8, N = 22,864, intercept = 43, 192.

a. Regression coefficients have been rounded to nearest whole dollars.
b. Housewives were given an occupational prestige score of 28.6 derived from a previous study by Rossi et al. (1974). Wives designated as housewives were also coded as a dummy variable. The regression coefficient for "housewife" is independent of the prestige ranking of housewife as an occupation.

the husbands-wives' earnings interaction. Interestingly, it is in cases where both spouses earn identical incomes that this compensatory effect is greatest.

The dollar value of equity. Implicit in the structure of earnings-fairness judgments, reflected in the regression analyses of Table 7.2, are dollar *increments* which are seen as *equally fair* for each unit increase in the household characteristic in question. The reader will recall that there was considerable tolerance for earnings variation displayed in the distribution of earnings-fairness judgments, as presented in Table 7.1. The implications of that tolerance for the present analysis is that variations in earnings can be offset by the dollar value of a unit of some characteristic of each household up to a point, at which more earnings must result in a shift in judgment toward overpayment. As such, if we were to regress the total earnings (in dollars) specified on each vignette on the remaining characteristics of the vignette, *holding rating constant,* we would have estimates of the fair earnings attributable to a unit of a given characteristic (whatever that unit may be). Table 7.3 presents the results of such a regression, along with the estimated *fair earnings difference* between having the least versus the most of a particular attribute. The regression coefficients may be interpreted as the "earnings sensitivity" of each of the characteristics, holding the other characteristics and fairness ratings constant. Only results for husband-wife household vignettes are presented. The estimates yielded in similar analyses for one-person vignettes were quite similar (see Alves and Rossi, 1978).[3] The first finding of note is that each unit of the fairness rating implies roughly $4150: In effect, an increment in total household earnings of that amount shifts the earnings-fairness judgment one unit toward overpayment. Actually, the coefficient puts things in the reverse—that is, a shift in the fairness rating one point in the direction of underpayment requires a $4150 income difference. Over the entire range of earnings-fairness ratings *equally fair* differences in earnings amount to roughly $33,000.

Second, we note that husbands' meritorious achievements provide more "fair dollars" than do wives' (almost 20 percent more in the case of occupational attainments, but more than *twice* in the case of educational achievement). If we examine the amounts of "equally fair" earnings implicit for the entire range of each characteristic of the vignettes, we note that occupational attainments dominate the fair dollar allocations (roughly $4500 for husbands' occupations and $3800 for wives'), with considerably less fair earnings being justified by educational attainments and number of children. The total possible contribution of educational achievements ($2222) is slightly larger than that for children ($1950).

The third, and final, finding of importance in Table 7.3 involves the *negative* fair earnings values implicitly attached to the welfare and housewife variables. In each case, by either specifying the family is "being on welfare" or the wife's occupation as "housewife," the household *loses* fair dollars (almost $2400 in the case of welfare families, and almost $10,000 in the case of families with house-wives). Put in a different way, a household which is not on welfare (or in which the wife is working outside the home) can earn roughly $2400 ($10,000) more than welfare or housewife family counterparts and still get the same income-fairness rating.

Estimating a fair distribution of earnings. From the preceding discussion it is clear that arriving at some overall impression of the fairness of a household's earnings involves *combining* various merit and need considerations. It is possible, in practice, for merit and need to come into conflict as earnings fairness judgments are made. If a society is to avoid conflict regarding the relative roles merit and need are to play in evaluating earnings, some "social minimum" earnings must be established: an amount of earnings under which the least meritorious and the most needy should not fall (see Boulding, 1958, 1962). A natural corollary is to suggest the possibility that a "social maximum" exists: an amount of earnings more than which no household would fairly earn. These earnings are limiting cases: They represent the amounts of earnings the least qualified and least needful household (social minimum) and the most qualified and most needful household (social maximum) can fairly earn.

Estimates of fair earnings were derived by setting linear versions of the equations presented in Table 7.2 to the value of a judgment of fair payment ("5") and specifying all characteristics for the described households except for earnings, which we then solved. The finding of most importance is that respondents implicitly defined a fair earnings distribution that had a higher mean and lower variance than is the case empirically. The estimated lower and upper bounds of fair earnings for one-person households are $2538 and $34,485, while similar boundaries for husband-wife households are $7211 and $44,466, respectively. It should be noted that the lower bounds describe the fair earnings for welfare families (see Table 5 in Alves and Rossi, 1978).

Additional insight into the fair earnings distribution estimated from the data can be gained from examining the figures in Table 7.4, which are estimated fair earnings for husband-wife households with varying combinations of meritorious achievements and need. The range of estimated fair earnings is $30,811, the difference between households with high merit and the most need and those with the least merit and least need. The range of fair earnings can be roughly decomposed into (a) the amount due to occupational achievements, (b) that due to educational achievements, and (c) that due to increased need (reflected by number of children in the household). This is done by comparing cases where the household is high on merit and need considerations to cases where the household is low on each factor in turn.[4] For example, the difference between the social maximum household (high on all three factors) and households high on education and children but low on occupation is $19,744— roughly 64 percent of the total range. The difference in estimated fair

TABLE 7.4 Estimated Fair Earnings for Households with Various Merit and Need Characteristics (Husband-Wife Households)[a]

Occupational Attainments	Educational Attainments	Number of Children	Estimated Fair Earnings	Welfare Estimates[d]
High[b]	High	High	44,468.	29,001.
High	High	Low[c]	39,401.	23,934.
High	Low	High	38,601.	23,134.
High	Low	Low	33,401.	17,934.
Low	High	High	24,723.	18,279.
Low	High	Low	19,523	13,079
Low	Low	High	18,723	12,279
Low	Low	Low	13,657	7,212

a. Estimates were computed by setting completely linear versions of the equation shown in Table 7.2 (Panel B) equal to "5" (a rating of "fairly paid"), setting vignette characteristics as indicated below, and solving for the implied earnings.
b. Where meritorious or need characteristics are indicated as "high," vignette characteristics were set at their *highest* values: occupations as "physicians," educational attainments as "college graduates," and number of children as "6", all maximum values used in design of the vignettes. Both husband and wife are assigned the same achievements.
c. Where meritorious or need characteristics are indicated as "low," vignette characteristics were set at their *lowest* values: no children, five years of education, and occupations shown as "garbage collector" for males and "laundry worker" for females (except for wives who are shown to be "housewives"), all minimum values used in design of the vignettes. Both husband and wife are assigned the same achievements.
d. Estimates are based on households designated by the same characteristics as those designated "low" on merit or need characteristics. Wives are shown as "housewife" in husband-wife vignettes. Occupation is described as "being on welfare."

earnings between households with high and low educational attainments (other factors held constant) is $5867, while the comparable figure for households differing in need is $5067. Occupational attainments clearly dominate contributions to estimated fair earnings, being roughly three to four times as great as contributions by educational achievements and need. A final finding is worth noting. If we compare the fair earnings estimates for various combinations of merit and need with comparable estimates for welfare families, we find that where occupational attainments are high, the difference is roughly $15,500, while in those cases where occupation is low the gap stands at slightly more than $6640. Once occupation is taken into account, differences in households' educational attainments and need do not seem to matter when adjusting fair earnings for families described as "being on welfare." The size of the welfare earnings figures are somewhat generous and perhaps reflect recognition on the part of respondents that any and all households may be subjected to the whims of the labor market and this should not be something that detracts too significantly from their *fair* earnings.

Consensus and dissensus in earnings-fairness judgments. Some amount of agreement regarding what relevant criteria are to be applied when evaluating earnings fairness is a necessary constraint for any empirical theory of distributive justice. While persons may disagree on exactly *how* rules apply in practice, they at least must agree on the rules themselves. We define consensus to mean that agreement regarding criteria for making earnings-fairness judgments exists among significant subgroups of a society. As a heuristic guide to aid in defining potentially significant subgroups from the perspective of earnings-fairness judgments, we regressed fairness ratings on vignette and respondent characteristics, as well as various interaction terms between vignette and respondent characteristics. Since the effects of respondent characteristics reflect overall differences in the *level* of fairness ratings given to the vignette households, it is in the interaction terms of vignette-respondent characteristics that we would expect to find evidence of subgroup variation. Finding that such variation was likely to exist between high- and low-status persons, we then divided our sample roughly in half using the mean value of respondent income. Table 7.5 presents the results of regressing fairness ratings on vignette and respondent characteristics for respondent income and sex subgroups. The findings for respondent sex subgroups are presented mainly because they indicate very little difference in the structure of earnings-fairness judgments of the two groups.

Examining the first four columns of Table 7.5, we find that higher income respondents give more weight to merit considerations (both occupational and educational achievements), while low-income respondents were more sensitive to need, as reflected in the larger coefficient for number of children in the low-income respondents' equation. We should note, however, that *both* income groups use both merit and need criteria in evaluating earnings fairness. It is simply the case that respondents tended to favor their cognates in the vignettes, while tempering this tendency when attainments get "too large." For example, as the respondent's income increases, there is a tendency to judge vignettes more in the direction of overpaid for each increment in vignette earnings. Yet, when a vignette household is characterized by high meritorious achievements, higher-income

TABLE 7.5 Regressions of Earnings-Fairness Ratings on Husband-Wife Household Vignette and Respondent Characteristics for Respondent Income and Sex Subgroups

Vignette Characteristics	High-Income[a] Respondents		Low-Income Respondents		Female Respondents		Male Respondents	
	b	t	b	t	b	t	b	t
1. Husband's gross earnings ($ hundreds)	-.0196	-29.1	-.0167	-25.4	-.0185	-18.5	-.0177	-17.7
2. Wife's gross earnings ($ hundreds)	-.0117	-24.1	-.0119	-25.4	-.0120	-12.0	-.0116	-11.6
3. Husband's occupation (NORC)	.0191	17.9	.0139	13.2	.0153	15.3	.0170	17.0
4. Wife's occupation (NORC)	.0184	15.1	.0128	10.8	.0163	16.3	.0146	14.6
5. Husband's education (years)	.0399	7.8	.0196	3.9	.0352	7.0	.0226	4.5
6. Wife's education (years)	.0218	4.2	.0117	2.3	.0157	3.1	.0163	3.2
7. Number of children (0-6)	.0471	6.6	.0984	14.1	.0895	12.8	.0612	8.7
8. Ethnicity	.0021	1.8	-.0005	-.4	-.0005	-.5	.0014	1.4
9. Husband's earnings squared	.00002	14.6	.00002	12.6	.00002	14.0	.00002	14.3
10. Wife's earnings squared	.00001	5.8	.00001	9.6	.00001	6.2	.00001	6.6
Respondent Characteristics								
11. Sex (1 = male, 2 = female)	-.0118	-.4	.1497	4.6	—		—	
12. Race (1 = white, 2 = black)	.3218	6.8	.3389	7.3	.0832	1.7	.5080	11.0
13. Age (years)	.0023	1.9	-.0045	-5.2	-.0026	-2.6	-.0033	-3.3
14. Education (years)	-.0337	-4.2	-.0035	-.6	.0034	.5	-.0254	-3.6
15. Income ($ thousands)	-.0069	-1.6	.0166	2.8	.0081	2.7	.0149	4.9
16. Household prestige[b]	-.0058	-4.2	-.0100	-7.1	-.0101	-10.1	-.0052	-5.2
Intercept	6.557		6.132		6.550		6.095	
R²	.503		.396		.433		.448	
N	9,411		11,418		10,298		10,531	

a. Income divided at $14,000 or more per year.
b. Household prestige as computed according to Rossi et al. (1974).

respondents tend to judge that household underpaid to a greater extent than do lower-income respondents. In sum, while there are systematic, subgroup differences in rating tendencies, those differences add little to predictions of earning-fairness ratings. Much the same pattern of findings results when we consider the results relating to the dollar value of equity and the fair earnings distribution in a similar fashion. Higher-status respondents allow more fair earnings per increment in merit characteristics (both education and occupation), while lower-income respondents allow greater fair earnings for each additional child. Interestingly, while higher-status respondents set the *maximum* earnings higher ("stretching out" the inequality) than their lower-status counterparts (who prefer to "shrink" the distribution), both groups tend to set the *same* minimum fair earnings. Finally, the coefficients for respondent characteristics in the bottom half of Table 7.5 indicate that various subgroups of respondents set overall earnings-fairness ratings higher (or lower) than their counterparts. For example, low-income women and blacks of each income group tend to set overall fairness ratings more in the direction of underpayment. On the other hand, older low-income respondents, as well as high-income persons with higher educational achievements, tend to set earnings-fairness ratings more toward overpayment. In any case, the differences noted do not overshadow earlier interpretations of earnings-fairness judgments.

Summary.   It is clear that the structure of distributive justice judgments regarding earnings fairness involves *combining* of socially relevant criteria (reflecting, at least minimally, merit, need, and status considerations) in arriving at an overall pattern of fair payment. Perhaps the most significant findings involve the tolerance Americans have for variation in earnings reflecting "fair payment," and the extent of judgmental consensus that exists regarding criteria appropriate for earnings-fairness evaluations. There are, however, some serious limitations to the findings discussed above. First, the results are limited by what was specified in the vignette descriptions. As such, we can expect that the judgments of earnings fairness made by our respondents were blunted by the relatively crude specification. More work needs to be done on developing a theoretical framework that would allow for specification of relevant fairness criteria and a suitable empirical test of just how relevant various criteria are. Second, we could not judge the relative sensitivity of respondents' judgments to need considerations as compared to those involving meritorious achievements. All we can be confident of at this point is that both need and merit are taken into account in arriving at earnings-fairness judgments.

The following questions may serve as a guide to the next stage of empirical research on distributive justice norms.

—What is the range of norms that exist in American society for fairly distributing social rewards and privileges?

—What counts as concrete dimensions in applying the various norms that exist for justifying inequality?

—Given that several criteria are used in making distributive justice evaluations, are the *same* norms used for justifying distributions of *all* types of social goods? Or are *different* norms used for *different* types of rewards and privileges?

—How are various distributional criteria "meshed" to produce fairness judgments? Do certain criteria "swamp" others? That is, does the presence of certain characteristics or performances indicate *sufficient* conditions for ignoring the presence or absence of others?

—To what extent do Americans agree on fairness evaluations? We should note that this could involve addressing the extent of consensus and dissensus regarding Americans' agreement on the overall fairness of the social goods possessed by specific individuals or households, the characteristics or performances that should be used to make such evaluations, and the relative importance of each characteristic or performance.

In the following section of this chapter we will examine some of the conceptual issues involved in following through a research program such as that indicated by the above questions. To illustrate how we might proceed, we will consider the question of earnings-fairness judgments in more detail.

Justifying Inequality

The central issue in distributive justice research concerns the question of justifying inequalities in distributions of social rewards and privileges in American society. This question involves two general, but related, aspects. On the one hand, there is concern for the *general* features of justification which involve, in some combination, a variety of *principles of equivalency* among individuals or households. For example, should differences in skills, achievements, personal characteristics, or family composition weigh into assessments of earnings fairness? On the other hand, it is fairly clear that there are *specific* aspects of social life which involve a series of "tradeoffs," as we thread a course through the life cycle. What is important for an adequate theory of distributive justice is whether those "tradeoffs" constitute *sufficient* justification for more or less reward or privilege. For example, should persons who forego autonomy in their choice of occupation have any more claim to greater earnings as a consequence of that choice? Or does the choice itself negate the claim? In the remaining discussion we largely concentrate on the issue of *general equivalency principles*. It seems sensible to understand the more general principles fully before attempting to understand how they are adjusted as the issue of individual choice comes into play.

If we are to shed light on how various characteristics and performances of individuals and households *actually* justify competing claims to shares of rewards or privileges, the question of *differential* justification will play a central role in future research. Some types of social rewards may not be justified in terms of certain distributional criteria. Further, it is not likely that any *single* criterion will be used to make distributive justice evaluations (in effect, concurring with Boulding, 1958, 1962). If one were to adhere strictly to merit characteristics as a sole criterion for justifying inequality, we would be denying the kind of loose sense of community implicit in our long-standing concern for those less fortunate than ourselves. Similarly, limiting our judgments of what is fair on the basis of need alone denies the fundamental economic problem of scarcity. Were it not probable that the sum of a society's needs will outweigh its productive output, the issue of distributive justice would be moot. Finally, there is no reason to believe that some intrinsic harmony will exist among possible distributive criteria (concrete or general). There is always the likelihood that some conflict will exist between individually *earned* shares and a "proper" share based on notions of the common good.

What Distributive Justice Norms Are There?

Some sense of the potential range of alternative norms that could guide judgments about fair distributions of social rewards and privileges in American society can be gleaned from a perusal of the disparate literature relating to distributive justice or equity processes. An initial foray into this literature reveals a number of general principles that could guide specification of research models, each of which we will consider briefly. In some cases we are more certain of the content of the norm described, while in others we are far from sure just how to proceed in empirically specifying them for research purposes. In any case, some idea of the potential norms that will have to be incorporated into any theory of distributive justice is evident from the list below.

1. *Strict Equality Norm:* This normative standard states that individuals or households have *equal claims* to shares of social rewards and privileges regardless of any other considerations (for example, equity in the form of meritorious achievement). While our research has started from observed inequalities in social goods and sought to unravel principles which justify those inequalities, there is more subtlety regarding this norm than first appears. As Jasso and Rossi (1977) correctly note, once we eliminate the possibility that strict equality is justifiable in a society, we must address the question of how much dispersion is allowable and whether that dispersion is simply random or justified in terms of specific normative principles. Yet, it is possible that an absence of effect attributable to various concrete characteristics of individuals or households may indicate an equality principle is operative in the society. For example, the lack of an effect attributable (generally) to ethnicity may indicate that the macro-structure of distributive justice judgments includes a precept that, all other factors held constant, equality between various ethnic groups should obtain if goods and privileges are to be considered fairly distributed.

2. *Merit Norm:* Distribution based on merit involves allocating fair shares of social rewards and privileges in terms of socially recognized and valued differences. In the most general sense, merit involves any and *all* entitlements based on a variety of "meritorious achievements": (a) behaviors seen by others as contributing to the collective effort either directly or indirectly; (b) behaviors seen by others as demonstrating personal sacrifice or exceptional effort in the performance of some role; or (c) personal characteristics with socially ascribed meanings. We will consider each type of behavior briefly.

All members of American society are expected to participate in its functioning to some degree. Goode (1978) notes, however, that some behaviors which are socially valued are so common that their social value is not an entitlement to reward or privilege. Thus, the issue of contribution involves performance above (or below) some "working norm." *Minimal* levels of performance are expected to be independent of any rewards. As such, "contribution" as a principle for justifying inequality reflects what is in excess of minimal expected levels of performance. Additionally, the issue of *past* versus *present* (or *future*) contributions to collective effort must be considered. To borrow Boulding's metaphor (1962), many sit down at the table of society who don't "deserve" to be there, and many eat from it who have made no contribution.

Our interpretation of "merit" goes beyond contribution to include any *compensation* of persons or households for the difficulties encountered or sacrifices made in performing social roles. Special payments are made to coal miners and are justified in terms of health risk. Cash transfers are given to single mothers and justified on the basis of children's special needs in such families. Yet, it is not clear what are the sources of compensation. What, if anything, should a person receive for a "loss" related to contribution to collective effort? For example, should the loss of a limb in an industrial accident be thought of in terms of dollar amounts or prosthetic equivalence?

3. *Need Norm:* Definitions of need typically refer to the *absence* of attributes or situations considered conducive to the "welfare" of individuals or households. Yet, "need" often shades into other issues of subjective evaluations. For example, we must clearly distinguish between *needs* and *wants*. From a distributive justice point of view, it is likely that "need" will refer to some *basic* deficiencies in individuals, households, or subgroups that are prior to felt needs which inevitably involve preference issues. In any case, differences in need are not simply fortuitous differences in individual or household requirements or circumstances. Rather, need reflects differences in the capacity of individuals or households to negotiate their social environments successfully. For example, level of needs can be stated in terms of ability to meet household consumption requirements (see Jacques, 1961).

This approach to the specification of "need" stresses its social character. That need is socially defined is evidenced by Rainwater's (1974) finding that people tend to believe that *any* job worth doing should pay an income that ensures, at the least, the jobholder does not have to live in poverty. Rainwater also found that popular conceptions of *fair minimum* earnings correspond to popular conceptions of the amount of earnings needed to provide some minimally adequate consumption budget for a household. Thus, specifying the determinants of household consumption (holding wealth and income constant) is a reasonable way of viewing "need." In sum, distinctions among need, felt need, and wants are social in origin. People integrate disparate knowledge of others' consumption in formulations of various "levels of living," including a minimal standard of living which may be considered as reflecting minimal survival needs (see Rainwater, 1974: especially chap. 8). It is worth pointing out here that the question of need also raises the issue of fair and reasonable precautions (alternatively, savings or investments) against the vagaries of social life likely to generate needy situations. That is, investments or precautions taken may influence assessments of degrees of need. Yet, investment alone is not likely to be enough in justifying distributions of rewards or privileges, since achievement seems to carry more weight. For example, Goode (1978) notes that prestige for performance is typically not given to someone whose competence is lower but whose costs or investments are higher. When assigning grades to term papers, instructors seldom weigh the relative ease with which two students may have completed the task.

Several additional norms potentially guide distributive justice judgments, but it is still not entirely clear how to specify these general principles. In particular, note the following:

4. *Custom Norm:* This principle involves justification of unequal rewards or privileges on the basis of traditional, well-proven, or well-entrenched ways of doing things.

5. *Compensatory Norms:* These principles justify unequal rewards or privileges in order to equalize or compensate individuals or households for "unusual" hardships, sacrifices, or unintended consequences of social action. In addition, there may be a compensatory mechanism involved in cases where access to desired social ends are evident. For example, one important aspect of occupational achievement involves an amount of moral rectitude that accrues by virtue of one's attainments. It may be that a norm operates such that persons are compensated for the loss of moral rectitude denied them by the vagaries of the labor market. The fascination and apparent "approval" that seems to accompany the "great robbers" or "Robin Hoods" of our folklore involve such a compensatory norm. Heroism and even

the "good samaritan" may be other examples.

6. *Legislative Norm:* This principle would evaluate as "fair" allocations derived from outcomes of the legislative process. In effect, members of any society may recognize "benefits" gained through legislative action as a necessary condition for effectively resolving the need for collective action.

7. *Control Over Scarce Resources:* This principle states that whoever commands scarce and needed goods and services has greater claims to social goods. It allows for the inclusion of power and its derivative processes into a theory of distributive justice.

8. *Trust and Intimacy:* This may operate as a distributive justice principle as a special form of compensatory norms. For example, as a family breaks up, or one works through the conflict involved in "turning someone in" versus intimacy of family ties, some form of fairness adjustment may be made.

9. *Loyalty Norms:* Though the hallmark of modern society is a rational, bureaucratic form of organization, a certain amount of "feudal loyalty" still seems to be in demand. This principle would justify inequalities on the basis of the loyalty exhibited by a person to his or her social role expectations.

10. *Life and Death Norm:* This principle would justify inequalities in allocations of social rewards or privileges by claiming a "sufficiency" status. For example, the fact that death may result from failure to receive, for example, kidney dialysis may be sufficient to ignore any lack of meritorious achievement.

This inventory of potential norms for evaluating the fairness of distributions of social rewards and privileges is not meant to be exhaustive. Indeed, we are not sure we can claim they are mutually exclusive. The main point to be gained from consideration of the possible normative principles that might guide distributive justice judgments is that such social evaluation processes are very complex in nature and involve understanding fully what concrete attributes or characteristics of individuals or households are to count as empirical referents of each of many principles, and how all these principles are combined and reconciled in practice.

Justifying Income Inequality

While inventories of potential distributive justice norms are useful, especially in clarifying the complexity of fairness judgments,

FIGURE 7.1   Sources of Individual and Household Income[a]

	Primary Income	*Redistributed Income*
Money Income	Wages and Salaries Property Income Proprietors' Incomes	Public Cash Transfers Private Cash Transfers (pensions and annuities)
Nonmoney Income	Employer Contributions to Public or Private Transfers	Public In-Kind Transfers (food stamps, medical care, and education)
	Net Imputed Rent of Owner- Occupied Housing	Private Transfers (employer- paid health insurance)
	Home Production and Leisure Corporate Profits Less Dividends	

a. Adapted from Danziger and Lampman (1978).

the underlying principles do not take us far in specifying those relevant characteristics which *actually* indicate the empirical *content* of distributive justice norms in any society. In this section of the chapter we will consider how we might go about studying justifications of inequality in income distributions. Before we consider income-fairness judgments per se, it would be useful to come to some agreement about what counts as "income." Fortunately, we can gain reasonable understanding of the concept "income" by examining the work of economists. Figure 7.1 is adapted for use in this chapter from Danziger and Lampman's (1978) work. We can see that "income" involves much more than wages and salaries from work, the subject of distributive justice studies to date. Although income does indeed derive from our occupational activities (for most of us this is true for the bulk of our income), it is clear from Figure 7.1 that control over scarce resources is also a major source of primary income. Of course, redistributed income must also be accounted for, both in the form of public income transfers (cash and in-kind) as well as private income transfers (such as employer-paid health benefits). In sum, "income" is a rather complex bundle of money and nonmoney resources which can be derived either from our efforts in the occupational world or through some form of government income transfer. A complete study

of justifications of income inequality, then, would require consideration of both earnings-fairness *and* the fairness of income transfers.

But income is also meant to be *used,* mainly in meeting the
consumption needs of a household. In trying to come to grips with the
problem of specifying *need* in the design of vignettes for studying
earnings-fairness judgments, both Rossi and I have resolved that a
useful *starting* point would be to use the determinants of household
consumption (holding, of course, income and wealth constant).
Danziger and Lampman (1978) have noted several uses of income:
(1) purchases by households (food, clothing, housing services,
medical care, education, and the like); (2) nonmarket consumption
behaviors (such as net housing services of owner-occupied housing,
as well as home production activities and leisure); (3) macro-
consumption activities on the part of government and employers (for
example, purchase of medical care and education); and (4) saving
behavior of households. Certainly Danziger and Lampman's first
category, household purchases, is relevant for our specification of
"need." Nonmarket consumption and savings behaviors of households also should be included in that specification, since it is likely
that compensatory norms will enter income-fairness judgments as
need, and status characteristics indicative of lifestyle differences are
considered in arriving at estimates of fairness. The macro-consump-
tion behavior of government would be relevant only in the case of
assessing the fairness of income transfers, while employer contributions to total income obviously are tied to work and rightly should be
specified as a characteristic of nonincome transfer households. In
any case, what the reader should appreciate is that income-fairness
judgments are likely to be very complex judgments involving a net
balancing of both the sources and uses of the income of any
individual or household.

It is likely that income fairness is tied to occupational attainments,
given that occupations are a major source of income (as well as
perhaps the major social role for channeling other social rewards).
Further, people can make the kind of discriminations among varying
incomes that we desire. Studies of occupational prestige indicate
widespread knowledge about occupations, as evidenced in research
showing that the location of an occupation in a prestige hierarchy
depends (at least in part) on how that occupation is articulated into

the wider division of labor in any society (Trieman, 1979; Hodge et al., 1966). A society's members have at least superficial knowledge of how politically important some occupations are—how important they are in the overall scheme of production—and are sensitive to the relative complexity of occupations, and thus requisite skills, performances, and responsibilities implicit in occupational titles (see Hodge et al., 1964). Sayles (1958) has found that factory workers "compute" the *fairness* of wages they are paid relative to other groups within the factory in terms of differences in the "importance" of their own work group versus others, where "importance" is equivalent to perceived investments of group members including skills, type of work, length of service, and similar factors. It should be noted here, however, that the kind of criteria relevant in the macrostructure of distributive justice judgments need not be equivalent (or mutually exclusive, for that matter) to those relevant within particular institutional settings such as firms. In a similar vein, Patchen (1961) found that workers in a firm cited several reasons for satisfaction with wage comparisons in which they earn less than others. Reasons cited are that others have superior qualities in what the job requires (for example, skills or education), seniority or experience, and selected personal qualities (though they weigh relatively little); that the persons making judgments of wage equity have *compensating* advantages relative to others, both financial and nonfinancial (benefit programs, steadier work, they like the work they do, cleaner jobs); or that they and others simply have *different* jobs.

What research should come next? First of all, it would be useful to consider the *entire* range of occupations and describe individuals and households in terms of merit and need considerations, where "merit" would be specified as the determinants of wages from which occupation-specific factors (degree of autonomy, size of firm typically practiced in, and the like) as well as other *local* factors (local labor market conditions, for example) have been stripped; and "need" would be specified as the determinants of household consumption, holding income and wealth constant. This way of specifying vignettes would reflect several considerations. To begin, studies on "human capital" focus on the importance of investments (education, migration, or job experience) on wages (Becker, 1964; Thurow, 1969). On the other hand, status attainment studies, beginning with Blau and

government programs and policies. Perhaps then we can attain convergence between what is and what is not just in American society.

NOTES

1. Several rationales guided both Jasso and Rossi (1977) and Alves and Rossi (1978) in the choice of earnings for an initial study of empirical distributive justice norms. Money is, to borrow from Galbraith (1975), something one worries about if they have it and if they don't! Earnings are the major source of income for most persons and, indeed, the major source of wealth for many. Other discussions of distributive justice typically involve earnings. For example, earnings have symbolic value in representing participation or membership in industrial society and the fruits of that participation or membership (see Rainwater, 1974). Validating ourselves as full and recognized members of society has important consequences to our sense of well-being and the quality of life. In addition, earnings are viewed in a number of ways in American society beyond an index of participation: as pay for the performance of work tasks, support for a family, a component of the social meaning of "Class," and an index of standard of living. Clearly, the social importance of earnings as a social reward cannot be understated. Finally, unlike many social rewards or privileges, earnings have a common, easily understood metric—the dollar.

2. Adults in each vignette could earn $2000 to $40,000. As such, vignettes in which two adults were specified could have a maximum earnings of $80,000. "Housewife" income was specified as $0.00.

3. It should be noted that the effect of ethnicity for one-person households is significant. Our analyses indicate that black males are penalized in such a fashion that their estimated "fair" payment is a net dissavings (that is, a negative amount).

4. There are several comparable comparisons implicit in Table 7.4, but all of which give comparable results. For example, one could obtain the estimate for "occupation" contribution by comparing those vignettes "high" on all three components with vignettes high on "education" and "children" but "low" on occupation. Similarly, one could compare those "low" on all three components, with the group "high" on "occupation" but "low" on the rest. The estimate is still roughly $19,000.

REFERENCES

Adams, J., 1965, "Inequity in social exchange," pp. 267-299 in L. Berkowitz (ed.) Advances in Experimental Social Psychology, Volume Two. New York: Academic Press.

Alves, W. and P. Rossi, 1978, "Who should get what? Fairness judgments of the distribution of earnings." American Journal of Sociology 84 (November): 541-564.

Becker, G., 1964, Human Capital. New York: Columbia University Press.

Berger, J. et al., 1972, "Structural aspects of distributive justice: a status value formulation," pp. 119-146 in J. Berger, M. Zelditch, Jr., and B. Anderson, Sociological Theories in Progress, Volume Two. Boston: Houghton Mifflin.

Blau, P. and O. Duncan, 1967, The American Occupational Structure. New York: John Wiley.

Boulding, K., 1958, Principles of Economic Policy. Englewood Cliffs, NJ: Prentice-Hall.

Boulding, K., 1962, "Social justice in social dynamics," pp. 73-92 in R. Brandt (ed.) Social Justice. Englewood Cliffs, NJ: Prentice-Hall.

Cook, K., 1975, "Expectations, evaluations and equity." American Sociological Review 40 (June): 372-388.

Curtin, R., 1977, Income Equity Among U.S. Workers. New York: Praeger.

Danziger, S. and K. Lampman, 1978, "Getting and spending." Annals of the American Academy of Political and Social Science, 435 (January): 23-59.

Galbraith, J., 1975, Money: Whence It Came, Where it Went. Boston: Houghton Mifflin.

Garfinkel, I., 1979, "Welfare reform: a new and old view." Journal of the Institute for Socioeconomic Studies 4 (Winter): 58-72.

Goode, W., 1978, The Celebration of Heroes: Prestige as a Control System. Berkeley: University of California Press.

Hodge, R., P. Siegel, and P. Rossi, 1964, "Occupational prestige in the United States, 1925-1963," American Journal of Sociology 70 (November): 286-302.

Hodge, R., D. Trieman, and P. Rossi, 1966, "A comparative study of occupational prestige," pp. 309-321 in R. Bendix and S. Lipset (eds.) Class, Status, and Power: Social Stratification in Comparative Perspective. New York: Free Press.

Homans, G., 1964, Social Behavior: Its Elementary Forms. New York: Harcourt Brace Jovanovich.

Jacques, E., 1961, Equitable Payment. New York: John Wiley.

Jasso, G., 1980, "A new theory of distributive justice." American Sociological Review 45 (February): 3-32.

1978, "On the justice of earnings: a new specification of the justice evaluation function." American Journal of Sociology 83 (May): 1398-1419.

Jasso, G. and P. Rossi, 1977, "Distributive justice and earned income." American Sociological Review 42 (August): 639-651.

Nozick, R., 1974, Anarchy, State, and Utopia. New York: Basic Books.

Patchen, M., 1961, The Choice of Wage Comparisons. Englewood Cliffs, NJ: Prentice-Hall.

Rainwater, L., 1974, What Money Buys: Inequality and the Social Meanings of Income. New York: Basic Books.

Rawls, J., 1971, A Theory of Justice. Cambridge: Harvard University Press.

Rescher, N., 1966, Distributive Justice. Indianapolis: Bobbs-Merrill.

Sayles, L., 1958, Behavior of Industrial Work Groups: Prediction and Control. New York: John Wiley.

Thurow, L., 1969, Investment in Human Capital. Belmont, CA: Wadsworth.
Trieman, D., 1977, Occupational Prestige in Comparative Perspective. New York:
    Academic Press.
Walster, E., G. Walster, and E. Berscheid, 1978, Equity: Theory and Research.
    Boston: Allyn & Bacon.

8

HOW MUCH IS TOO MUCH?
Popular Definitions of Alcohol Abuse

LAWRENCE J. O'BRIEN
PETER H. ROSSI
RICHARD C. TESSLER

A critical issue in the understanding of alcohol abuse is the measurement of how individuals define what constitutes abuse and how such definitions vary with the drinking habits and social characteristics of the individuals involved. A more complete understanding of this issue would also address how such definitions become established and the extent to which they can be modified through experience and by the intervention of educational campaigns. This chapter proposes a technique for measuring popular conceptions of alcohol abuse and illustrates its use with results from a sample survey of undergraduates from two New England universities. Because alcohol abuse has been a continuing concern on many campuses, and since alcohol-related problems reported by youths are predictive of problems with alcohol later in life (Jellinek, 1946; Fillmore, 1974, 1975), students are more relevant as a study population than in many areas of study for which they have been used as subjects.

Over the past fifteen years the trend has been to define alcoholism less as a disease entity and focus more on the epidemiology of drinking problems. The shift in emphasis recognizes that wide variations exist in the amount of alcohol consumed and in the effects of consumption on the persons in question. Prompting this shift were various conceptual, methodological, and epidemiological difficulties

Authors' Note: We would like to thank Dr. Sonia Wright and Dee Weber-Burdin for their assistance. Address all communications to Lawrence O'Brien, Department of Sociology, University of Massachusetts, Amherst, MA 01003.

(Knupfer, 1967; Plaut, 1967; Cahalan, 1970). As a consequence, knowledge concerning the prevalence and incidence of drinking problems in the population at large has become increasingly refined (Cahalan, 1970; Cahalan et al., 1969; Cahalan and Room, 1974).

However, this epidemiological tradition has not been without its own problems. Typically, the definition of drinking problems applied to the assessment of consumption has been based on standards established in physiological research—that is, so many ounces of alcohol leads to such and such impairments of functioning. For a further understanding of drinking patterns, a social psychological dimension must be added to these epidemiological concerns that describes how individuals define excessive alcohol consumption and how they define the point at which alcohol use turns into abuse. As in so many other areas of social activity, the line between the acceptable and the unacceptable, the normal and the deviant, is not clear-cut. For example, when does drinking become viewed as problem drinking? Does this depend solely on the amount of alcohol consumed per unit of time? Or, are there elements in the person (for example, behavioral consequences) or, in the drinking situation (for example, social as opposed to solitary drinking) that indicate whether the drinking in question is viewed as problematic?

The method employed in our research was to provide subjects with short vignettes, each describing a hypothetical person's drinking pattern along with certain descriptive attributes. Subjects rated how seriously they regarded the drinking pattern described in each of the vignettes. The way vignettes were constructed allows for the precise assessment of how each of the constituent features of the vignettes contributed to the seriousness assessment. In effect, the vignette method allows the researcher to simulate the attribution processes used by subjects in making judgments about alcohol abuse.

Especially of interest in studying such attribution processes is determining the degree to which such processes are idiosyncratic or consensual. Indeed, if everyone had their own particular way of making such judgments, then attribution becomes of minor interest. Whether judgments indicate the existence of a normative order underlying the attribution process is of special concern. In short, for attribution of alcohol abuse to be of theoretical or practical significance, some degree of consensus must exist concerning what constitutes a serious drinking problem. Hence, the first question we raise in this research is whether or not a consensual, normative framework can be discerned in the process generating seriousness ratings.

A second and related concern examines how the specific features of the vignette influence seriousness ratings. Each of the vignettes describes an individual in terms of sex, social class, age, amount of drinking, frequency of drinking, some behavioral consequences of drinking, and whether or not the individual has sought help for his or her drinking problem. Of course, it is to be expected that the amounts of alcohol and frequency of drinking will dominate in their influence on the ratings. Beyond this, however, we ask, for example, whether males will be allowed to drink more than females to achieve the same level of seriousness. Or do the consequences of drinking sharply modify seriousness—for example, can a person who "holds his liquor" drink more without being regarded as having a serious drinking problem?

Third, since the ratings are made on a 9-point scale, ranging from "least serious" (1) to "most serious" (9), we are able to designate the upper reaches of the scale (7) through (9) as representing very serious drinking problems. We seek to determine whether there are certain features describing individuals which clearly drive the ratings into the very serious drinking problems area—that is, whether or not a threshold effect exists. Here the question is whether the effects of amount and frequency of drinking on perceptions of severity are linear in form. Severity ratings may remain fairly constant across low to medium levels of amount and frequency of alcohol consumption and then jump significantly when a tolerance threshold is reached and exceeded. To probe for threshold effects of this type, several levels on these two variables were included in the experimental design, and regression coefficients associated with each level will be reported.

A final concern of this chapter is subgroup differences in the attribution process, a topic closely related to that of consensus. Consensus is compatible only with some kinds of subgroup differences. If there are some subgroups that use different attribution principles in arriving at judgments of seriousness, then the evidence for consensus is weakened. However, subgroups may vary in their thresholds without departing from attribution principles. For example, men may be more tolerant of drinking than women but put the same weight on behavioral consequences, sex, age, and so on as do women in arriving at their more tolerant judgments.

FIGURE 8.1   Examples of Vignettes

Mary P.   23 years old
Comes from a Middle-Class Background
Drinks an Average of 9 Beers
Drinks the Above Amount Once a Month
Is Able to Relax After Drinking

Craig L.   19 years old
Comes from an Upper-Middle-Class Background
Drinks an Average of 5 Beers
Drinks the Above Amount Once or Twice a Week
Worries Less about School After Drinking
Currently Sees a Health Counselor about Drinking

Method

Measures of seriousness were obtained by presenting subjects with brief accounts of drinking situations (vignettes) describing fictitious individuals. Subjects were asked to rate how seriously they regarded the drinking pattern for each of the individuals described. These accounts, printed on computer cards, were constructed by combining items drawn from lists of characteristics selected on the basis of previous literature. The vignettes were created by a computer program which assembled each vignette by randomly choosing one value from each of the lists of characteristics (see Figure 8.1). Seven lists were employed as follows.

1. *Sex*—two values, either a male or female first name and the first initial of a last name (Bose, 1973). Sex was used as a descriptor even though the evidence drawn from previous literature is mixed on the effect of drinker's gender on tolerance of deviance. Lawrence and Maxwell (1962) and Knupfer (1964), using survey questionnaire data, found a greater intolerance toward drunkenness in women. In contrast, Stafford and Petway (1977), using semantic differential scales, reported an absence of sex differences.

2. *Social Class*—values range from lower class through upper class as follows: lower class, middle class, upper middle class, and upper class. Alcoholism or serious abuse has been described as a lower-class characteristic (Warner, 1963). Labeling theorists would predict a greater likelihood for lower class individuals to be identified as alcohol abusers' given that lower class is an indication of a less powerful position in society (Scheff, 1970).

3. *Age*—measured in years, ranging from 17 to 29. Given that our society is in many respects age stratified (Parsons, 1942, 1961) and

that drinking is often seen as a "rite of passage" (Jessor and Jessor, 1975), we felt that the age of the fictitious actors might influence attributions of seriousness regarding drinking behavior.[1]

4. *Consumption*—defined as how much, on the average, one drinks. Consumption could be of two types: beer (ranging from 1 to 13 drinks) and scotch (ranging from 2 to 8 drinks.)

5. *Frequency*—defined as how often, on the average, one drinks the amount described above. Frequency could be one of the following: every day, nearly every day, once or twice a week, two or three times a month, about once a month, or about once every other month.

6. *Consequence*—incorporates 20 behavioral consequences of drinking, 13 of which were to represent negatively valued drinking outcomes and 7 as positive. On one-fifth of the vignettes no consequence statement was printed. Blizard (1969) concluded that social consequences (the extent to which others were harmed) were the most important quality affecting levels of perceived seriousness of drinking (for a complete list of these values, see Table 8.3).

7. *Help Sought*—specified as seeking help for drinking at a student health clinic. This statement appeared on a randomly selected 20 percent of the vignettes. On the remainder, blank spots appeared in the appropriate space alloted (see Figure 8.1). In light of the strong norms of self-reliance in our culture, one would predict that if help had been sought, a given actor's drinking might be perceived as more serious. Support for this hypothesis is found in a study by Phillips (1963) in which it was found that individuals exhibiting identical behavior were increasingly rejected, as they were described as relying on various sources (no help, clergyman, physician, psychiatrist, and a mental hospital). On the other hand, indicating help sought raises the possibility of certain respondents recognizing that little can be done to help a "problem drinker" until that drinker defines the situation as problematic and decides to seek help. Such a situation may seem less serious compared to an individual experiencing similar problems with drinking but who does not elect to seek help.

Since the vignettes were constructed by random combinations of statements assembled from each of the seven lists, the total set of vignettes rated have two important statistical qualities. First, each variable is rectangularly distributed and therefore possesses larger variance than would be the case for a descriptive survey.[2] Hence, the *standardized* regression coefficients in the vignette method are useful for comparison *within* the sample but differ from "real-world" betas in this important respect. Second, the correlations among vignette characteristics hover around zero, in contrast to the usual real-world problem of multicollinearity. This orthogonality allows more precise estimates of the effects of the independent variables on seriousness ratings. Indeed, the statistical advantages of this method resemble those of a fully crossed experimental design (Alves and Rossi, 1978).

Data were collected from 152 college students in sophomore- and junior-level sociology classes at two northeastern universities. Roughly half were female (52.8 percent), most were white (89.5 percent), and the mean age of the sample was 20.8 years. Respondents were asked to execute two tasks: to rate a sample of 30 vignettes *and* to fill out a questionnaire assessing sociodemographic information, respondents' specific drinking habits, and, in lesser detail, the drinking habits of their friends, families, and relatives.[3]

Each respondent was asked to judge how serious the drinking situation was for the fictitious actor portrayed in the vignettes. The seriousness continuum consisted of a rating scale ranging from 1 as "least serious" to 9 as "most serious," with the ratings in between representing intervening levels of seriousness. If respondents felt unable to rate a given vignette on the seriousness scale, they marked it 0. Of the total 4560 vignettes presented, subjects produced usable ratings for 4521 (99 percent). The vignettes not rated did not differ systematically from those included in the analysis.

Overall Findings

The analysis was accomplished by regressing the seriousness ratings on the seven variables incorporated into the vignettes. The individual *vignette* was treated as the *unit of analysis*. This approach allows for the assessment of independent contributions of each vignette characteristic on attributions of seriousness.

Table 8.1 presents in Panel A the intercorrelations among the vignette characteristics and in Panel B correlations between each of the vignette characteristics and the seriousness ratings. Intercorrelations among vignette characteristics cluster around zero by design.

Two of the seven correlations presented in Panel B of Table 8.1 are negligible (not statistically significant); neither the sex nor the social class of the fictitious persons depicted in the vignettes significantly

TABLE 8.1   Zero-Order Corrections Among Vignette Characteristics and
Vignette Characteristics with Seriousness Rating

Panel A: Zero-Order Correlations Among Vignette Characteristics:

	Sex	Age	Social Class	Consumption	Frequency	Consequence
Age	-.025					
Social class	-.002	-.016				
Consumption	.009	-.031	-.022			
Frequency	.003	.031	.003	.011		
Consequence[a]	-.017	.013	-.013	.013	.014	
Help sought[b]	-.016	-.004	.001	.028	.032	-.026

Panel B: Correlations of Vignette Characteristics with Seriousness Rating:

	Sex	Age	Social Class	Consumption	Frequency	Consequence
Rating	.081	-.026*	-.018	.378*	.153*	.081*

*Significant at the .05 level.
a. Treated dichotomously; the blank spot (that is, when no consequence measure appeared on the vignettes) was recoded as zero. Codes one through twenty were all recoded equaling one—that is, when a consequence measure appeared on the vignettes.
b. Treated dichotomously; the blank spot (when no help-seeking measure appeared) was recoded as zero. The presence of a help-seeking measure ("is currently seeing a health counselor about drinking") was recoded as one.

TABLE 8.2   Regression of Seriousness Ratings on Vignette Characteristics

Independent Variables	Dependent Variable Is Seriousness of Drinking			
	b	SE	Beta	sig.
Sex	.008	.062	.002	N.S.
Social class	-.016	.028	-.006	N.S.
Age	-.029	.011	-.032	.005
Consumption	.313	.010	.368	.000
Frequency	.780	.018	.494	.000
Consequence[a]	1.05	.076	.157	.000
Help sought[b]	.392	.076	.059	.000
Constant	5.63			.000
$R^2 =$	.415			.000
N =	(4521)			

a. Treated dichotomously; the blank spot (when no consequence measure appeared on the vignettes) was recoded as zero. Codes one through twenty were all recoded equaling one (when a consequence measure appeared on the vignettes).
b. Treated dichotomously; the blank spot (when no help-seeking measure appeared) was recoded as zero. The presence of a help-seeking measure, ("is currently seeing a health counselor about drinking") was recoded as one.

influenced the seriousness ratings. The remainder of the correlations in Panel B are all statistically significant. These effects are more appropriately examined in terms of the results presented in Table 8.2.

Several overall findings emerge from the regression analysis presented in Table 8.2. First, the R^2 of .415 makes it abundantly clear that, taken as a set, the vignette characteristics strongly affect the seriousness ratings. Second, as anticipated, the amount and frequency of drinking are the two strongest determinants of seriousness (see the standardized coefficients). Indeed, it appears that frequency is more important than the amount consumed during a given bout of drinking. The unstandardized coefficients provide concrete meaning to the effects of amount of alcohol consumed. The findings indicate that each additional beer or scotch consumed increases seriousness ratings by nearly a third of an interval on the seriousness scale. An increase in frequency of one unit, as for example between descriptors "drinks X amount once a month" and "drinks X amount two or three times a month," leads to over three-quarters of a unit increase in seriousness.

Third, neither sex nor social class make the drinking described in a vignette appear more or less serious. The null finding with respect to gender has also been noted in previous research (Stafford and Petway, 1977) and may reflect recent trends in the relative statuses of the sexes.[4] Caution should be taken in explaining the null finding for social class, in that its measurement in this study was somewhat crude. In addition, it was the social class of the fictitious drinker's family of orientation that was manipulated. Different findings might have resulted if direct social class descriptors of drinkers had been written into the vignettes.

Fourth, more tolerance is shown for the drinking behavior of older persons. Each additional year led to a reduction of nearly .03 in seriousness ratings. Since the age range used was 17 to 29, the drinking patterns of the oldest persons described in the vignettes were judged as a third of an interval less serious than the same drinking patterns of the youngest persons described in the vignettes.

Finally, the presence of the description of either consequences or help-seeking behavior significantly increased the seriousness ratings. Since the consequences used consist of negative outcomes mixed with some positive outcomes, full explication of the meaning of the finding that consequences in general increase seriousness is postponed until we can look at the impact of specific consequences in the

TABLE 8.3 Regression of Seriousness Ratings on Consequences

"Positive" Values of Consequence	Dependent Variable is Seriousness of Drinking[a]			
	b	SE	Beta	sig.
1. "more considerate of others after drinking"	-.095	.208	-.007	N.S.
2. "has a great sense of humor after drinking"	-.098	.210	-.007	N.S.
3. "more friendly after drinking"	-.205	.217	-.014	N.S.
4. "able to relax after drinking"	.251	.209	.018	N.S.
5. "appears much happier after drinking"	.486	.209	.035	.020
6. "worries less about school after drinking"	.613	.208	.045	.003
7. "can speak to members of the opposite sex only after drinking"	1.06	.218	.074	.000
"Negative" Values of Consequence				
8. "regularly misses morning classes"	.569	.205	.043	.006
9. "noisy at night in the dorm after drinking"	.723	.210	.053	.001
10. "appears withdrawn"	.717	.207	.053	.001
11. "grade point average has dropped"	.924	.216	.065	.000
12. "recently placed on academic probation"	1.14	.220	.078	.000
13. "language gets abusive after drinking"	1.10	.212	.079	.000
14. "drinking resulted in losing a friend"	1.47	.205	.110	.000
15. "lost license to drive because of drinking"	1.72	.212	.124	.000
16. "gets into heated arguments in the dorm after drinking"	1.75	.212	.126	.000
17. "has been in two fights in the dorm after drinking"	1.97	.206	.146	.000
18. "destroyed some dorm property after drinking"	2.00	.207	.148	.000
19. "stopped twice by police for drunken driving"	2.18	.218	.152	.000
20. "drinks and drives"	2.18	.211	.158	.000
Constant	4.71			.000
$R^2 =$	.085			.000
$N =$	(4521)			.000

a. Omitted value is no consequence shown on the vignette.

next section. The interpretation of the effect of help sought may follow Phillips's observation that seeking help is confirmation in the eyes of others that one has a serious problem (1963). The policy implications of this finding are noteworthy for campaigns against drinking that suggest persons come to clinical centers for counseling or other help.

Specification of the Effect of Consequences

In order to gain a finer appreciation of the effect of consequences of drinking on seriousness, we have coded each consequence as a dummy variable and regressed the seriousness ratings on the resulting set of 20 dummy variables. The results are shown in Table 8.3.[5] The coefficients in that table indicate how much more (or less) serious a vignette is rated when the consequence in question appears. Thus for example, the coefficient, .486 associated with the consequence "appears much happier after drinking" means that the vignettes with this consequence were regarded as .486 points more serious than vignettes which had no consequence printed at all (constant).

Eight and a half percent of the variance in seriousness ratings can be explained by the descriptions of drinking consequences. Clearly, the consequences of drinking modify seriousness attributions.

The first seven consequences of Table 8.3 were intended to designate positive outcomes of drinking. None had such effects. In fact, the three consequences with statistically significant effects indicate such consequences *increase* the seriousness judgment. One plausible interpretation of these counterintuitive findings is that what we had considered to be positive drinking outcomes may have seemed to respondents to mean that the drinking was symptomatic of a much deeper personal problem. For example, "appears happier" and "worries less" may connote psychological dependency on alcohol—that is, that the person described *needs* to drink, relying on alcohol to lighten his or her mood.

The remaining 13 consequence descriptors were each constructed to represent negatively valued outcomes of drinking. All regression coefficients are statistically significant, and in the expected direction. Those descriptors which emphasize the failure of the drinker to meet the normative expectations of the student role ("regularly misses morning classes," "g.p.a. has dropped," "recently placed on academic probation") are substantively less important than the remaining consequences, which focus on social threats rather than personal loss. The strongest effects were obtained for consequences 14 through 20, each of which concerns effects of drinking that are predominantly social and potentially threatening to other persons. Three of these descriptors involved drinking and driving. Others involved were "fighting," "gets into heated arguments," and "destroys dorm property." Overall these findings indicate that the *social* consequences of drinking, more than the *personal* consequences, enhance the seriousness of drinking alcohol in the eyes of subjects.

TABLE 8.4   Regression of Seriousness Ratings on Consumption

Value of Consumption[a]	Dependent Variable Is Seriousness of Drinking			
	b	SE	Beta	sig.
3 beers	1.08	.174	.115	.000
2 scotch	1.58	.171	.171	.000
5 beers	1.87	.176	.195	.000
4 scotch	2.39	.172	.264	.000
7 beers	2.42	.173	.267	.000
9 beers	3.05	.175	.320	.000
6 scotch	3.06	.175	.321	.000
11 beers	3.06	.174	.325	.000
13 beers	3.50	.173	.372	.000
8 scotch	3.69	.172	.402	.000
Constant[b]	3.17			.000
R^2	.157			.000
N =	4521			

a. These values appeared on the vignettes as, for example, "drinks an average of."
b. Constant equals the deleted category "one beer."

Specifying the Effect of Amount of Alcohol

The amount of alcohol vignette persons usually drank at a sitting was expressed in terms of numbers of beers, ranging from 1 to 13, or numbers of scotches, beginning with 2 and ending with 8. The full set of drinking amounts is shown in Table 8.4, where seriousness ratings are regressed on each of the amounts coded as dummy variables.

The purpose of the regression analysis was to estimate the imputed differences between beer and scotch as well as the increment in seriousness accompanying each step in the amount of each beverage imbibed. The amount of drinking accounts for 15 percent of the variance in seriousness ratings, as shown by the R^2. Note that this is approximately twice the amount of variance explained by the consequence variable.

The objective amount of alcohol in a typical scotch on the rocks is roughly equivalent to that contained in one beer. However, respondents attached more seriousness to scotch, a hard liquor, than warranted by its alcoholic content. When a dummy variable coded 0=beer, 1=scotch was included, the resulting b=.54 indicated that for equivalent numbers of drinks, scotch was seen as a half-point more serious.

TABLE 8.5   Regression of Seriousness Ratings on Frequency

Value of Frequency[a]	Dependent Variable Is Seriousness/Drinking			
	b	SE	Beta	sig.
Every day	3.41	.118	.478	.000
Nearly every day	3.52	.119	.485	.000
One or twice a week	1.75	.119	.241	.000
Two or three times a month	.86	.117	.122	.000
About once a month	.34	.122	.045	.006
Constant[b]	3.86			.000
$R^2=$	.267			.000
N =	4521			

a. These values are prefaced on the vignettes with "drinks the above amount."
b. Constant equals the deleted category "about once every other month."

The existence of a threshold effect was investigated by looking for discontinuities in the regression coefficients associated with varying levels of alcohol consumption. No threshold effect could be discerned. Drinking increasing amounts is more serious, given equal increments, at the lower and higher levels of drinking, but the amount consumed by itself did not automatically place a person into the very serious category (designated as ratings 7 through 9).

Specifying the Frequency of Alcohol Consumed

The frequency with which an amount of alcohol was consumed was captured in terms of days, ranging from every day to about once every other month. Table 8.5 is a dummy variable regression analysis of the full range of values associated with this variable.

The frequency of drinking, as evidenced by the R^2, accounts for nearly 27 percent of the variance in seriousness ratings. In terms of the amount of variance explained, this respectively reflects a three-fold and nearly a two-fold increase when compared to the variables consequence and consumption.

Despite the slight reversal between the values "every day" and "nearly every day," these data show a trend in the anticipated direction. The two values expressing the highest rates of frequency, every day and nearly every day, markedly affect seriousness ratings, exhibiting regression coefficients of 3.41 and 3.52; where these values appear on the vignettes, the predicted values of seriousness (7.27 and 7.38) place an individual into the very serious category (ratings 7 through 9).

TABLE 8.6 Regression of Seriousness Ratings on Respondent Characteristics

Independent Variables	Dependent Variable Is Seriousness of Drinking			
	b	SE	beta	sig.
Do any of your relatives have a problem with drinking? 0 = no; 1 = yes	-.251	.096	-.041	.009
Do any of your friends have a problem with drinking? 0 = no; 1 = yes	-.209	.095	-.039	.028
Usually having a drink at least twice a day[a].	.433	.065	.278	.000
Having eight or more drinks in a day last month[b].	-.103	.030	-.079	.000
Do you drink? 0 = no; 1 = yes	-3.55	.495	-.356	.000
Religion[c]				
Protestant 0 = no; 1 = yes	-.892	.167	-.123	.000
Jewish 0 = no; 1 = yes	-.713	.163	-.109	.000
Catholic 0 = no; 1 = yes	-.473	.139	-.088	.000
Constant	7.23			.000
$R^2 =$	.061			.000
N =	(4133)			

a. In the past three months, how often have you had some kind of drink containing alcohol? (Include wine, beer, liquor or any other kind of drink). 1 = usually twice a day; 7 = less than once a month.
b. On how many days last month did you have eight or more drinks in the course of the day? 1 = 1 day; 7 = 7 days or more.
c. Deleted category includes those of other religions and those declaring no religious preference.

As opposed to consumption, an apparent threshold effect is demonstrated in the consideration of the frequency variable. Discontinuities in the regression coefficients associated with varying levels of frequency are revealed by noting the marked gap between the respective predicted values for every day (7.27) and once or twice a week (5.61). Clearly, the values every day and nearly every day are interpreted by respondents as *substantially* more serious than other values and have the effect of placing those persons who drink at these frequencies into the area on the scale designated as very serious drinking problems.

Effects of Respondent Characteristics

Up to this point we have considered only the effects of vignette characteristics on perceived seriousness. The fact that the vignette characteristics account for so large a proportion of the variance in ratings indicates that, to a large degree, respondents were reacting in similar ways to the descriptions given. Substantial variance remains unexplained, however, and it remains to be seen whether consideration of respondent characteristics will be of explanatory value.

This topic is relevant in two ways: First, if large amounts of the variance in seriousness can be explained by taking into account respondent characteristics, the evidence for consensus across subjects is weakened.[6] Second, the existence of subgroup differences would also be revealed by such analyses, especially if subgroup membership characteristics such as religion were shown to affect ratings. It should be borne in mind that the tests made with these data are limited because of the homogeneity of subjects; all are undergraduates and hence relatively similar with respect to age, socioeconomic background, and educational attainment as compared to the general population.

Table 8.6 presents the results of the analysis of the effect of respondent characteristics on seriousness ratings.[7] The resulting R^2 of .061 indicates that only modest amounts of the variance in seriousness ratings are accounted for by respondent characteristics, particularly when contrasted with the more than 40 percent of the variance explained by the seven vignette descriptors. Table 8.6 contains only respondent characteristics which turned out to be statistically significant. Other characteristics, such as age, sex, institution, ethnicity, and marital status, were not significant. Respondent characteristics which were statistically significant consist of items that relate to the respondent's own drinking habits, acquaintance with persons with drinking problems such as friends or relatives, and religious affiliation.

Perhaps the most striking result presented in Table 8.6 pertains to whether the respondent drinks at all. Teetotalers and imbibers are separated by 3.5 points on the 9-point scale of perceptions of seriousness, with the former group considering the vignettes *that much more serious* on the average. Furthermore, the more subjects reported drinking, the less seriousness they imputed to the drinking of the fictitious persons in the vignettes. This set of findings indicates that nondrinkers, light drinkers, and heavy drinkers apparently agree on the relative seriousness of drinking but add or subtract to the ratings a constant that makes them relatively tolerant (or intolerant) of the same descriptions. Whether this constitutes a pattern of convenient denial on the part of drinkers or of militant temperance on the part of teetotalers cannot be determined from our data.

Subjects professing religious affiliation in any one of the three major religious groups—either Protestant, Catholic, or Jewish—are more tolerant of drinking than those who belong to other religions or who profess no religious affiliation at all. Of the three major religious groups, Protestants are the most tolerant and Catholics the least.

The findings concerning the influence of respondent characteristics are somewhat puzzling. First, the amount of variance explained is relatively small. In that regard the findings support the contention that respondents tend toward a generalized consensus over what constitutes relatively serious drinking problems. On the other hand, there do appear to be structured differences among subjects according to their own drinking habits and of the drinking habits of those closely related to them. While both teetotalers and drinkers may agree, for example, that drinking a lot frequently with potential social harm is more serious than the opposite condition, it takes substantially more in that direction to elicit an attribution of very serious from drinkers as compared to nondrinkers. In short, there appears to be consensus concerning *how to* assess drinking problems but dissensus concerning *what should be* society's level of tolerance for those drinking problems.

Conclusions

This chapter has sought to add to the already rich epidemiological tradition of research into drinking problems a social psychological dimension addressing how individuals define what constitutes excessive alcohol use and the points at which use shades into abuse. In order to simulate the process of attribution employed by students in making judgments about alcohol abuse, a vignette method was used—a method whereby one value from each of the lists of characteristics is randomly assigned to construct a controlled stimulus.

Several findings are noteworthy. First, the vignettes were not rated in a random or idiosyncratic manner—five of the seven descriptors were, in varying degrees, associated with seriousness ratings. The coefficients of amount and frequency of drinking proved to be the most substantively powerful predictors of seriousness. While respondents were most influenced by these cues, other variables also contributed to the prediction of seriousness. In terms of their explanatory power, these were, respectively, the presence of a consequence descriptor, evidence of help sought, and age of the fictitious person described on the vignette. The coefficients associated with the vignette actor's sex and social class position were insignificant.

Second, to the extent that the vignette descriptors explained a large portion of the variance (42 percent) in seriousness ratings and respondent characteristics did not (6 percent), the data support the existence of consensus underlying these attributional processes. This result seemed tempered by the additional finding of structured differences among respondents according to their religious preference, their drinking habits, and the drinking habits of particular significant others. Although these structured differences do not call into question the presence of consensually agreed-upon principles employed in making attributions of seriousness, they do illuminate a degree of dissensus concerning what should be society's level of tolerance for drinking behavior.

We conclude with a brief set of comments about directions for further research. The vignette methodology applied in this study illustrates the potential of such an approach for the investigation of social psychological issues concerning the societal reaction to alcohol abuse. Some of the findings from the present study require replication in more heterogeneous samples, as well as more focused inquiry. The absence of an effect due to gender is provocative, but caution should be taken in interpreting this "finding" until it is corroborated in other studies. Future studies of the perception of alcohol consumption might also take into account such dependent variables as desired social distance and recommendations for help. Finally, it seems worth exploring whether the same factors observed to affect "other perception" also affect "self-perception" as far as alcohol consumption is concerned.

NOTES

1. The restricted age range used was especially appropriate for undergraduate students. Note also that the age range spans the legally defined drinking ages of the two states involved.

2. For example, the vignettes contain proportionately more heavy drinkers than would be found in a sample of undergraduates.

3. The instructions used to elicit respondents' ratings were as follows: "In part one you are asked to rate a stack of cards on which there appear short statements about specific drinking situations. Rate the cards on a nine-point scale of seriousness. Numbers one through nine represent varying degrees of seriousness between least and most serious. Use one for the least serious and nine for the most serious situations. If you feel a situation is moderately serious, you might rate it a 4, 5, or 6. If you feel it was less serious but not least serious, you might rate it a 2 or 3, or if you feel it was more serious but not most, you might rate it a 7 or 8. If you feel unable to rate any given card, please mark that card with a zero. If you change your mind about the rating you have assigned, just scratch out your initial rating and rerate the card."

4. Suspecting that the findings concerning gender might conceal an important interaction effect, separate regressions were run for vignettes of each sex. Findings indicated that the structures (that is, regression coefficients and R^2s) were essentially identical in the resulting two equations.

5. Note that because vignette characteristics are orthogonal to each other (by design), it is not necessary to hold other vignette characteristics constant in the regression equation.

6. In addition, we tested for differences between the two institutions from which students were selected. No differences between institutions were found.

7. Since vignette characteristics are, by design, orthogonal to respondent characteristics, it is not necessary to put in the former to get unbiased estimates of the latter.

REFERENCES

Alves, W. M. and P. Rossi, 1978, "Who should get what?: fairness judgments of the distribution of earnings." American Journal of Sociology 84: 541-564.

Blizard, P., 1969, "Public image and social rejection of the alcoholic." Quarterly Journal of the Study of Alcohol 30: 686-697.

Bose, C., 1973, "Jobs and gender: sex and occupational prestige." Ph.D. thesis, Johns Hopkins University.

Cahalan, D., 1970, Problem Drinkers. San Francisco: Jossey-Bass.

Cahalan, D. and R. Room, 1974, Problem Drinking Among American Men. Monograph No. 7. New Brunswick, NJ: Rutgers Center of Alcohol Studies.

Cahalan, D., I. Cisin, and H. Crossley, 1969, American Drinking Practices. Monograph No. 6. New Brunswick, NJ: Rutgers Center for Alcohol Studies.

Fillmore, K. M., 1974, "Drinking and problem drinking in early adulthood and middle age: an exploratory 20-year follow-up study." Journal of the Study of Alcohol 35: 819-840.

Jellinek, E. M., 1946, "Phases in the drinking history of alcoholics: analysis of a survey conducted by the official organ of Alcoholics Anonymous." Quarterly Journal of the Study of Alcohol 7: 1-88.

Jessor, R. and S. Jessor, 1975, "Adolescent development and the onset of drinking." Journal of the Study of Alcohol 36: 27-51.

Knupfer,G., 1967, "The epidemiology of problem drinking." American Journal of Public Health 57: 973-986.

1964, "Female drinking patterns." Presented at the annual meetings of the North American Association of Alcohol Programs, Washington, D.C.

Lawrence, J. and M. Maxwell, 1962, "Drinking and socio-economic status," in D. Pittman and C. Snyder (eds.) Society, Culture, and Drinking Patterns. New York: John Wiley.

Parsons, T., 1961, "Youth in the context of American society." Daedalus 91: 97-123.

1942, "Age and sex in the social structure of the United States." American Sociological Review 7: 604-616.

Phillips, D., 1963, "Rejection: a possible consequence of seeking help for mental disorders." American Sociological Review 28: 968-972.

Plaut, T., 1967, "Some major issues in developing community services for persons with drinking problems." Washington, DC: U.S. National Clearinghouse for Mental Health Information.

Scheff, T., 1970, "Schizophrenia as ideology." Schiophrenic Bulletin I: 15-20.

Stafford, R. and J. Petway, 1977, "Stigmatization of men and women problem drinkers and their spouses." Journal of the Study of Alcohol 38: 2109-2121.

Warner, W. L. (ed.), 1963, Yankee City. New Haven: Yale University Press.

ABOUT THE AUTHORS

Wayne M. Alves is currently Assistant Professor in the Department of Neurological Surgery, University of Virginia Medical School, Charlottesville. He formerly was Assistant Professor of Sociology at Virginia, and prior to that an NIMH postdoctoral scholar in Mental Health Evaluation Research at UCLA. Dr. Alves's current research includes the study of social competence following damage to the central nervous system, and evaluating new methods of managing patients with minor head injuries. Related research involves the study of social-historical aspects of congenital skull and facial anomalies routinely treated by neurosurgeons.

Andy B. Anderson is Associate Professor of Sociology at the University of Massachusetts, Amherst, where he teaches statistics, research methods, and social psychology. His research interests include mathematical models of social judgment and choice and evaluation research. He currently is co-principal investigator, with Anthony Harris, on a project entitled "Perception of Criminal Risk," a study using factorial surveys to model decision making in criminal actions. Prior to coming to the University of Massachusetts, Anderson was involved in negative income tax experimentation, first as co-principal investigator during the last half of the Gary, Indiana Income Maintenance Experiment and then as Senior Scientist to the Manitoba income maintenance project.

Richard A. Berk is Professor of Sociology at the University of California at Santa Barbara. He has published widely in the fields of evaluation research and the sociology of law. His two most recent books are *Money, Work and Crime: Experimental Evidence* (with Peter H. Rossi and Kenneth J. Lenihan) and *Water Shortage: Some Lessons in Conservation from the Great California Drought, 1976-1977* (with Thomas Cooley, C. J. LaCivita, and Kathy Sredl).

Karen Garrett received her Master's degree in sociology from the University of Massachusetts, Amherst. She is currently working toward her Ph.D. at the University of California at Berkeley. Her present research is focused on the sociopolitical history of child welfare legislation in the United States. She is also co-editor of a forthcoming anthology, *Biological Rhythms and Social Relations.* In addition to her academic work, she is also a research consultant for Levi-Strauss in San Francisco.

Jeffrey K. Liker is a research associate in the Department of Human Development and Family Studies at Cornell University. He is interested in the linkages between economic factors, psychological health, and the quality of family interactions. With Glen H. Elder, Jr., he is investigating the influence of economic loss during the Great Depression on personality and family patterns over time. In this work, they find influences of the Depression as long as forty years after the losses occurred. Liker is also working with Greg Duncan on the impact of income fluctuations on feelings of personal control for black and white men in the Panel Study of Income Dynamics at Michigan.

M. Bonner Meudell, a sociologist by training, is currently a research methodologist at the Southern California Kaiser-Permanente Medical Care Program. In this position she is primarily involved with applied social science research. Specifically the position involves evaluating the feasibility and effectiveness of various health care programs and procedures. Recently, the major emphasis of her work has been focused on a National Cancer Institute-funded study of a hospice program within the Kaiser-Permanente Medical Care system. In conjunction with her interest in the content and delivery of health care she also has been involved in the area of mental health research. In addition, she has just concluded a pilot study for the National Institute of Alcohol Abuse and Alcoholism. This study explored the way older persons used alcohol as a coping mechanism for stressful life events.

Steven L. Nock is currently Assistant Professor of Sociology at the University of Virginia, Charlottesville. He received his Ph.D. in sociology in 1976 from the University of Massachusetts, Amherst, where he studied with Peter Rossi. In addition to his research on family social standing, his published works deal with the consequences of various family life cycle transitions. His current research interests focus on the balancing of family and work life in two-earner families.

Lawrence J. O'Brien received his B.A. degree (1976) from the University of Delaware in sociology and in education. Since the fall of 1977, he has been a graduate student in sociology at the University of Massachusetts, Amherst, earning a M.A. in the spring of 1979. At present he is a Ph.D. student in sociology, pursuing as well a Master's degree in business administration, also at Amherst. Current areas of interest include medical sociology and organizational sociology.

Peter H. Rossi is Professor of Sociology and Director of the Social and Demographic Research Institute at the University of Massachusetts, Amherst, and co-editor of *Social Science Research*. He has been on the faculties of Harvard University, Johns Hopkins University, and the University of Chicago, where he also served as Director of the National Opinion Research Center. His research has largely been concerned with the application of social research methods to social issues, and he is currently engaged in research on natural disasters and criminal justice. In 1979-1980 Professor Rossi was president of the American Sociological Association, and in 1981 he received the Evaluation Research Society's Myrdal Award for contributions to evaluation research methods.

Richard C. Tessler received his Ph.D. in sociology in 1972 from the University of Wisconsin. Following a year as a postdoctoral fellow at Wisconsin, he joined the sociology faculty at the University of Massachusetts, Amherst, where he currently holds the rank of Associate Professor. He has published numerous articles in medical sociology and social psychology, and is now completing his first book entitled *The Chronically Mentally Ill: Assessing Community Support Programs*. This book grows out of his association with the National Institute of Mental Health, where he worked for 13 months in 1979-1980 while on leave from the University of Massachusetts. For the last two years, he has been an associate editor of the *Journal of Health and Social Behavior.*